THE RAINBOW
PEOPLE
OF GOD

The Making of a Peaceful Revolution

IMAGE BOOKS

DOUBLEDAY

New York London Toronto Sydney Auckland

THE RAINBOW PEOPLE OF GOD

DESMOND TUTU

Edited by John Allen

N

AN IMAGE BOOK
PUBLISHED BY DOUBLEDAY

a division of Random House, Inc.
1540 Broadway, New York, New York 10036

IMAGE, DOUBLEDAY and the portrayal of a deer
drinking from a stream are trademarks of Doubleday,
a division of Random House, Inc.

Design by Bonni Leon-Berman

The Rainbow People of God was originally published
in hardcover by Doubleday in October 1994.

Library of Congress has cataloged the Doubleday
hardcover as follows:

Tutu, Desmond.
   The rainbow people of God: the making of a
peaceful revolution / Desmond Tutu; edited by John
Allen.
        p. cm.
   Includes bibliographical references and index.
   1. South Africa—Race relations. 2. Sermons,
English—South Africa. 3. Church of the Province of
Southern Africa—Sermons. 4. Anglican
Communion—South Africa—Sermons.   I. Allen,
John.   II. Title.
DT1756.T88   1994
968.06′—dc20   94-16011
                                                                      CIP
ISBN-13: 978-0-385-48374-2
ISBN 0-385-48374-0

146119649

AT HOME IN South Africa I have sometimes said in big meetings where you have black and white together: "Raise your hands!" Then I've said, "Move your hands," and I've said, "Look at your hands—different colors representing different people. You are the rainbow people of God."

And you remember the rainbow in the Bible is the sign of peace. The rainbow is the sign of prosperity. We want peace, prosperity and justice and we can have it when all the people of God, the rainbow people of God, work together.

> —Desmond Tutu,
> preaching in Tromsö, north of
> the Arctic Circle in Norway,
> December 5, 1991

Contents

Foreword
xi
Chronology
xiii
Terminology
xix
Editor's Preface
xxi

Part One:
THE SCHOOLCHILDREN REBEL:
South Africa's Watershed

1. A Growing Nightmarish Fear:
An open letter to Prime Minister B. J. Vorster (1976)
3
2. Oh, God, How Long Can We Go On?:
Address at the funeral of Steve Biko (1977)
15

Part Two:
CHURCH CONFRONTS STATE:
The South African Council of Churches

3. We Drink Water to Fill Our Stomachs:
Address to the Provincial Synod of the Church of the
Province of Southern Africa (1979)
25
4. A Deep and Passionate Love for Our Land:
Transcript of remarks to P. W. Botha and members
of his cabinet (1980)
41

5. Why Did Mr. Botha's Courage Fail Him?:
Extract from a presentation to a Johannesburg study group (1981)
47

6. The Divine Imperative:
Evidence to the South African government's commission of inquiry
into the South African Council of Churches (1982)
53

7. Not Even Invited to the Party:
Remarks on proposals for a new constitution (1983)
81

8. Apartheid's "Final Solution": Nobel Lecture (1984)
85

Part Three:
"THERE IS NO PEACE":
The States of Emergency

9. You Don't Reform a Frankenstein: Extract from an address to the
Political Committee of the UN General Assembly (1985)
97

10. Punitive Sanctions: Press statement (1986)
105

11. Agents of Transfiguration: Charge on enthronement as
Archbishop of Cape Town (1986)
113

12. Perhaps Even to Die: Sermon on the eve of a return
to controversy in South Africa (1987)
129

13. You Give Yourself a Left Hook:
Address at a prayer service for peace in Natal (1987)
133

14. You Will Bite the Dust!: Extracts from a sermon at a service
held to replace a banned rally (1988)
139

15. Your Policies Are Unbiblical, Unchristian, Immoral and Evil:
A letter to P. W. Botha (1988)
145

Contents

16. All That Has Changed Is the Complexion of the Oppressor:
Extract from a sermon in Mobutu's Zaire (1989)
157

17. You Are Not God!: Sermon in Noriega's Panama (1989)
161

Part Four:
"WE ARE UNSTOPPABLE":
The Defiance Campaign and the Release of Nelson Mandela

18. They Have Power but No Authority:
The beginning of the Defiance Campaign in Cape Town (1989)
169

19. Straighten Up Your Shoulders!:
Remarks to victims of police brutality (1989)
179

20. We Are the Rainbow People!: The Cape Town march (1989)
185

21. We Have Seen Some Extraordinary Things:
Sermon at a thanksgiving service for the release of
Nelson Mandela (1990)
191

22. Why I Believe This Is Happening:
Lecture to cadets at the U.S. Military Academy (1990)
199

23. I Am Not a Politician:
Interview on a new role for Desmond Tutu (1990)
203

Part Five:
A KIND OF ROLLER-COASTER RIDE:
The Violence of Transition

24. The Nadir of Despair:
Extracts from addresses on the Transvaal township war (1990)
209

25. We Forgive You:
Contributions to the Rustenburg church conference (1990)
221

Contents

26. Something Has Gone Desperately Wrong:
Homily during Holy Week (1991)
227

Part Six:
A SPIRITUALITY OF TRANSFORMATION:
Toward Democracy

27. Nurturing Our People:
Extract from Charge to the Anglican Synod of Bishops (1992)
235
28. On the Brink of Disaster:
Sermon on the Boipatong Massacre (1992)
241
29. We Offer to You These Children:
Prayer at the site of the killing of six children (1993)
249
30. His Death Is Our Victory:
Sermon at the funeral of South African Communist Party leader
Chris Hani (1993)
251
31. The Bottom of Depravity:
Address at an interfaith rally after a massacre at St. James Church,
Cape Town (1993)
255
32. A Miracle Unfolding:
Sermon on and thanksgiving for South Africa's first
free election (1994)
259

Editor's Acknowledgments
270
Bibliography
272
Index
273

Contents

Foreword

President Nelson Mandela

The struggle against apartheid required and itself produced men and women of courage. Archbishop Desmond Tutu is one such outstanding patriot.

This collection of speeches and writings mirrors the most important milestones in almost two decades of struggle against apartheid, racism and injustice. For a person whom history put among those at the epicenter of these efforts, a collection of his pronouncements becomes at once an epitome of a given historical period.

The Archbishop's speeches and writings display his deep understanding of the sufferings to which the majority of South Africans were subjected, of their aspirations, courage, determination and spirit of sacrifice. From the address at the funeral of Steve Biko, representations to the apartheid governments of the day, to the Nobel Peace Prize lecture and his call for sanctions against apartheid South Africa—these pronouncements reflect his astute political insight.

Such is the character of a fighter against apartheid that he was "public enemy number one" to the powers-that-be. And it is tribute to his independent mind that what he said was not always popular.

The negotiations process and South Africa's first democratic elections in April 1994 have vindicated the struggles and sacrifices of peace-loving South Africans, among whom Archbishop Tutu will remain an eminent example.

This book is an important contribution to the growing collection of literature on the history of the anti-apartheid struggle. Without it, we could not justifiably claim to have the total picture.

NELSON MANDELA

Chronology

1910	Formation of the Union of South Africa
1912	Founding of the South African Native National Congress, predecessor of the African National Congress
1913	Natives Land Act imposes territorial segregation and sets aside most land for white ownership; further segregation laws follow
1931	Birth of Desmond Tutu in Klerksdorp, a gold-mining town west of Johannesburg
1948	White electorate votes the National Party into power with a mandate to introduce apartheid
1949	Passage of the Prohibition of Mixed Marriages Act extends prohibition on marriages between whites and Africans to outlaw unions between whites and all other races
1950	Population Registration Act enforces classification of all individuals by race
	Suppression of Communism Act outlaws the Communist Party of South Africa; marks the beginning of severe erosion of civil liberties
	Immorality Amendment Act introduces stricter provisions into the law prohibiting sex between persons of different races
	Group Areas Act provides for segregated urban areas
1951	Tutu enters teacher training college
1952	Defiance Campaign in protest against apartheid laws
1953	Bantu Education Act establishes control by the central government over African schools
1955	Tutu marries Leah Nomalizo Shenxane
1958	Tutu leaves teaching to train for the priesthood
1959	University segregation imposed
	Founding of the Pan Africanist Congress
1960	Sharpeville Massacre
	ANC and PAC outlawed
	Tutu ordained a deacon

1961	Declaration of the Republic of South Africa
	South Africa leaves the British Commonwealth
	Nelson Mandela goes underground
	ANC President-General Albert Luthuli awarded the 1960 Nobel Peace Prize
	ANC and PAC resort to armed struggle
	Tutu ordained a priest
1962	Sabotage Act, General Laws Amendment Act and other draconian laws further restrict civil liberties and stipulate heavy penalties to crush resistance
	Mandela arrested and jailed for five years
	Tutu begins theology studies at King's College, London
1964	ANC leaders jailed for life
	Mandela had been brought from prison to join leaders who had been arrested at Rivonia, outside Johannesburg
1965	Tutu awarded a bachelor of divinity (honors) degree
1966	Tutu graduates with a master's degree in theology
1967	Tutu returns to South Africa to teach at St. Peter's College, Federal Theological Seminary, Eastern Cape
	Terrorism Act provides for indefinite detention without trial
	ANC begins guerrilla warfare
1969	South African Students' Organization founded
1970	Tutu becomes a lecturer at the Lesotho campus of the University of Botswana, Lesotho and Swaziland
1972	Black People's Convention formed
	Tutu becomes Associate Director for Africa, Theological Education Fund, World Council of Churches
1973	Wave of strikes beginning in Durban marks the start of a new upsurge of labor organization
1974	Military coup in Portugal prepares the way for Angolan and Mozambican independence
1975	Tutu appointed as Dean of Johannesburg
	Inkatha, a Zulu cultural organization of the 1920s, reconstituted by Mangosuthu Buthelezi as a political movement open to all Africans
1976	Tutu writes Prime Minister John Vorster warning of the potential for violence

	Soweto uprising
	Tutu elected Bishop of Lesotho
	Transkei becomes the first "independent" bantustan
1977	Steve Biko killed in detention
	Banning of twenty black consciousness organizations and newspapers and detention of leaders and black journalists
	Bophuthatswana bantustan becomes "independent"
1978	Tutu appointed General Secretary of the South African Council of Churches
	Azanian People's Organization founded by black consciousness supporters
	P. W. Botha replaces Vorster as Prime Minister
1979	SACC supports civil disobedience
	Tutu visits victims of forced removals at Zweledinga, Eastern Cape, and supports a Danish boycott of South African coal
	Legal recognition given to nonracial trade unions
	Venda bantustan becomes "independent"
1980	Zimbabwean liberation war ends in independence from Britain
	New surge of protests, strikes and school boycotts in South Africa
	Church leaders, including Tutu, arrested while protesting at the detention of a colleague and jailed overnight
	Church leaders meet Botha
	Government inaugurates President's Council to make recommendations on constitutional change
1981	Appointment of the "Eloff commission of inquiry" into the SACC
	Ciskei bantustan becomes "independent"
1982	Right wing of the National Party breaks away to form the Conservative Party
	The National Party announces proposals for a new constitution allowing white, "Colored" and Indian representation in a parliament of three chambers
	Tutu gives evidence to the Eloff commission

1983	The Labor Party, representing Coloreds, agrees to participate in the new constitutional dispensation
	Formation of the National Forum Committee to fight the government's new constitutional proposals
	Launching of the United Democratic Front to fight the proposals
	White electorate approves the constitution
1984	Protests against Indian and Colored elections
	New constitution comes into effect; P. W. Botha becomes Executive President
	Protests over rent increases erupt and troops are ordered into townships
	Nobel Peace Prize awarded to Tutu
1985	Tutu enthroned as Bishop of Johannesburg
	Declaration of a state of emergency
	Foreign banks refuse to extend loans; P. W. Botha dashes hopes of reform; value of South African rand collapses; white business leaders meet ANC leaders in exile
1986	State of emergency lifted under international pressure
	Tutu declares support for sanctions; elected Archbishop of Cape Town
	Repeal of the pass laws
	New state of emergency declared (to be reimposed annually thereafter)
1987	Controversy over Tutu's visit to Mozambique
	Natal violence escalates
1988	Government restricts seventeen organizations, including United Democratic Front and Azanian People's Organization; church leaders arrested during an illegal protest march; Tutu clashes with Botha during meeting; Tutu writes to Botha defending his position
1989	Tutu visits Angola and Zaire
	Tutu visits Nicaragua and Panama
	Launching of Defiance Campaign
	P. W. Botha resigns
	Police shoot demonstrators during election protests; F. W. de Klerk takes power; Cape Town march, followed by

	marches all over the country; ANC "Rivonia trialists" and a PAC leader freed; church leaders meet de Klerk
1990	De Klerk unbans ANC, PAC and South African Communist Party; Nelson Mandela released
	Namibia becomes independent
	Upsurge of violence in Natal
	ANC and South African government meet
	ANC suspends armed struggle; Transvaal township war begins
	Rustenburg Church Conference
1991	Nelson Mandela and Mangosuthu Buthelezi meet for the first time after Mandela's release; violence continues and Tutu warns: "Something has gone desperately wrong"
	Key segregation laws repealed
	Signing of a National Peace Accord
	Convention for a Democratic South Africa (CODESA) begins constitutional talks
1992	De Klerk wins mandate for constitutional talks in white referendum
	CODESA deadlocks; Boipatong massacre; Tutu calls for new Olympic boycott of South Africa; ANC withdraws from CODESA
	Bisho massacre
1993	Constitutional talks resume at the Multiparty Negotiating Forum
	Massacre of six children at Table Mountain, Natal
	Assassination of Chris Hani
	Election date for 1994 set; Tutu and Methodist Presiding Bishop Stanley Mogoba broker talks between Buthelezi and Mandela
	Massacre at St. James Church, Cape Town
	Establishment of Transitional Executive Council ends exclusive white rule; Parliament approves democratic interim constitution
1994	First democratic elections
	First democratically elected legislature meets
	Nelson Mandela inaugurated as President

Terminology

South African laws have grouped people into four broad racial categories: white, African, Indian and "Colored" people. Whites are the descendants of settlers who migrated to South Africa from different parts of Europe in successive waves since 1652. Although a number of whites now regard themselves as being Africans rather than Europeans, the term "African" is customarily used to refer to those of purely African descent. The Indian community was founded by laborers brought in to work on white settlers' sugar plantations in Natal from 1860. The people who have come to be called Colored are a community of mixed origin, descended variously from the Khoisan (hunter-gatherers and herders who were indigenous to the west of the country), from whites and from slaves brought from the East by Dutch colonists.

African, Indian and Colored people came to be referred to collectively as "black" with the development of black consciousness in the 1970s. Desmond Tutu identified with this nomenclature, and it is adopted as standard in this collection. However, some references to "blacks" apply only to black people of purely African descent.

Editor's Preface

This collection sketches the story of South Africa through the eyes of Desmond Tutu from 1976, when the oppression of apartheid was at its peak, to the birth of democracy in the 1994 elections.

It opens with a letter that marked the rise to public prominence of the newly appointed Anglican Dean of Johannesburg, written shortly before the watershed event in recent South African history, the 1976 Soweto youth rebellion. The first three sections cover the period to 1989, during which the country experienced steadily growing resistance to apartheid while the government futilely attempted to come to grips with this challenge and intensified repression under states of emergency. It covers the escalating confrontation between the state and the church and the campaign of nonviolent direct action against apartheid. (Two pieces here reflect Tutu's advocacy of human rights internationally.) The fourth section deals with the culmination of a campaign of civil disobedience in 1989 and the euphoria following the release of Nelson Mandela from prison in 1990, and the last sections chart the confusion and violence of the ensuing transition to democracy.

The material comprises key speeches, letters, sermons, interview extracts, submissions to government and off-the-cuff remarks. Since some of Desmond Tutu's most articulate commentary is extemporaneous, the audiotape archives of the Church of the Province of Southern Africa have been a rich source of material.

In the period covered by this collection, Dean Tutu went on to serve as Bishop of Lesotho, as General Secretary of the South African Council of Churches, as Bishop of Johannesburg and as Archbishop of Cape Town. He has announced that he will retire as Archbishop of Cape Town in 1996, when he turns sixty-five.

I want to put formally on record that we could not hope in this book to do justice to the contributions which other people of faith have made to the struggle for democracy in South Africa. There are countless numbers of these, but as I write I think particularly of Simeon Nkoane of the Community of the Resurrection, the much-loved Anglican Bishop Suffragan of Johannesburg, who died shortly before that which he had been striving for began to be realized.

John Allen
Cape Town, 1994

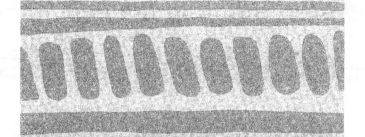

Part One

THE
SCHOOLCHILDREN
REBEL

South Africa's Watershed

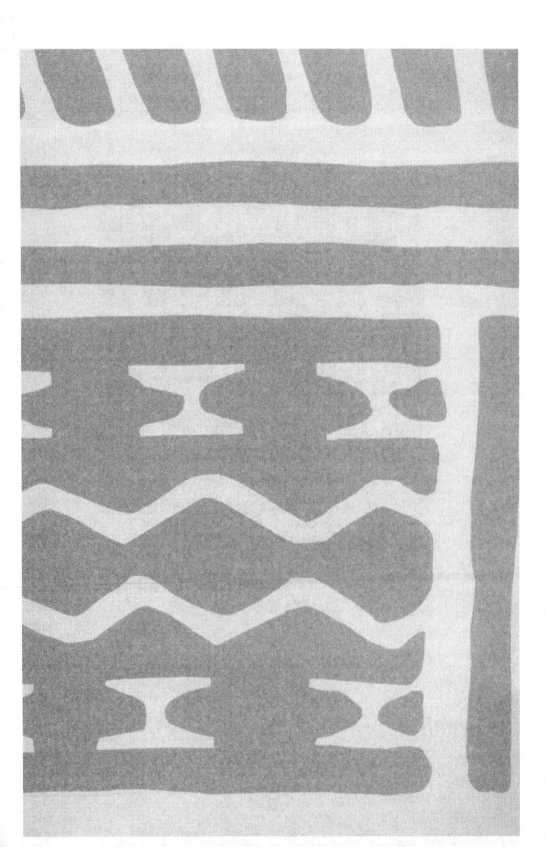

1
a Growing Nightmarish Fear
(1976)

DESMOND MPILO *Tutu was born on October 7, 1931, in Klerks-dorp in the Transvaal, twenty-one years after the formation of the Union of South Africa. The union was formed when two former Afrikaner republics—the South African Republic (the Transvaal) and the Orange Free State, established in the 1850s by descendants of Dutch, German and French settlers but occupied by the British during the Anglo-Boer War in 1900—joined two British colonies—the Cape Colony and Natal—to create the modern South African state. The subjugation of the country's indigenous people, which had started after the first Europeans settled in the Cape in 1652, was confirmed at the foundation of the union in 1910. Under the constitution of the new state, the franchise laws of each province remained in force. Because black South Africans in the Transvaal and the Orange Free State had no vote at all, because the franchise in Natal was so highly qualified that less than 1 percent of the voters' roll were black, and because the nonracial franchise in the Cape was so qualified that only 15 percent of the voters' roll were people of color, colored and black South Africans were for all practical purposes disenfranchised. In addition, only whites could be members of the union parliament. The act establishing the union was approved by legislators of the colonial power, Britain, who rejected the appeals of a predominantly black group of South African leaders which traveled to London to lobby against the racist basis of the constitution of the state.*

From the first years of union and in the face of opposition from the

South African Native National Congress (later the African National Congress), whites of Boer and British descent combined to legislate for segregation in a wide range of fields. The Natives Land Act of 1913 caused particular suffering; it set aside rural reserves covering 7.5 percent of the country for Africans, who then constituted 68 percent of the population, and barred them from buying or leasing other land. Combined with laws which provided for segregated townships for Africans working in urban areas, the Land Act effectively established separate white and black areas. As Allister Sparks, a leading South African journalist, notes in his The Mind of South Africa (Mandarin Paperbacks, 1991), the law began "the most comprehensive system of labour coercion on a racial basis that has been devised since slavery." Among the coercive measures used to channel African workers to where their labor was required and to enforce segregation were the "pass laws," which had their origins in eighteenth-century laws. To move from the reserves, later called homelands, or between urban townships, Africans had to carry a "pass book" identifying them and showing they were entitled to be in "white" areas. Thousands defied the laws, however, to seek work or join their families. Since no housing was provided for the influx of people, the system led to the growth of shanty settlements. An average of 250,000 people a year were arrested for violations of the pass laws between 1916 and 1981.

As Tutu completed his schooling at Johannesburg Bantu High School, more popularly called Madibane High after its principal, pressure against racism and colonialism was mounting in most of the international community, partly as a result of World War II. In South Africa, however, hard-line Afrikaner nationalists replaced an administration representing both Afrikaans- and English-speaking voters in 1948. The new National Party government took power with a mandate to ensure white supremacy in perpetuity and passed, over the next fifteen years, systematic, comprehensive and relentless legislation that would separate South Africans and hold them apart—apartheid, or "apartness." Every individual was to be classified by race—white, African, Indian, or Colored (of mixed origin); interracial sex and marriage were banned; separate public facilities were enforced; urban segregation and separation in the workplace were intensified; and multiracial trade unions were prohibited. Blacks finally lost any semblance of a right to

The Rainbow People of God

vote in national political structures, despite the fact that their influence had been minimal. "By far the most deadly" of the laws, in the view of anti-apartheid campaigner and Anglican priest Trevor Huddleston, was that which imposed government control on African education (Naught for Your Comfort, Collins, 1956, 1977). Until 1953 most African education had been provided by church schools. In speeches to parliament in 1953 and 1954, Hendrik Verwoerd, the minister responsible for black education, said, "There is no place for . . . [Africans] in the European community above the level of certain forms of labor" and that existing schooling misled the black child "by showing him the green pastures of European society in which he is not allowed to graze." This takeover of the educational system led Desmond Tutu to abandon his first career as a teacher—he had followed in the footsteps of his father—and to enter the Anglican priesthood.

Apartheid was implemented in the face of campaigns of defiance, and the government responded to growing militancy by abandoning key civil liberties and suppressing opposition. After sixty-nine Africans were massacred at a demonstration against the pass laws in Sharpeville, south of Johannesburg, in 1960, the government outlawed the two key movements defying it, the African National Congress and the Pan Africanist Congress, which had broken away from the ANC in 1959 and was organized on the principle of black control of the struggle against apartheid. Some members went underground or into exile and resorted to armed rebellion, but they were dealt a serious blow by the arrest and jailing for life of many of their key leaders, including Nelson Mandela. In 1961, further isolating itself from the international community, the South African government declared a republic and simultaneously withdrew from the British Commonwealth, partly in response to criticism of apartheid from African member states, which was supported by Canada and India. By the mid-1960s the government had crushed efforts to stop apartheid.

Between his ordination in 1961 and 1975, the then Father Tutu had been a curate in the Diocese of Johannesburg, studied in London, lectured in theology in South Africa and Lesotho, then returned to London to work for the Theological Education Fund of the World Council of Churches. In South Africa the black consciousness movement was emerging as a political force during the late 1960s and 1970s, and a

The Making of a Peaceful Revolution　　　5

new, strong anti-apartheid trade union movement was beginning, but when Tutu returned from England in 1975, open mass resistance to the government remained suppressed.

At a time when many black political leaders were jailed, were in exile, or were restricted from political activity, Tutu became Dean of St. Mary's Cathedral in Johannesburg, the first black South African to hold such a high post in his church in South Africa's major metropolitan area. Refusing to seek government permission to live in the deanery in an exclusive white suburb, he went to live with most of Johannesburg's black residents in the city's South Western Townships, or Soweto. Early the following year he wrote an open letter to the Prime Minister of the time, B. J. Vorster, warning of the possibility of bloodshed.

May 6, 1976

The Hon. Prime Minister
Mr. John Vorster
House of Assembly
Cape Town
8000

Dear Mr. Prime Minister:
This will be my second letter ever to you. In 1972 after I had been refused a passport to take up a post as Associate Director of the Theological Education Fund, I appealed to you to intervene on my behalf with the appropriate authorities. Your intervention was successful because, soon thereafter, the then Minister of the Interior changed his mind and granted me and my family our passports. I am writing, therefore, optimistically in the hope that this letter will have similar happy results for all of us.

I am writing to you, Sir, in all deep humility and courtesy in my capacity as Anglican Dean of Johannesburg and, therefore, as leader of several thousand Christians of all races in the Diocese of Johannesburg. I am writing to you as one who has come to be accepted by some blacks [Africans, Indians and Coloreds] as one of their spokesmen articulating their deepest aspirations, as one who shares them with equal steadfastness. I am writing to you, Sir, because I know you to be a loving and caring father and husband, a doting grandfather who has experienced the joys and anguish of family life, its laughter and gaiety, its sorrows and pangs. I am writing to you, Sir, as one who is passionately devoted to a happy and stable family life as the indispensable foundation of a sound and healthy society. You have flung out your arms to embrace and hug your children and your grandchildren, to smother them with your kisses, you have loved, you have wept, you have watched by the bed of a sick one whom you loved, you have watched by the deathbed of a beloved relative, you have been a proud father at the wedding of your children, you have shed tears by the graveside of one for whom your heart has been broken. In short, I am writing to you as one human person to another human person, gloriously created in the image of the selfsame God, redeemed by the selfsame Son of God who for all our sakes died on the Cross and rose triumphant from the dead and reigns in glory now at the right hand of the Father; sanctified by the selfsame Holy Spirit who works inwardly in all of us to change our hearts of stone into hearts of flesh. I am, therefore, writing to you, Sir, as one Christian to another, for through our common baptism we have been made members of and are united in the Body of our dear Lord and Saviour, Jesus Christ. This Jesus Christ, whatever we may have done, has broken down all that separates us irrelevantly—such as race, sex, culture, status, etc. In this Jesus Christ we are forever bound together as one redeemed humanity, black and white together.

I am writing to you, Sir, as one who is a member of a race that has known what it has meant in frustrations and hurts, in agony and humiliation, to be a subject people. The history of your own race speaks eloquently of how utterly impossible it is, when once the desire for freedom and self-determination is awakened in a people, for it to be quenched or to be satisfied with anything less than freedom and that self-determination. Your people, against tremendous odds, braved the unknown and faced up to daunting challenges and countless dangers rather than be held down as a subjugated people. And in the end they emerged victorious.* Your

*A reference to Afrikaner resistance to British imperialism. Boers trekked north and east from the Cape after 1836 to escape British colonial control, eventually establishing their own republics. The republics were defeated by the British in the Anglo-Boer War (1899–1902).

people, more than any other section of the white community, must surely know in the very core of their beings, if they were unaware of the lessons of history both ancient and modern, that absolutely nothing will stop a people from attaining their freedom to be a people who can hold their heads high, whose dignity to be human persons is respected, who can assume the responsibilities and obligations that are the necessary concomitants of the freedom they yearn for with all their being. For most blacks this can never be in the homelands because they believe they have contributed substantially to the prosperity of an undivided South Africa. Blacks find it hard to understand why the whites are said to form one nation when they are made up of Greeks, Italians, Portu-guese, Afrikaners, French, Germans, English, etc., and then by some tour de force blacks are said to form several nations—Xhosas, Zulus, Tswanas, etc. The Xhosas and the Zulus, for example, are much closer to one another ethnically than, say, the Italians and the Germans in the white community. We all, black and white together, belong to South Africa against a visiting Argentinian [rugby] side. The South African team won hands down and perhaps for the first time in our sporting history South Africans of all races found themselves supporting vociferously the same side against a common adversary. The heavens did not fall down. Is it fanciful to see this as a parable of what will happen when all South Africans together are given a stake in their country so that they will be ready to defend it against a common foe and struggle for its prosperity vigorously and enthusiastically?

I write to you, Sir, because our Ambassador to the United Nations, Mr. [R. F. "Pik"] Botha, declared [in the UN Security Council in 1974] that South Africa was moving away from discrimination based on race. This declaration excited not only us but the world at large. I am afraid that very little of this movement has been in evidence so far. It is not to move substantially from discrimination when some signs are removed from park benches. These are only superficial changes which do not fundamentally affect the lives of blacks. Husbands and fathers are still separated from their loved ones as a result of the pernicious system of migratory labor which a Dutch Reformed Church synod once castigated as a cancer in South

African society, one which had deleterious consequences on black family life, thus undermining the stability of society which I referred to earlier.* We don't see this much-longed-for movement when we look at the overcrowded schools in black townships, at the inadequate housing and woefully inadequate system of transport, etc.

I write to you, Sir, to give you all the credit due to you for your efforts at promoting détente and dialogue [with black African countries and within neighboring white-ruled states]. In these efforts many of us here wanted to support you eagerly, but we feel we cannot in honesty do this, when external détente is not paralleled by equally vigorous efforts at internal détente. Blacks are grateful for all that has been done for them, but now they claim an *inalienable right to do things for themselves,* in cooperation with their fellow South Africans of all races.

I write to you, Sir, because, like you, I am deeply committed to real reconciliation with justice for all, and to peaceful change to a more just and open South African society in which the wonderful riches and wealth of our country will be shared more equitably. I write to you, Sir, to say with all the eloquence I can command that the security of our country ultimately depends not on military strength and a Security Police being given more and more draconian power to do virtually as they please without being accountable [by law] to the courts of our land, courts which have a splendid reputation throughout the world for fairness and justice. That is why we have called and continue to call for the release of all detainees or that they be brought before the courts where they should be punished if they have been found guilty of indictable offenses. There is much disquiet in our land that people can be held for such long periods in detention and then often either released without being charged or, when charged, usually acquitted; but this does not free them from police harassment. Though often declared innocent by the courts, they are often punished by being banned [again without

*The white Dutch Reformed Church (Nederduitse Gereformeerde Kerk) was the principal church of the Afrikaner ruling elite. The migratory labor system denied African families the right to live with breadwinners in areas designated "white." Most migrant workers were housed in single-sex hostel complexes.

recourse to the courts] or placed under house arrest or immediately re-detained.

How long can a people, do you think, bear such blatant injustice and suffering? Much of the white community by and large, with all its prosperity, its privilege, its beautiful homes, its servants, its leisure, is hag-ridden by a fear and a sense of insecurity. And this will continue to be the case until South Africans of all races are free. Freedom, Sir, is indivisible. The whites in this land will not be free until all sections of our community are genuinely free. Then we will have a security that does not require such astronomical sums to maintain it, huge funds which could have been used in far more creative and profitable ways for the good of our whole community, which would take its rightful place as a leader in Africa and else-where, demonstrating as it will that people of different races can live amicably together. We need one another and blacks have tried to assure whites that they don't want to drive them into the sea. How long can they go on giving these assurances and have them thrown back in their faces with contempt? They say even the worm will turn.

I am writing to you, Sir, because I have a growing nightmarish fear that unless something drastic is done very soon then bloodshed and violence are going to happen in South Africa almost inevitably. A people can take only so much and no more. The history of your own people which I referred to earlier demonstrated this, Vietnam has shown this, the struggle against Portugal has shown this. I wish to God that I am wrong and that I have misread history and the sit-uation in my beloved homeland, my mother country South Africa. A people made desperate by despair, injustice and oppression will use desperate means. I am frightened, dreadfully frightened, that we may soon reach a point of no return, when events will generate a momentum of their own, when nothing will stop their reaching a bloody denouement which is "too ghastly to contemplate," to quote your words, Sir.

I am frightened because I have some experience of the awfulness of violence. My wife and I with our two youngest children stayed for two months in Jerusalem in 1966 and we saw the escalating vio-lence and the mounting tensions between Jew and Arab which pre-

ceded the Six-Day War. I was in Addis Ababa when there was rioting in the streets, a prelude to the overthrow of the dynasty of Haile
Selassie. I was in Uganda just before the expulsion of the Asians
from that country and have returned there since and experienced
the fear and the evil of things there. I have visited the Sudan, ad-
mittedly after the end of the seventeen years of civil strife, but I
could see what this internecine war had done to people and their
property. I have visited Nigeria and the former Biafra and have seen
there the awful ravages of that ghastly civil war on property and on
the souls of the defeated Biafrans. Last year I was privileged to address the General Assembly of the Presbyterian Church in Ireland
in Belfast—and what I saw shook me to the core of my being. We
saw daily on television in Britain horrific pictures of the pillage and
destruction being perpetrated in Vietnam: children screaming from
the excruciating agony of burns caused by napalm bombing, a people rushing helter-skelter, looking so forlorn and bewildered that
one wanted to cry out, "But is there no God who cares in heaven?"
No, I know violence and bloodshed and I and many of our people
don't want that at all.

But we blacks are exceedingly patient and peace-loving. We are
aware that politics is the art of the possible. We cannot expect you
to move so far in advance of your voters that you alienate their support. We are ready to accept some meaningful signs which would
demonstrate that you and your government and all whites really
mean business when you say you want peaceful change. First, accept the urban black as a permanent inhabitant of what is wrongly
called white South Africa, with consequent freehold property
rights. He will have a stake in the land and would not easily join
those who wish to destroy his country. Indeed, he would be willing
to die to defend his mother country and his birthright. Secondly,
and also as a matter of urgency, repeal the pass laws which demonstrate to blacks more clearly than anything else that they are third-
rate citizens in their beloved country. Thirdly, it is imperative, Sir,
that you call a National Convention made up of the genuine leaders
(i.e., leaders recognized as such by their section of the community)
to try to work out an orderly evolution of South Africa into a nonracial, open and just society. I believe firmly that your leadership is

The Making of a Peaceful Revolution   *11*

quite unassailable, that you have been given virtually a blank check by the white electorate and that you have little to fear from a so-called right-wing backlash. For if the things which I suggest are not done soon and a rapidly deteriorating situation arrested, then there will be no right-wing to fear—there will be nothing.

I am writing this letter to you, Sir, during a three-day clergy retreat in Johannesburg, when in the atmosphere of deep silence, worship and adoration and daily services of the Lord's Supper we seek to draw closer to our Lord and try to discover what is the will of God for us and what are the promptings and inspirations of God's Holy Spirit. It is during this time that God seemed to move me to write this letter.

I hope to hear from you, Sir, as soon as you can conveniently respond, because I want to make this correspondence available to the press, preferably with your concurrence, so that all our people, both black and white, will know that from our side we have done all that is humanly possible to do, to appeal, not only to the rank and file of whites but to the highest political figure in the land, and to have issued the grave warning contained in my letter. This flows from a deep love and anguish for my country. I shall soon become Bishop of Lesotho, when I must reside in my new diocese. But I am quite clear in my own mind, and my wife supports me in this resolve, that we should retain our South African citizenship no matter how long we have to remain in Lesotho.

Please may God inspire you to hear us before it is too late, and may he bless you and your government now and always.

Should you think it might serve any useful purpose, I am more than willing to meet with you to discuss the issues I raise here, as you say in Afrikaans, *onder vier oë* [face to face].

Since coming to this Cathedral last year, we have had a regular service, praying for justice and reconciliation in this country, every Friday. And at all services in the Cathedral we pray:

> God bless Africa
> Guard her children
> Guide her rulers and
> Give her peace,
> For Jesus Christ's sake.

And:

> O Lord, make us instruments of Thy peace
> Where there is hatred, let us sow love
> Where there is injury, pardon
> Where there is despair, hope
> Where there is darkness, light
> Where there is sadness, joy.

> O divine Master, grant that we may not so much seek
> to be consoled as to console
> To be understood as to understand
> To be loved as to love;
> For it is in giving that we receive
> It is in pardoning that we are pardoned
> It is in dying that we are born to eternal life.
> Amen.

And we mean it.

Yours respectfully,
Desmond Tutu

During the first few months of 1976 there had been increasing tension between government officials on the one hand and black parents and pupils on the other over attempts to enforce a policy that Afrikaans, regarded as the language of the oppressor, should be an official medium of instruction alongside English in Soweto secondary schools. On May 17 the first students went on strike. Further boycotts followed, and some pupils refused to write exams. There were isolated incidents of violence. Approaches to the Deputy Minister of Bantu Education, Dr. Andries Treurnicht, to defuse the crisis failed. On June 16 pupils at Soweto schools organized a protest march. Armed white police confronted them on their way to Orlando West High School in an attempt to stop them. When the students waved their fists in response, the police launched tear gas into the group. The students responded with stones, and the police opened fire, killing thirteen-year-old Hector Peterson. Rioting spread throughout Soweto, then to other areas, and by June 24 the official death toll was 140. Unrest began to break out in other areas of the country. The years of quiet resistance had come to an end.

In his reply to Tutu's letter, Vorster suggested that the white opposition in parliament had put him up to writing it.

The Rainbow People of God

2
Oh, God, How Long Can We Go On?
(1977)

O N E   O F   the factors which contributed to the spirit of protest among
black pupils was black consciousness, which became a powerful force in
black political debate and activity in South Africa. Advocates had begun to propound black consciousness in the late 1960s, strongly com-
mitting themselves to building black pride, self-reliance and defiance
in the face of state oppression. In 1969 they founded the South African
Students' Organization (SASO), whose first president was Stephen
Bantu Biko, a medical student, and in 1972 they formed the Black
People's Convention (BPC) as an umbrella body. The leaders of the
movement faced continual detention, restriction and other harassment,
culminating in a two-year-long show trial in Pretoria which ended
with five- and six-year jail sentences for nine leaders at the end of
1976.

On August 18, 1977, Steve Biko, who had not been put on trial
but had given evidence for the defense, was detained near Grahamstown in the Eastern Cape. On August 19 he was handed into the
custody of the Security Police in Port Elizabeth. He was denied
exercise and kept naked in a police cell for eighteen days without being questioned, according to police. Interrogation began on September
6. By 7 A.M. on September 7 he had suffered a brain injury, the consequence of at least three blows to the head according to a neurologi-
cal pathologist. He was transported 750 miles naked on the floor of
a police van to Pretoria, where he died on September 12, at least
the tenth political prisoner to die in custody that year. The Minister of

Police, Jimmy Kruger, told a party congress that Biko's death "leaves me cold."

Biko's death focused international attention on racial oppression in South Africa and fueled the domestic unrest which had begun in 1976. The UN Security Council imposed a mandatory arms embargo on South Africa, its first against a member state. The United States sent a large delegation to his funeral and diplomatic representatives of other major Western democracies attended. The government blamed black consciousness for the continuing unrest and, in a move reminiscent of its action against the African National Congress and the Pan Africanist Congress in 1960, it outlawed twenty black consciousness organ-izations and supporting groups, including SASO and the BPC. Most of the organizations' leaders were detained, the major black news-paper, The World, *was banned, and its editor, Percy Qoboza, and other senior black journalists also detained. White sympathizers, notably C. F. Beyers Naudé, a dissident Afrikaner church leader, and Donald Woods, a newspaper editor who had befriended Biko, were also banned. (Woods fled the country and later recorded his story in* I Found My Brother: Steve Biko. *Biko was the subject of a widely shown British television documentary and a play, and in 1987, ten years after his death, Sir Richard Attenborough released* Cry Freedom, *a film about Biko and Woods's friendship, with the American actor Denzel Washington playing Biko.)*

More than 15,000 people attended Biko's funeral in King William's Town in the Eastern Cape on September 25. Desmond Tutu, now Anglican Bishop of Lesotho, was one of the speakers.

When we heard the news "Steve Biko is dead" we were struck numb with disbelief. No, it can't be true! No, it must be a horrible nightmare and we will awake and find that really it is different—that Steve is alive even if it be in detention. But no, dear friends, he is dead and we are still numb with grief and groan with anguish, "Oh, God, where are you? Oh, God, do you really care? How can you let this happen to us?"

It all seems such a senseless waste of a wonderfully gifted person, struck down in the bloom of youth, a youthful bloom that some wanted to see blighted. What can be the purpose of such wanton destruction? God, do you really love us? What must we do which we have not done, what must we say which we have not said a thousand times over, oh, for so many years—that all we want is what belongs to all God's children, what belongs as an inalienable right: a place in the sun in our own beloved mother country. Oh, God, how long can we go on? How long can we go on appealing for a more just ordering of society where we all, black and white together, count not because of some accident of birth or a biological irrelevance, where all of us, black and white, count because we are human persons, human persons created in your own image.

In our grief and through our tears, we recall. Let us recall, my dear friends, that nearly two thousand years ago a young man was done to death and hung like a common criminal on a cross outside a city where they jeered at him and made fun of him. Let us recall how his followers were dejected and quite inconsolable in their grief. It all seemed so utterly meaningless, so utterly futile. This young man, God's own son, Jesus Christ, had come preaching the good news of God's love for all his children. He came seeing himself as one who fulfilled the glorious prophecy of Isaiah:

THE SPIRIT OF the Lord God is upon me; because the Lord hath anointed me to preach good tidings unto the meek; he hath sent me to bind up the brokenhearted, to proclaim liberty to the captives, and the opening of the prison to them that are bound;

To proclaim the acceptable year of the Lord, and the day of vengeance of our God; to comfort all that mourn;

To appoint unto them that mourn in Zion, to give unto them beauty for ashes, the oil of joy for mourning, the garment of praise for the spirit of heaviness; that they might be called trees of righteousness, the planting of the Lord, that he might be glorified.

And they shall build the old wastes, they shall raise up the former desolations, and they shall repair the waste cities, the desolations of many generations.

(Isaiah 61:1–4)

The Making of a Peaceful Revolution   *17*

Because Jesus saw himself as the son, the great liberator, God himself, the God who had sided with a miserable, oppressed and disorganized group of slaves. And this God had taken their side against their oppressors—this great God of the Exodus, with power and might, with an outstretched arm he had led this group of slaves victoriously out of their slavery in Egypt to the freedom of the Promised Land.

Yes, the God Jesus came to proclaim was no neutral sitter on the fence. He took the side of the oppressed, the poor, the exploited, not because they were holier or morally better than their oppressors. No, he was on their side simply and solely because they were oppressed. Yes, this was the good news Jesus came to proclaim—that God was the liberator, the one who set free the oppressed and the poor and exploited. He set them free from all that would make them less than he wanted them to be, fully human persons as free as Jesus Christ showed himself to be. And so all the mighty works which Jesus performed, healing the sick, opening the eyes of the blind, forgiving the sins of all sinners, were to set them free so that they could enjoy the glorious liberty of the children of God. And his followers believed he would restore the kingdom again to Israel. He would set them free from being ruled by the Romans and give them back their political independence. They had placed their hopes on him. And look at him now. This young man in his thirties who had said, "I have come that all might have life and that they might have life in all its fullness," look at him, dead, and all our hopes, said his followers, lie shattered with his death.

The powers of darkness, of evil and of destruction had done their worst, they had killed the Lord of life himself. But that death was not the end. That death was the beginning of a glorious life, the resurrection life. That death was the death of death itself—for Jesus Christ lives for ever and ever. The grave could not hold captive such a gloriously free life. Jesus burst the very bonds of death and what had seemed like an ignominious defeat and complete meaninglessness was proved to be a splendid victory and an event giving meaning to all history. Life has triumphed over death. Light and goodness and love reign forevermore, over hatred and evil and darkness.

We too, like the disciples of Jesus, have been stunned by the death of another young man in his thirties. A young man completely dedicated to the pursuit of justice and righteousness, of peace and reconciliation. A young man completely committed to radical change in our beloved land. Even his worst enemies and detractors knew him as a person of utmost integrity and principle. And those who knew him better loved him as a warmhearted man with a huge sense of fun and yet with a massive intellect. God called Steve to be his servant in South Africa, to speak up on behalf of God, declaring what the will of this God must be in a situation such as ours, a situation of evil and injustice, oppression and exploitation.

God called him to be the founder father of the black consciousness movement, against which we have had tirades and fulminations. It is a movement by which God, through Steve, sought to awaken in the black person a sense of his intrinsic value and worth as a child of God, not needing to apologize for his existential condition as a black person, calling on blacks to glorify and praise God that he had created them black. Steve, with his brilliant mind that always saw to the heart of things, realized that until blacks asserted their humanity and their personhood, there was not the remotest chance for reconciliation in South Africa. For true reconciliation is a deeply personal matter. It can happen only between persons who assert their own personhood and who acknowledge and respect that of others. You don't get reconciled to your dog, do you? Steve knew and believed fervently that being pro-black was not the same thing as being anti-white. The black consciousness movement is not a "hate white movement" despite all you may have heard to the contrary. He had a far too profound respect for persons as persons to want them under ready-made, shop-soiled, secondhand categories.

I want again to appeal, with all the eloquence that I can muster, to our white fellow citizens and our white fellow Christians. We who today still advocate peaceful change and still talk about reconciliation and justice are in grave danger. The danger is that our credibility is being seriously eroded; for while we speak of peace and nonviolence we have the quite inexplicable action of the authorities in stopping those coming to mourn at Steve's funeral, an action that is most provocative. Why? We are answered by bulldozers which destroy the homes of squatters, leaving them without shelter in drenching rain. We thank God for the many whites who have shown compassion to these poor folk [and sheltered them on church property]. We talk of nonviolence but we have the legalized violence that separates husband and father from his wife and family. We have long periods of detention without trial and deaths in detention. We have bannings and banishments.

I want to say, with all the circumspection and sense of responsibility that I can muster, that people can take only so much . . . I have seen too much violence to talk glibly about it, but I do want to issue a serious warning, a warning I am distressed to have to make . . . Please, please for God's sake listen to us while there is just a possibility of reasonably peaceful change. Nothing, not even the most sophisticated weapon, not even the most brutally efficient police, no, nothing will stop people once they are determined to achieve their freedom and their right to humanness. For God's sake let us move away from the edge of the precipice. We may, all of us, black and white, crash headlong to destruction. Oh, God, help us! We cry for our beloved country which has been so wanton in wasting her precious human resources.

We weep with and pray for Ntsiki [Mrs. Biko] and all of Steve's family. We weep for ourselves. But that can't be the end of the story, because despite all that points to the contrary, God cares. He cares about right and wrong. He cares about oppression and injustice. He cares about bulldozers and detentions without trial. And so, paradoxically, we give thanks for Steve and for his life and his death. Because, you see, Steve started something that is quite unstoppable. The powers of injustice, of oppression, of exploitation, have done their worst and they have lost. They have lost because they are immoral and wrong and our God, the God of the Exodus, the liberator God, is a God of justice and liberation and goodness. Our cause, the cause of justice and liberation, must triumph because it is moral and just and right. Many who support the present unjust system in this country know in their hearts that they are upholding a system that is evil and unjust and oppressive, and which is utterly abhorrent and displeasing to God. There is no doubt whatsoever that freedom is coming. Yes, it may be a costly struggle still. The darkest hour, they say, is before the dawn. We are experiencing the birth pangs of a new South Africa, a free South

Africa, where all of us, black and white together, will walk tall; where all of us, black and white together, will hold hands as we stride forth on the Freedom March to usher in the new South Africa where people will matter because they are human beings made in the image of God.

We thank and praise God for giving us such a magnificent gift in Steve Biko, and for his sake and for the sake of ourselves, black and white together, for the sake of our children, black and white together, let us dedicate ourselves anew to the struggle for the liberation of our beloved land, South Africa. Let us all, black and white together, not be filled with despondency and despair. Let us blacks not be filled with hatred and bitterness. For all of us, black and white together, shall overcome, nay, indeed have already overcome.

If God is on our side, who can be against us? What can separate us from the love of Christ? Can affliction or hardship? Can persecution, hunger, nakedness, peril or the sword? We are being done to death for they sake all day long, as the scripture says; we are being treated like sheep for slaughter—and yet in spite of all, overwhelming victory is ours through him who loves us.

Part Two

CHURCH
CONFRONTS STATE
The South African Council of Churches

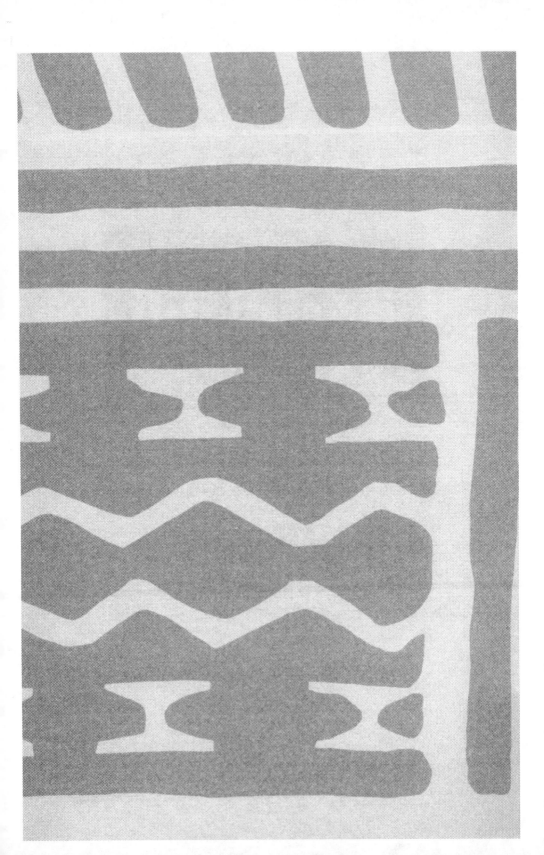

3

We Drink Water to Fill Our Stomachs

(1979)

*DESMOND TUTU returned to South Africa from Lesotho soon af-
ter the crisis brought about by the killing of Steve Biko. In March 1978
he became General Secretary of the South African Council of Churches,
a post he held until 1985. The SACC included the multiracial churches
which had grown out of missionary work and many indigenous African
churches but not the white Afrikaans reformed churches which provided
scriptural justification for apartheid. All told, the council had twenty
member churches and four observer member churches, claiming to represent nearly 15 million Christians.*

*Sections of the churches represented in the SACC joined the upsurge
of resistance after 1976. In 1979 the national conference of the SACC
approved a resolution that advocated civil disobedience as a response to
racist laws. Tutu had been deeply affected by an encounter with a
young victim of forced relocation in Zweledinga in the Eastern Cape on
a visit in June 1979, as noted in his report to the SACC national conference in July:*

I MET THIS little girl who lives with her widowed mother
and sister. I asked whether her mother received a pension or
any other grant and she said, "No." "Then how do you live?" I
asked. "We borrow food," she said. "Have you ever returned

the food you have borrowed?" "No." "What happens if you can't
borrow food?" "We drink water to fill our stomachs."

Tutu began to call for economic pressure on the government. In September 1979 he stated, in an interview on Danish television, that it was "rather disgraceful" for Denmark to buy South African coal, provoking a furor. In October he was called to a meeting with the Minister of Justice, A. L. Schlebusch, and Piet Koornhof, Minister of Cooperation and Development (who was responsible for administering the lives of black people under apartheid), and told to withdraw the statement or have action taken against him. He refused and later that month told the conference of the Methodist Church of Southern Africa, "I will do all I can to destroy this diabolical system [of forced removals] whatever the cost to me." With his increasing activity Tutu came into prominence, and the editor of this collection observed in an article on the national conference that the new General Secretary "appears destined to be known as one of the country's great churchmen."

In the face of rising domestic and international pressure, the government began a retreat from hard-line apartheid, adjusting some policies but not conceding in any way white control of the country. In September 1978, P. W. Botha had become Prime Minister, succeeding B. J. Vorster, who resigned in the wake of a scandal over the misappropriation of public funds, used for pro-apartheid propaganda by the government's Department of Information. Botha pursued reform, alienating the right wing of his party but enlisting the support of business leaders who believed elements of apartheid stunted economic growth. The objective of eventually removing African people from "white" areas was gradually abandoned and their permanent residence in urban areas was accepted. The independent labor movement forced legal recognition of nonracial unions. The law underpinning the reservation of jobs for whites was abolished. The government began to improve the physical conditions of African urban residents in the hope of co-opting a black middle class. But "grand apartheid," which denied black South Africans any role in the central government, remained. Despite the opposition of most homeland leaders, four ethnic homelands were given "independence" between 1976 and 1981—the Transkei, Bophuthatswana, Venda and Ciskei—and their inhabitants, as well as black Africans living elsewhere but assigned to them, lost their South African citizenship and thus the right to any say in the government.

In December 1979, Desmond Tutu gave the ruling body of the Anglican Church in Southern Africa, its Provincial Synod, a wide-ranging overview of what motivated the SACC and of what it was doing. Among the activities he listed were those which were leading to conflict with the government.

The Transcendent God

The God whom we worship is wonderfully transcendent. The Psalmist exclaims in Psalm 139 that his ways are too wonderful for him and somewhere the prophet Isaiah hears God saying, "My thoughts are not like your thoughts and your ways are not like my ways." This God is utterly unlike anything or anyone else and so even to behold his face is an impossibility for a human person because to do so would result in the death of the beholder.

It is because of this utter holiness and otherness of God that Israel is forbidden to make an image of God. There is nothing that can be a fitting symbol and image for such a supreme being. And so St. John in his gospel sums it all up by saying, "God is spirit."

This God dwells in light inaccessible, so that the very angels veil their eyes in his presence. He is unknowable except insofar as he makes himself known.

Jesus, the Man for Others

And yet when this God wanted to intervene decisively in the affairs of his creature, man, he did not come as a spiritual being. He did not come as an angel. The Epistle to the Hebrews says, "It is not angels, mark you, that he takes to himself but the sons of Abraham." No, he became a human being. It further says, "He was like unto us in all things, sin excepted." He came in a really human and physical way.

His mother became pregnant and he was born as a helpless baby depending on mother and father for protection, for feeding, for love and teaching. When they looked for him in the houses of kings and the high and mighty, he was born in a stable as one of the lowly and the despised.

He worked as the village carpenter, knowing what it meant for a mother to lose her only coin and have to light a candle and sweep out the house diligently to find the coin and to rejoice at the finding. He walked this earth as we walk it. He grew tired, so that he could fall asleep out of sheer exhaustion in a boat even in the middle of a raging storm. He thirsted, so that he broke social conventions and asked for a drink from a woman, and a Samaritan woman at that. He was so fully human that he yearned for human companionship and feared that his best friends would also desert him because of the hardness of his teaching. "Will ye also leave me?" was his wistful question. And he went about doing good. He did the most physical and materialistic things. When people were hungry, he did not just say, "Pray about it." No, he ordered his disciples to feed them. He took bread and fish, gave thanks, broke and gave. He forgave sins; he healed the sick; he cleansed lepers; he opened the eyes of the blind and the ears of the deaf; he made the lame whole again, raised the dead to life and preached the good news of God's love for all his children and about the coming kingdom of this God.

Do you recall the answer he sent back to John, who was in prison? John wanted to know whether Jesus was the long-expected Messiah. Jesus told his disciples to tell John the things that they heard and saw. These were the signs of the kingdom of his father and the proof of who he was for those with eyes to see.

In his first recorded sermon, in chapter 4 of Luke's gospel [referring to God's choosing him to "preach good tidings unto the meek"], he used the words found in Isaiah 61. They appear to be the words he used to characterize his own ministry. He had been sent therefore, according to those words, to preach the gospel to those whom we call the marginalized ones of society, the scum and riffraff, to bind up the brokenhearted, proclaiming freedom to captives and liberty to prisoners, to comfort those who mourn.

There is nothing that might be called otherworldly about this ministry of Jesus. He scandalized the religious leaders of his day, the prim and proper ones, because he consorted with the social and religious pariahs of his day: the tax collectors who were despised and hated because they collaborated with the Romans. His friends were the ladies of easy virtue who went about with uncovered heads, who made public spectacles of themselves at parties, clutching the feet of strange young men and weeping copiously over them and wiping them with their long hair, having wastefully poured expensive oil on the heads of these young men. Such were his friends, the ones who were looked down upon. No wonder one of the favorite titles for Jesus today, which captivates so many, is calling him *the man for others.* You will recall, too, in his parable of the last judgment, his describing what will determine whether we are fit or not fit for heaven. And the criteria have nothing about them that you could call religious or otherworldly in the narrow sense. We qualify ourselves for heaven by whether we have fed the hungry, clothed the naked, or visited the sick and those imprisoned. And Jesus says that to do these things to the least of his brethren is to have done them as to him.

What we note, therefore, is that we could not accuse our Lord of using religion as a form of escapism from the harsh realities of life as most people live and experience it. The gibe of the Marxist, that religion is an opiate of the people, promising them "pie in the sky when you die," could not apply to him. He knew that people want their pie here and now, today and not in some future tomorrow. A postmortem pie is an oddity in any case.

We need to remind ourselves constantly that Jesus was heir to the prophetic tradition. You can't read any of the major prophets such as Isaiah, Amos, Hosea and Jeremiah without being struck by at least one thing. They all condemned as worthless religiosity a concern with offering God worship when we were unmindful of the sociopolitical implications of our religion. Such worship and religion they condemned roundly as quite unacceptable to God and for that reason worthless and an abomination. For Jesus, as for them, all of life belongs as a whole to God, both its secular and its sacred aspects. They could not have understood our peculiar habit of compartmentalizing life, nor could he . . .

The Making of a Peaceful Revolution   **29**

Jesus, the Man of God, the Man of Prayer

But having said all that about Jesus Christ, it is important to stress that that was only half the truth about him. An equally important truth was that he was a man of prayer, a man of God. Right at the outset of his public ministry, he was baptized in the river Jordan by John the Baptist when he saw the heavens opened and the Holy Spirit descending on him as a dove. Luke records that at that moment Jesus was praying. So we are given some glimpses of our Lord's intimate communion with his father, which formed his lifeblood. Thus we can understand his cry of dereliction and anguish, "My God, why hast thou forsaken me?" when our sins blotted out for him his experience of the nearness of God the Father. Prayer and communion with the father were like breathing to him. And we see him going into a forty-day retreat there to learn something about the nature of his vocation as a messiah, that people needed more than just bread or spectacular miracles. Luke especially tells us of several other occasions when Jesus prayed, as on the Mount of Transfiguration, as on the night before he chose the Twelve, as in the garden before his arrest and as on the Cross.

So we conclude that prayer and spirituality were central in the life of our Lord and that indeed he could have been the man for others only because first and foremost he had been the man of God.

Consequences for the Church and the Council of Churches

For us, his followers, it cannot be otherwise. This twofold movement and pattern in our Lord's life must be ours as well. And so for the Council of Churches an authentic spirituality is central and crucial. Prayer and worship and the sacraments and Bible reading take first place in the life of the South African Council of Churches. Our belief is that a relevant and authentic spirituality cannot but constrain us to be involved, as we are involved, in the sociopolitical realm. It is precisely our encounters with Jesus in worship and the sacraments, in

Bible reading and meditation, that force us to be concerned about the hungry, about the poor, about the homeless, about the banned and the detained, about the voiceless whose voice we seek to be. How can you say you love God whom you have not seen and hate the brother whom you have? He who loves God must love his brother also.

We declare the Lordship and Kingship of God—we declare that he is Lord of all life, that his writ runs everywhere.

And so our daily staff prayers are not optional extras. They are an integral part of the timetable in Diakonia House, Braamfontein [in Johannesburg], when we read the scriptures and sing praises to God. Once a month we have a Eucharist celebrated in the house. At the two-day executive committee meetings every three months, we start with a substantial Bible study and on the second day we always have a Eucharist. Once a year the senior executive staff have a two- to three-day retreat. We want to affirm that it is not our political creed that makes us be involved as we are with the families of political prisoners and those detained without trial, or the people who lead a twilight existence as banned persons. No, it is not our politics. It is our Christian faith that says, "Thus saith the Lord."

Nearly everything we do is approved either by the national conference which is held annually and where all the member churches can voice their disagreement at the direction, programs and policy of the council. Quarterly the churches have another means of control through the executive committee, which vets our financial conduct through a finance committee that meets twice a month. Our accounts are audited by a reputable firm in Johannesburg. These are tabled in the conference and are always available for anybody who wants to inspect them. Mr. [Jimmy] Kruger [the former Minister of Police] made some innuendo last year saying we should account for how we spent R7 million [US $8.3 million at 1979 exchange rates] we had received from overseas over three years. One of my sadnesses is that 90 percent of our financial support comes from overseas and only 10 percent from local sources. In part it is because our churches are hardly self-supporting. My own church still receives a fair amount of support in people and money from overseas. Secondly, I think it is because many people are uneasy about what they call our political involvement. But that involvement is dictated to us by our Lord. We are obeying the command of Jesus Christ, who said the two great commandments of the law are that we love God with all our being and our neighbor as ourselves. We had much rather obey God than man.

The churches have a further opportunity of controlling the council in the divisional committees which determine the policy and program of each of the fourteen divisions of the council. For instance we have the Division of Mission and Evangelism. It is concerned with spreading the Gospel of Jesus Christ and helping the churches win people for our Lord. It is engaged in unity matters, to try to help reunite the broken body of Christ. In this division is to be found our unemployment project, which is there to help the churches develop programs for combating the escalating unemployment in our midst.

We have the African Bursary Fund, which handles bursaries at the secondary school level for children in rural areas. This is because urban children are relatively better served with the availability of scholarships. We also have in this division the University and Technical Bursaries Program. You know that last year we had eight hundred applicants and could give only seventy scholarships. Recently we were able to obtain R50,000 [US $59,000] a year for three years from German churches to mount a crash program to train black professionals. We will be able to give six scholarships a year for five years to enable people to train as doctors, dentists, vets, chartered accountants, etc., in addition to those who benefit from the other university bursary fund.

Our communications cluster produces *Kairos*, a monthly newspaper, and *The Journal of Theology for Southern Africa*, a prestigious journal much respected in academic circles. The Department of Theological Education; Choir Resources; and Ecumenical Education—we have many divisions that deal with largely churchy affairs. People may be surprised to learn that we are in fact so ecclesiastical.

We have other divisions—for example, Home and Family Life, which is concerned about the sanctity of marriage, about the deleterious effects of the migratory labor system, about illegitimacy and prostitution, and is involved in youth work. This division has the part-time services of that outstanding Christian person Sheena Duncan to help set up advice offices all over the country and to train black women to staff them, helping people to claim what residual rights they have.

The Dependents' Conference (DC), which serves banned persons and their families as well as the dependents of political prisoners, is currently looking after about seven hundred families of political prisoners, who receive a maximum of the piffling amount of R57 [US $67] a month. This means that for this class of persons we disburse from this division alone nearly R40,000 [US $47,000] per month or R480,000 [US $566,000] a year. I believe it is possible to raise the grants to about R100 [US $118] per month. I have received, unusually, R50 [US $59] from a black parish for this work. If we could find a thousand churches or congregations to do likewise, that would bring in R50,000 [US $59,000]. It can happen and I know that you can let it happen and so I want to ask, if a thousand why not ten thousand, which could bring in R500,000 [US $590,000]. I think that too could happen. There are more than ten thousand parishes and congregations of all denominations in the Republic [of South Africa]. The Dependents' Conference also arranges for relatives to visit their folk on Robben Island [where black political prisoners were jailed]. You can imagine what a visit from a wife or other relative must mean for someone sentenced to a minimum of five years or even to life imprisonment. Through the generosity of the Diocese of Cape Town, DC has been able to lease at a very nominal rent Cowley House as a hostel to accommodate these visitors who come from all over the country and Namibia. They can usually fit in two visits during their stay—two visits for the whole year.

Jesus said, "When I was in prison you visited me." That is our mandate for this work. DC also tries to rehabilitate released political prisoners by helping them set up self-help projects. We helped a man who had seven children. He died and we continued to help his family. Now the widow has died and DC is the only source of sustenance for the orphaned children. It is strange that it is for work such as this, when we are trying to obey our Lord, that the SACC is in bad odor.

Fortunately those who control the SACC, its executive and national conference, believe there can be no argument whose laws must be obeyed when there is a clash between God's laws and those of man. We constantly reiterate we are not looking for any confrontation with the state. . . .

The Making of a Peaceful Revolution   33

The Asingeni Fund came into existence in June 1976 to provide relief and help with funeral expenses to families affected by the uprisings of that year. Most of the funds have been used to provide legal aid. We do not necessarily support the accused or condone their alleged crimes, but we believe firmly in the principle that each person is entitled to the best legal defense possible. We are assisting in the proper administration of justice and deserve to be commended rather than to be vilified. We have had some significant statistics. In those cases where we have provided legal assistance we have notched up an acquittal rate of between 70 and 75 percent. Where people have been undefended the conviction rate has been as high as 80 percent. Recently through legal services that the SACC provided, a man sentenced to twelve years on Robben Island was acquitted on appeal. One such case is justification enough for our continuing this work.

My dear friends, what are we as Christians doing about the arbitrary curtailment of individual freedoms that happen through bannings? Do we say, as a letter in the *Rand Daily Mail* on Tuesday, December 4, said, that there is no banning without a reason—there can't be smoke without fire? Are we ready to accept this serious erosion of the rule of law without so much as a whimper? If there is a reason for relegating our brothers and sisters to a twilight existence as nonpersons [through bannings], why is this reason not produced and tested in an impartial court of law? Do you really think the Nationalist government would consign Mrs. Winnie Mandela [an activist and the wife of the imprisoned ANC leader, Nelson Mandela] to Brandfort [a remote rural town] if they had evidence which would vindicate them before the world, evidence which would satisfy a court of law? Supposing we granted that that might be the case with people who are banned who have been outside prison—can you really believe that there is a reason for banning someone who has just completed a twelve-year prison sentence on Robben Island? Why want him to be a prisoner at his own cost? . . .

My friends, is it being emotional or melodramatic to say that it is becoming increasingly criminal to be a Christian in South Africa? Well, try employing a so-called illegal black—you are told it is better to increase the unemployment figures and to consign people to the scrap heap of discarded people in the resettlement camps or the home-lands.* What is the church of God doing about it? What are we doing about it all? I believe we should tell people who are banned to ignore their banning orders and let us support them when there are conse-quences. I think the churches should mount a massive campaign of support through positive noncooperation with the implementation of immoral, unchristian and unjust laws. Perhaps I should say that churches should first urge the government to lift all banning orders forthwith, and failing this to make it impossible to apply unchristian and immoral laws.

The SACC tries to maintain links between our South African churches and the worldwide community . . . We hope we can share . . . experiences and insights with our fellow Christians in South Africa. We are linked with many Christians in other lands in very strong and close bonds of fellowship. They are linked with you as well in the body of our Lord and Saviour Jesus Christ.

The General Secretary is not always merely negative and critical of the authorities. He often sends congratulatory messages to the government—most recently we assured Mr. [P. W.] Botha of our prayers for his meeting with business leaders. We have com-mended him publicly for his courage and praised Dr. [Piet] Koornhof, of whom I am quite fond, for his reprieve of Crossroads and Alex-andra Township.† Dr. Koornhof always writes back apprecia-tively . . .

We believe passionately in the future of a nonracial South Africa and as an earnest of this we have called for a Pilgrimage of Hope, due to take place next July. Last August I was at Taizé in the South of France, the home of the ecumenical Protestant religious community headed by Brother Roger. When I was there about 5,000 young peo-

*The government had increased the fines levied on employers convicted of hiring black people who were in "white areas" illegally. The "resettlement" camps were the areas in the homelands to which Africans were forcibly removed under the policy of racial separation.
†When Koornhof took office late in 1978 the government was intent on destroying the Crossroads settlement in Cape Town, in which people defying the pass laws lived, and was also removing families from Alexandra Township in Johannesburg and turn-ing the area into one of single-sex hostels for migrant workers. In 1989 Koornhof's de-partment backed down from these positions after protest campaigns.

The Making of a Peaceful Revolution   35

ple from all over the world were at Taizé. One Sunday morning I attended the Eucharist in the packed Church of Reconciliation in a service held in several languages. I had a vision of young South Africans of all races in Taizé, loving, playing, worshipping, working and roughing it together for the sake of racial harmony. I even had the number in the party—144, from the 144,000 marked with God's seal in Revelation 7. We plan to spend a week in the Holy Land and about two weeks in Taizé and Geneva. The community have generously already said they will foot the bill for the whole party during their ten-day stay in Taizé. Please pray for God's blessing on this pilgrimage.

We in the SACC believe in a nonracial South Africa where people count because they are made in the image of God. So the SACC is neither a black nor a white organization. It is a Christian organization with a definite bias in favor of the oppressed and the exploited ones of our society. In a small way we in the SACC offices are first fruits of this new South Africa. We have nearly all the races of South Africa, belonging to most of the major denominations, working together as a team headed by a General Secretary who happens to be black. The sun, so far as I can make out, still rises in the east and sets in the west. I have not noticed that the sky has fallen because whites might have to take instructions from blacks. They are not whites or blacks, no, they are Wolfram, Thom, Anne, Margaret, Father Tutu. If it can happen there, as it has happened, say, at St. Mary's Cathedral [in Johannesburg] or the Federal Theological Seminary [in the Eastern Cape], why can't it happen more universally?

We are committed to liberation. This is not the other side of the coin to apartheid. No, the obverse of liberation is damnation. Liberation is what the Gospel of Jesus Christ spells out in a situation of injustice, oppression and deprivation, such as most blacks experience in the land of their birth. Liberation is through and through biblical and evangelical. You would have to scrap a substantial section of the biblical and Christian tradition if you marginalized liberation. The divine act of salvation par excellence in the Old Testament was the Exodus, an act of redemption, an act of liberation which was the founding act for the establishment of Israel as a people. You can't understand the Old Testament at all if you discount this primordial act of deliverance which God effected, first through Moses and then through Joshua.

The Gospel according to Matthew depicts Jesus as the second and greater Moses, who also goes to a mountaintop to deliver God's law, this time contained in the Sermon on the Mount. The name Jesus is from the Greek form of Joshua, so he is to be the second Joshua to lead God's people from their bondage to sin and to all that makes us less than what God intended us to be, into the promised land of what Romans calls the glorious liberty of the children of God. Jesus describes himself as the ransom, and the ransom is paid to set free those who are kidnapped. It is more than just a picturesque figure of speech, because in John's Gospel we hear him say, "If the son sets you free you will be truly free." He says, "The truth will make you free." Even his mighty works, his miracles, are actions to set God's children free from all kinds of bondage. So when a woman is cured of a disease he exclaims that this daughter of Abraham has been liberated from the chains of Satan.

Luke describes the subject of Christ's conversation with Moses and Elijah on the Mount of Transfiguration as concerning his departure to be accomplished in Jerusalem. Perhaps coincidentally, the Greek word to describe this departure is Exodus—does it ring a bell? We are told in Galatians that we must be free with the freedom which Christ has given us, this Christ who has led captivity captive, who has bought us with his blood to be priests and kings to his God, so that we are no longer our own, because we have been bought with a price. To excise the liberation theme from the Bible would be to leave us with a more truncated Bible than Marcion's. [Marcion, a heretic who died in A.D. 160, rejected the Old Testament and reduced the New Testament to Luke's Gospel and ten edited letters from Paul.] It would be an emasculated Gospel utterly unacceptable to me because it would have nothing to say to my condition and to that of most blacks. Such a Gospel I reject.

Indeed the liberation is to be set free from sin, the most fundamental bondage, but Jesus was a Jew and he would have known nothing about an ethereal act of God—God's liberation would have to have real consequences in the political, social and economic spheres or it was no Gospel at all. It was liberation from bondage and liberation for the service of God and of his creation, liberation so that we might become fully human with a humanity to be measured by nothing less than the humanity of Christ himself.

It is a glorious prospect and to help bring this about is the task of God's church. But we must not be starry-eyed. We must face up to harsh reality. We are, in Jesus Christ, completely one with a unity that transcends all sorts of barriers—of race, sex, color, culture, etc. But existentially we know we are divided. You can be sure that the bulk of white Christians [in South Africa] and the bulk of black Christians are on opposite sides on quite crucial matters and these tensions are putting our unity to strenuous testing. Most white Christians execrate the World Council of Churches [for giving humanitarian grants to liberation movements in exile]. Most black Christians sing its praises. Most white Christians believe you must do your military service and defend South Africa. Most black Christians believe South Africa is indefensible morally and, therefore, militarily under the present dispensation. Most white Christians think that our [the liberation movements'] "boys on the border" are terrorists. Most black Christians believe them to be truly freedom fighters [serving in the liberation movements]. Most white Christians support more foreign investment in South Africa. Many blacks (I won't put it higher because they are not free to say what they really believe) would want economic sanctions to be applied to South Africa if this will bring about fundamental change reasonably peacefully. Most whites see black political prisoners as justly condemned criminals, whereas the vast majority of blacks regard them as heroes and as their leaders. Most whites are dazzled by what they believe to be real change happening in South Africa under the scintillating performances of the Prime Minister. Most blacks do not think so yet.

And it is futile to think that blacks will be satisfied with economic and social advancement—surely crumbs, even though they could be substantial crumbs of concessions from the master's table. These economic and social privileges will always be at risk because they depend on the whim of those who wield political power. There will be no real security, peace and justice until blacks have a significant part in political decision making in an undivided South Africa. Anything else is really fiddling while Rome burns.

God is good and in his mercy he has provided us with an object lesson on how not to solve the political and racial crisis of a country. That object lesson is Rhodesia [where there was a bloody liberation war before the creation of an independent Zimbabwe in 1980].

There will be no security, peace, justice or reconciliation while we chase the chimera of independent homelands and while we cause untold and unnecessary suffering, utterly diabolical . . . [by removing people and resettling them there]. I myself will forever be haunted by the specter of the little girl in Zweledinga who said, "We drink water to fill our stomachs" when they could not borrow food. That suffering is what has tipped the scales for me in calling for economic pressure on this country. Frankly, I am not impressed by a sudden upsurge of white altruism about a possible future suffering of blacks that might happen as a result of such pressures. Many white people benefit from present black suffering in cheap labor, in migratory labor, without their losing too much sleep over the matter. And the government could stop this policy immediately if they wanted to. Until they do, I will certainly do all I can to muster international support for that pressure to get us to the negotiating table.

I love to be loved and it has been a horrible pain to experience the hatred, vituperation and hostility of whites because of my Denmark coal statement. (I am thankful for the many white friends who have supported me even when they disagreed with what I said.) If I could have released only a fraction of the feeling against resettlements and population removals that my Danish statement did, I would sing Alleluia. It is almost as if I had said, "Black men, go on the rampage and rape white women."

Conclusion

Humanly speaking, it seems quite hopeless. But we are not alone. Man, this is God's world. He is in charge. The kingdoms of this world are becoming the Kingdom of our God and of his Christ and he shall reign for ever and ever. Hey, man, we have been given the ministry of reconciliation, of liberation, of justice, of peace and of love. And I believe passionately with all my being in that ministry and in him who has called us to his service. We are they who believe in the resurrection from the dead. That is our guarantee that no encircling gloom can snuff out the light of Christ, the light of love, joy, peace, justice and reconciliation.

The resurrection of Jesus is our guarantee that right has triumphed and will triumph over wrong, that good has triumphed and will triumph over evil; is our guarantee that love has triumphed and will triumph over hate. You and I know that Jesus has broken down all kinds of walls of separation. You and I know despite all the evidence to the contrary that we, black and white together, are one in the Lord, we, black and white together, are one in the Spirit. You and I know that we will hold hands, black and white together, with our heads held high as we stride into the glorious future which God holds out to us, black and white together, as we work with him for the fulfillment of the vision of St. John the Divine:

AFTER THIS I looked, and there was an enormous crowd—no one could count all the people! They were from every race, tribe, nation, and language, and they stood in front of the throne and of the Lamb, dressed in white robes and holding palm branches in their hands.

They called out in a loud voice: "Salvation comes from our God, who sits on the throne, and from the Lamb!"

All the angels stood round the throne, the elders, and the four living creatures. Then they threw themselves face downward in front of the throne and worshipped God, saying, "Amen! Praise, glory, wisdom, thanksgiving, honor, power, and might belong to our God for ever and ever! Amen!"

(Revelation 7:9–12)

4

A Deep and Passionate Love for Our Land

(1980)

I n 1 9 8 0 *there was a new surge of school boycotts around the country. Pupils from Colored schools played a more prominent part than in the 1976 unrest, and a fifteen-year-old schoolboy was killed in a Cape Town protest in May, sparking a complete boycott in the area. Church leaders themselves took part in an illegal march in Johannesburg in May, protesting the detention of a colleague from a community where there was a school boycott, and spent a night in jail awaiting their court appearance. The exiled ANC, its ranks swelled by young activists who fled the country after the unrest of 1976 and 1977, was able to launch renewed sabotage attacks. Percy Qoboza, who had emerged from detention to edit a new newspaper, began a campaign for the release of jailed political leaders by making a front-page "Free Mandela" appeal.*

In June, the SACC asked for a meeting with Prime Minister Botha because of "a rapidly deteriorating situation—spreading strikes and boycotts, explosive church-state confrontation and mounting hard-arm tactics by the police against peaceful demonstrators . . ." Despite opposition from some churches and after wrangling over the terms of the meeting, a delegation of leaders, led by SACC president Sam Buti, met Botha and key members of his cabinet in Pretoria on August 7.

This was Desmond Tutu's contribution, delivered in two sections during the proceedings.

Thank you very much, Mr. Prime Minister. I, too, wish to express the depth of my gratitude for your agreement to meet with us and I want to reiterate what I mentioned in my letter to you, Sir, that this meeting is a meeting which is surrounded by the prayers of many Christians, both in South Africa and in other parts of the world. We have come in the same spirit of Christian and brotherly love.

We are moved by a deep and passionate love for our land. We are moved by a true patriotism. As I said in the speech which you have quoted, Sir, we certainly have no political axes to grind and I think that that should be underlined. The same Gospel of Jesus Christ which compels us to reject apartheid . . . or whatever else it may be called, as totally unchristian, is the selfsame Gospel that constrains us to work for justice, for peace and for reconciliation. God has given us a mandate to be ministers, as well, of his reconciliation.

We thank God that you and your government have come to recognize that the destiny of the peoples of South Africa cannot be decided by one group alone. We want to urge you, Sir, yet again, to do what I think you have recognized, to negotiate for orderly change by calling a national convention where our common future can be mapped out by the acknowledged leaders of every section of our South African population. To this end we believe fervently that the political leaders in jail, in detention and exile must be permitted to attend such a convention. After all, your predecessor, Mr. Vorster, counseled Mr. Ian Smith [the Prime Minister of Rhodesia] to release black political leaders and sit around a conference table with them to try to hammer out a solution for their country.

It was your government which tried out a scheme similar to this in the Turnhalle talks relating to Namibia.* Why should this way of dealing with apparently intractable problems be one that is for export only? We want to stress that the churches made this call for a national convention long before it became official Progressive Federal Party policy [the official opposition party in the white parlia-

*From 1975 to 1977 white and black members of the ethnically based governing structures set up by South Africa in the former trust territory of Namibia, a bordering state, held meetings to draw up a plan for interim government of the territory. The meetings took place at the Turnhalle building in the Namibian capital, Windhoek, and excluded the territory's principal liberation movement, Swapo.

ment]. I myself made such a call to Mr. Vorster in my letter to him before the outbreak of the Soweto uprising in 1976.

We believe that there can be no real peace, Sir, in our beloved land until there is fundamental change. General [Magnus] Malan [the Minister of Defense] has said that the crisis in South Africa is 20 percent military and 80 percent political. You yourself have very courageously declared [in a 1979 speech] that whites must be ready to adapt or die. This adapting, or change, has to go to the heart of the matter, to the dismantling of apartheid and not dealing with what many consider peripheral matters where we seem to be working only for an improvement in the situation rather than changing it fundamentally.

Please believe us when we say that there is much goodwill left, although we have to add that time and patience are running out. Hatred, bitterness and anger are growing. Unless something is done to demonstrate your intentions and those of your government to bring about fundamental change leading to political power sharing, then we are afraid that the so-called ghastly alternative will be upon us. We recognize, Sir, that this kind of fundamental change cannot happen overnight and so we suggest that only four things need to be done to give real hope that it is going to happen. We can assure you that if we go along this route, you, Sir, will gain most of South Africa and the world while losing some of your party dissidents.

One, please let the government commit themselves to a common citizenship for all South Africans in an undivided South Africa. If this does not happen, then I am frightened, we are frightened that we will have to kiss goodbye to peaceful change.

Two, please abolish the pass laws. Nothing is more hateful in a hateful system for blacks than these laws. Yes, let it be a phased process because none of us want to have a chaotic country. But, Sir, I wish God could give me the words that could describe the dramatic change that would occur in relationships in this country if . . . the real abolition of the pass laws were to happen.

Third, please stop immediately all population removals and the uprooting of people. It is in my view totally evil and has caused untold misery.

Fourth, please set up a uniform educational system. We are glad to note, Sir, that you have agreed to the setting up of a commission to look into this matter. We want to suggest in relation to this that all universities be declared open and that black universities should appoint blacks who have credibility in the black community. Otherwise we fear that the unrest in these institutions will remain endemic.

Those are the four points. If these four things were done as starters we would be the first to declare out loud: "Please give the government a chance, they seem in our view now to have embarked on the course of real change." I certainly would be one of the first to shout this out from the rooftops. Then in that process we would all have real security. Not a security that depends on force for its upholding. What a wonderful country we can have when we all, black and white, will walk with our heads high to this glorious future together. Because we will have a nonracial society, a just society where everyone, black and white, will count because each, black and white, is a child of God, as we all believe, created in his image. And you, Sir, will go down in history as a truly great man.

If this does not happen now, urgently, I fear that we will have to say we have had it. But God is good and God loves all of us and God has filled this country with his Holy Spirit. Let us be open to that Holy Spirit and share our fears and anxieties. Thank you. . . .

I want to reiterate here that I have a very deep love for my country and I refuse to take second place to anyone on this point. I am committed to finding and helping us all to find a way through our impasse. I have said what one seeks is viable ways which will enable us in this country to come together and really talk about real change. I have indicated in my presentation what these steps are . . . I do not want our country destroyed. I want to reiterate: I don't want it destroyed either by internal forces or by external forces. If . . . we were going to be seen to move in the direction of that change, I have pledged myself, and I pledge myself again here, to say quite firmly . . . that we are now moving and please give the country a chance.

I do not wish to be the one who is going to provoke the revolution, precisely because all of us will be destroyed in that. That is my position . . . I have said, and some of your colleagues, Mr. Prime Minister, have agreed, that some of the changes that have happened at home have happened because there have been pressures, peaceful pressures of various kinds. That is to be underlined.

The church leaders said afterward that there had been a very wide gulf between the two sides but at least they had met. "We were talking different languages but we were talking in the same room," said one. The prospect of further discussions was raised, but then Botha invited the leaders to visit South African Defense Force bases in neighboring Namibia. The church leaders, refusing to give legitimacy to South Africa's illegal occupation of Namibia, declined the invitation and the dialogue collapsed.

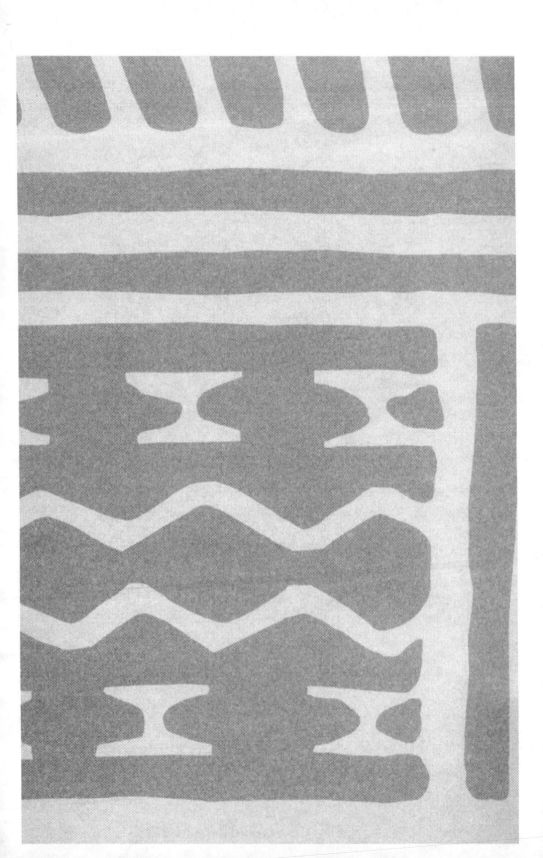

5

Why Did Mr. Botha's Courage Fail Him?

(1981)

AN EXPLANATION of why Prime Minister Botha's reforms did not meet even the minimum expectations of black South Africans was given in this extract from an address to a study group in Johannesburg in October 1981.

It would be fair to say that everybody in South Africa was taken aback (some pleasantly and others rudely shaken) at the first utterances of Mr. P. W. Botha soon after he became Prime Minister. We couldn't quite believe our ears—had we heard correctly? Did he really say that whites would have to adapt or die? That was quite incredible. Nobody had ever dreamed to hear a Nationalist Prime Minister utter such epoch-making sentiments. He certainly sent shudders through many a good Nationalist person. Had he really dismissed several of the Afrikaners' sacred cows, declaring that he would not want to be sent to the stake, as it were, for things which most of us had thought to be central pillars of Nationalist thinking? And he sounded so decisive after the dithering last days of a [Prime Minister] Vorster paralyzed by his unmanning fear of causing a split in the ranks of Afrikanerdom. Mr. P. W. Botha was prepared to beard the lion in his den, taking the fight to some of those he could regard as redoubtable opponents of reform, because he spoke so intrepidly in the Transvaal Congress of his party [its most conservative wing].

Those were heady days. Many of us were loud in our praise and admiration of this new broom that was going to get rid of all the cobwebs and open the windows to let in the fresh air and light of real change through reform. He got stuck into reforming the colossus of state bureaucracy. People believed that we would not recognize the South Africa that could evolve from the impetus Mr. P. W. Botha had given to change and reform. He promised so much and most South Africans wished him well in this exhilarating endeavor. He seemed to realize that to embark on reform and change would mean a drastic realignment of political forces. He seemed to realize that he could not rely any longer on the traditional allies of a Nationalist Prime Minister—the white blue-collar worker and the farmers and miners who had been pampered and spoiled by decades of white rule that ensured their position through color-bar legislation. Consequently, Mr. P. W. Botha performed a veritable tour de force in his engagement with leaders of the private sector at the Carlton Hotel [in Johannesburg] in November 1979 [where he spelled out his plans to adjust government policies to meet business needs]. They were dazzled by his scintillating footwork and promised to work hand in glove with him. We thought reform would now take off. Mr. Botha's stocks were high all around. A survey of black opinion at that time showed that a substantial percentage of blacks had a positive attitude toward him.

Things have changed, very sadly. Apart from some good and some bad things in the labor dispensation (much like the curate's egg, good in parts), we have not had much else in translating the rhetoric of reform into tangible and concrete reality. If anything, we see a veritable retreat on nearly all fronts. It seemed as if people were ready to accept even a touch of autocracy if that would turn the trick à la De Gaulle. So very few tears were shed with the passing away of the Senate and the advent of nominated members of parliament.* It was thought the

*The whites-only upper house of parliament was replaced by the President's Council, an advisory body set up in 1980 to make recommendations on, inter alia, constitutional change. Provision was also made for a limited number of members of the white parliament to be nominated instead of elected. Membership in the President's Council was extended to people designated as Colored, Indian or Chinese under the race classification law but Africans were excluded.

Prime Minister would thereby jettison his dyed-in-the-wool *verkramptes* [the "narrow-minded," or supporters of full-scale apartheid]. If need be, he could bypass parliament if that body might hamper his momentum for change. There was excitement in the air with the appointment of the President's Council. Up to then whites had thought they had a divine and unshared right to determine the constitutional future of this land. Now it was being conceded that South Africa's future would be decided by all its people. It is horridly tragic that what would have been a truly revolutionary innovation was vitiated by two fatal flaws—the exclusion of blacks and a nominated rather than an elected membership. Having got so far, why, oh, why, did Mr. Botha's courage fail him?

The wind has apparently been taken out of the sails of reform and change. We were given a taste of things to come in the extraordinary business of schoolboy rugby relating to Craven Week [an annual national school tournament]. The Prime Minister declared that it was up to the organizers to decide whether so-called Coloreds could participate or not. The government would not interfere. Dr. [Andries] Treurnicht, nothing daunted, declared that Craven Week would remain a lily-white affair. Subsequently the Prime Minister backed down, having been humiliated publicly. We are one of the few countries in the world where such momentous issues as to whether schoolboys can play rugby together are discussed by the cabinet. We are told the Prime Minister had to give in to Dr. Treurnicht because he was warned that if he took this matter to his party caucus he would be defeated. So he succumbed to right-wing pressure, and that sadly has set the pattern for where we are today.

The [April 1981] election happened. During the campaign it became clear from the poor attendances at Nationalist gatherings that the faithful were disillusioned both on the right and on the left; the former worried that the party was abandoning the cause of white privilege and *swart gevaar* politics [literally "black peril" politics] and the latter disillusioned that we were still being regaled with antediluvian racist thinking when the time called for boldness and statesmanship. The Nationalist leadership was rattled, so that you could hear cabinet ministers actually boasting that they were spending ten times as much on a white child's education as on a black—this in 1981 after June 16,

1976. The party was trying very hard to redress the balance and to show that reform did not mean any significant departure from traditional, well-tried apartheid—things would change but they would remain the same. We live in an Alice in Wonderland world, of course, with words meaning whatever we want them to mean.

The election revealed a deeply divided white electorate. What is more, it showed a deeply divided Afrikanerdom. Mr. Botha lost on both right and left and that election mauling has left its marks. It has determined what must now be done. You see, he had two options. He still has. Either he would pander to the right and try to woo the lost dissidents and so restore what is an obsession for all Nationalist Prime Ministers—Afrikaner unity—or he would go all out for reform. The point is that the election has shown him that there is no longer any such entity as Afrikaner unity. He has been relieved of an albatross which destroyed his predecessor, who suffered a terminal paralysis when he had a massive parliamentary majority that could have allowed him to do virtually anything he wanted . . . No Nationalist Prime Minister wants to go down in history as the man who splintered the party . . . and consequently led to its loss of political power. For this reason a whole nation has been held to ransom in order to maintain the myth of Afrikaner unity. There is nothing Mr. Botha can do which will satisfy the right. They will always raise the ante each time he kowtows to them.

He must ignore the [extreme right wing] Herstigte Nasionale Party, the Afrikaner Weerstandsbeweging and Aksie Eie Toekoms, nail his colors firmly to the mast of fundamental change and thereby lose a few, perhaps many, on the right. But he will be set to gain most of South Africa, black and white, and the whole free world, which is eager to welcome South Africa back into the fold of respectable nations as soon as apartheid is dismantled. . . .

For a former Defense Minister, Mr. Botha can be faulted for using inappropriate strategies. He should have secured his power base before embarking on reformist talk, demonstrating first that he was a "tough cookie" not to be trifled with. He is sadly now trying to prove that he is a man of iron. That is why all reform and even talk of reform has dried up. That is why we have been fed on a diet of *kragdadigheid* [powerful hard-line action] against the trade unions, with a spate of banning orders returning us to the dark ages of Dr. Verwoerd and Jimmy Kruger. We have had the callousness of the treatment of the Nyanga squatters with Dr. Koornhof, the erstwhile *verligte* [advocate of "enlightened" apartheid], outverkramping even Dr. Treurnicht with his heartless statement about being too humane.* I think his credibility has gone for a loop. He is unrecognizable as the man of Crossroads and Alexandra Township, with talk of blacks swamping whites and the government taking appropriate action. Add to that [Minister of Community Development] Pen Kotze's assertion that the Group Areas Act [the principal law used to implement relocation to racially pure suburbs] will be applied more vigorously and more strictly, all of it being capped by the Prime Minister's repeated declaration that his policy is actually "white domination" unadulterated and unabashed. Can you imagine what feathers would have flown if, say, Dr. [Nthato] Motlana [a popular Soweto civic leader] had announced that the purpose of the liberation struggle is black domination? So for the present it has all put paid to any hope of evolutionary change leading to political power sharing, which is the name of the game.

Yet it is not all entirely gloomy and unrelieved somberness. There has been the splendid showing of the Progressive Federal Party in the last election. Even more heartening has been the awakening of Afrikaner youth to the morality or immorality of the situation. It must be quite something when students at Stellenbosch University [the cradle of Afrikaner political leaders] give Dr. Motlana a rousing welcome and give the Prime Minister a roasting. Something is happening. We should not be overly euphoric, because, come the crunch, these young Afrikaners would most likely bolt into the tribal laager [literally a circle of ox wagons]. But we should also not be unduly cynical—they are asking questions about what the future holds for them if things go on in this way. They are saying, unbelievably, that apartheid, judging from Nyanga, has failed. I have spoken at all the Afrikaans university campuses and I must say I am surprised at my reception.

I am quite certain if the authorities were more generous in their

*More than 1,000 people were arrested in raids at Nyanga, Cape Town, in July and August 1981 and their shelters destroyed. Many were banished to the nominally independent Transkei homeland, hundreds of miles away, and there was a public outcry.

The Making of a Peaceful Revolution

definition of conscientious objection that South Africa would be shattered at the number of white South Africans who would prefer to do alternative forms of national service. They don't believe that South Africa is fighting a just or a justifiable war on the border. Some of them go so far as to believe that South Africa as presently ordered is not defensible. That gives blacks some hope that patriotism does not mean "my country right or wrong," especially when blacks remember that many Afrikaners were opposed to the Allied war effort during World War II, when blacks had to face up to Rommel's troops armed splendidly with assegais [light spears].* And that white Dutch Reformed churches used to expel from their services anyone wearing the South African Defense Force uniform. It is galling to have to be read lessons in patriotism by people who had to be interned during the last world war.† We must doff our hats to others in the white community who want a better South Africa and the palm must surely go to those splendid women of the Black Sash [an organization founded by white women opposed to apartheid] who have gone on in the face of ridicule and worse.

---

*South Africans, black and white, were among the Allied troops who fought the forces of German general Erwin Rommel in North Africa during World War II. However, Africans, who were laborers, drivers and stretcher bearers, were not allowed to carry arms, only assegais.

†Some Afrikaner nationalists who opposed the country's entry into World War II on the side of the British joined the paramilitary Ossewa Brandwag (Ox Wagon Sentinels) and attempted to sabotage the war effort. B. J. Vorster was one of the OB leaders interned under security laws.

6

The Divine Imperative

(1982)

THE BOTHA administration's policy has been described by commentators in the South African Review as having a "reform-repression characteristic" (Ravan Press, 1983). With one hand the government introduced limited reform, with the other it tried to eradicate opposition which fell outside the narrow parameters prescribed by that reform, and beyond the country's borders it carried out a ruthless program of destabilization in the neighboring black-ruled states to stop them from giving sanctuary and providing military bases to its opponents. Botha had been Minister of Defense before becoming Prime Minister and under his rule the country's military leadership gained prominence. It developed a National Security Management System, which set up military parallels to civilian organs of government. The new "securocrats" believed the government had to develop a "total strategy" to combat a Communist-inspired "total onslaught" from internal and external enemies. One of the internal enemies was identified as the South African Council of Churches.

The council had been experiencing problems over its finances since 1977. In October 1981, after a number of auditing investigations, it announced the appointment of a commission of inquiry. The SACC did not receive public funds but the following month the government announced the appointment of its own commission of inquiry into financial irregularities. When the terms of reference of the government's commission were revealed, however, it was clear that they were far wider

*than the keeping of the accounts: the whole of the council's work was to
be investigated.*

*A Transvaal judge, C. F. Eloff, headed the commission and hearings
began with Desmond Tutu's evidence in September 1982. In his statement Tutu refers to the Dutch Reformed Church (NGK), the biggest of
the white Afrikaans churches. In its missionary work the church had created three other segregated churches, intended for Africans, Coloreds
and Indians, but because of the NGK's support of apartheid, these
churches were turning against it. In August 1982 the World Alliance of
Reformed Churches, meeting in Ottawa, suspended the NGK and
elected Dr. Allan Boesak, a leader of the Dutch Reformed Mission
Church, president of the world body.*

Preamble

My Lord and members of the Eloff commission, I want to start by ex-
pressing the appreciation of the South African Council of Churches to
the commission and its officers in their dealings with the council.
They could very well have hamstrung our operations by taking away
our books and records. Instead they examined our records in such a
way as to dislocate our work as little as possible. For this we are grateful.

Secondly, I want to indicate briefly at the beginning what I hope to
elaborate in the body of my submission.

My purpose is to demonstrate from the scriptures and from hallowed
Christian tradition and teaching that what we are as the South African
Council of Churches, what we say and what we do, all of these are determined not by politics or any other ideology. We are what we are in
obedience to God and in response to the gracious Gospel of his Son
our Lord and Saviour Jesus Christ. We owe ultimate loyalty not to any
human authority, however prestigious or powerful, but to God and to
his Son our Lord Jesus Christ alone, from whom we obtain our mandate. We must obey the divine imperative and word whatever the cost.

Everything we do or say and everything we are must be tested by
whether it is consistent with the Gospel of Jesus Christ or not, and not
by whether it is merely expedient or even acceptable to the govern-

ment of the day or whether it is popular. To understand the nature of the council, its aims, objectives and activities, requires that you appreciate the theological raison d'être of its existence. Without this biblical and theological justification you will almost certainly misunderstand what we are about. Consequently, I want to underline that it is not the finances or any other activities of the SACC that are being investigated. It is our Christian faith; it is the Christian churches who are members of the SACC who are on trial. It is our Christianity, it is our faith and therefore our theology that are under scrutiny. The central matters at issue are profoundly theological. As a commission you are being asked to determine whether our understanding and practice of the Christian faith can pass muster. We are under trial for being Christian and that by a government which claims to be Christian. It may be that we are being told that it is an offense to be a Christian in South Africa. That is what you are asked to determine and that is a theological task through and through.

I will show that the Bible describes God as creating the universe to be a cosmos and not a chaos, a cosmos in which harmony, unity, order, fellowship, communion, peace and justice would reign and that this divine intention was disturbed by sin. The result was disunity, alienation, disorder, chaos, enmity, separation. In the face of this, God then sent his Son to restore that primordial harmony to effect reconciliation.

By becoming a real human being through Jesus Christ, God showed that he took the whole of human history and the whole of human life seriously. He demonstrated that he was Lord of all life, spiritual and secular, sacred and profane, material and spiritual. We will show that scripture and the mainstream of Christian tradition and teaching know nothing of the dichotomies so popular in our day which demand the separation of religion from politics. These I will demonstrate are deeply theological matters which affect the nature, work and attitudes of the SACC. Our God cares that children starve in resettlement camps, the somewhat respectable name for apartheid's dumping grounds for the pathetic casualties of this vicious and evil system. The God we worship does care that people die mysteriously in detention. He is concerned that people are condemned to a twilight existence as nonpersons by an arbitrary bureaucratic act of banning them without giving them the opportunity to reply to charges brought against them.

I will show this from the Bible. I might add that if God did not care about these and similar matters, I would not worship him, for he would be a totally useless God. Mercifully, he is not such a God.

I will show that the central work of Jesus was to effect reconciliation between God and us and also between man and man. Consequently, from a theological and scriptural base, I will demonstrate that apartheid, separate development or whatever it is called is evil, totally and without remainder, that it is unchristian and unbiblical. It has recently been declared a heresy by a world body of responsible Christians, a body to which the white Dutch Reformed churches belong and which can therefore not be dismissed as a so-called left-wing radical body . . . If anyone were to show me that apartheid is biblical or Christian, I have said before, and I reiterate now, that I would burn my Bible and cease to be a Christian. I will want to show that the Christian Bible and the Gospel of Jesus Christ our Lord is subversive of all injustice and evil, oppression and exploitation and that God is on the side of the oppressed and the downtrodden, that he is the liberator God of the Exodus, who leads his people out of every kind of bondage, spiritual, political, social and economic. Nothing will thwart him from achieving the goal of the liberation of all his people and the whole of his creation.

The SACC and its member churches, we will show, are not a tuppenny-ha'penny fly-by-night organization. We belong to the Church of God, a church that is found universally spread throughout the face of the whole inhabited universe. That is what the Greek word from which we find "ecumenical" means. It is the body of Jesus Christ of which we are members and it is a supernatural, a divine fellowship brought into being by the action of God himself through his Holy Spirit. It is not merely a human organization that is limited by national or ethnic boundaries. It transcends time and space, race, culture and sex, nationality and all the things that men sometimes think are important. I am a bishop in the Church of God—that is what was pronounced over me when I was consecrated—so that I am a bishop of the church when I go to Timbuktu, when I go to Korea; I am a bishop of the church in Russia and in the United States. We belong to something which includes the living in what is called the church militant, which includes the dead in what is called the church quiescent, which includes the saints in glory in what is called the church triumphant. Theologically

I have brothers and sisters whom I have never met physically and will probably never meet, but ontologically we are one in our Lord Jesus Christ and I know that they are upholding us with their prayers, with their love, with their caring concern, even now. Your investigators will know that from their recent visit in the United States. Because of this theological fact of the nature of the church we express our oneness in all kinds of ways—in our prayers for one another, in making up what is lacking in the resources of another church and so on. When one church gives to another church either personnel or material or money resources, that is in fact nothing remarkable.

It is as it should be. It is an expression of Christian fellowship, of *koinonia* in our Lord. We might want local churches to be more self-supporting but it is no aberration for a more affluent part of the church to give of its wealth, of which it is only a steward on behalf of God, from whom all things come. It gives and it receives. There is the mutuality of giving and receiving as of a loving family. Those who criticize the SACC for depending so greatly on overseas support show their woeful ignorance of ecclesiology, the theology of the nature of the Church of God—when one part suffers the whole suffers with it and when one part rejoices the whole rejoices with it.

I have already said we owe our ultimate loyalty and allegiance only to God. With due respect I want to submit that no secular authority or its appointed commissions have any competence whatsoever to determine how a church is a church or what is the nature of the Gospel of Jesus Christ. When secular authority tries to do this, it is then usurping divine prerogatives and the prerogatives of the church itself. With respect, we do not recognize the right of this commission to inquire into our theological existence, and therefore into any aspect of our life as a council, since every other aspect of our existence is determined by theological facts, as I have already pointed out. Only our member churches can call us to task. If we have contravened any laws of the country, then you don't need a commission to determine that. There is an array of draconian laws at the disposal of the government and the courts of law are the proper place to determine our guilt or innocence. This commission, with respect, is totally superfluous. We have agreed to appear before it only because we have nothing to hide, which does not mean that we are infallible. Our written submission to the commission acknowledges that we are fallible and have made mistakes. Equally we have taken steps to correct those mistakes, but it is our member churches and not the government or any other secular authority who is the proper judge of that. And to reveal that we are sinners as if some major scientific discovery was being made is to become quite ridiculous in Christian terms, for it is to belabor the obvious. We are always justified and we are always sinners. We depend not on our goodness but on the gracious mercy of God. And again the government or any other secular body has no competence whatsoever to pass judgment on this. God alone can do that. And when the government usurps God's prerogative, then it becomes not just wrong but blasphemous.

The government appointed this commission for a reason that is perfectly obvious and totally unsubtle. It has used commissions before to deal with awkward customers. I don't impugn the integrity of this commission and its members in any way, but I want the government to know now and always that I do not fear them. They are trying to defend the utterly indefensible. Apartheid is as evil and as vicious as Nazism and Communism and the government will fail completely, for it is ranging itself on the side of evil, injustice and oppression. The government is not God, just ordinary human beings who very soon, like other tyrants before them, will bite the dust. When they take on the SACC they must know that they are taking on the Church of God and those who have done so in the past, the Neros, the Hitlers, the Amins of this world, have ended up, as I have said before on another occasion, as the flotsam and jetsam of history. Christ has assured us that his church is founded on a rock and not even the gates of hell can prevail against it. The Resurrection of our Lord and Saviour declares for all to know that life will triumph over death, that light will triumph over darkness, that goodness will triumph over evil, that justice will triumph over injustice and that freedom will triumph over tyranny. I stand before you as one who believes fervently what Paul wrote when he said, "If God be for us, who can be against us?"

The Divine Intention

In the constitution of the SACC . . . under the heading "3. Objects" we read, "The principal objects of the Council shall be: 3.1 To foster that unity which is both God's will for all mankind and his gift to the Church . . ." I want to point out that this first object permeates all the other objects as stated in paragraphs 3.2 to 3.5, reflected in expressions such as "to coordinate the work in Southern Africa of churches," "to undertake on behalf of churches . . . joint action and service . . . and to encourage joint action and service," "to do all such things, to encourage all such things . . . calculated to reduce divisive factors . . ." and "by developing dialogue with people of other faiths and ideologies."

It can be said that the search for the unity of the churches and of humankind is a central concern of the SACC. But is unity a central biblical concern or is it just peripheral to the life of faith, something to be engaged in as an optional extra by those who are temperamentally suited to do so? I want to show that the SACC and its member churches have their agenda and their programs in this matter determined by what the scriptures have revealed as the will of God, the God and Father of our Lord Jesus Christ. I want to stress that this concern for unity is not something that was introduced by the ecumenical movement from its inception. No, the scriptures declare that unity, the unity of the entire creation was God's intention from the very beginning of creation. The SACC is thus caught up in a divine mission; it is a fellow worker with none other than God himself; it is an agent of the divine mercy and compassion. Its concern is not just for the world and not just for human beings, but for the whole of creation.

Let us start at the beginning where the Bible seems to start and that is with the creation of all there is. We find our sources in the sublime stories contained in the first eleven chapters of Genesis. Some have sought to dismiss these stories as myths, meaning that their truth content was no more than that of fairy tales. But those who do so are dull, unimaginative souls who would ask Wordsworth, writing about a host of golden daffodils "dancing in the breeze": "Which band was playing, and who were their dancing partners?" No, in these chapters we have the evocative, imaginative, highly symbolical language of poetry conveying to us some of the most profound theological or, if you like, spiritual and existential truths about God, about ourselves and about the rest of God's creation. No advances in technology or science will be able to produce anything to contradict those truths—true science cannot contradict true religion.

The first creation narrative reaches a climax in Genesis 1:26, when God says, "Let us create man in our image and likeness to rule . . ." Human beings are created, so St. Augustine of Hippo tells us, by God, like God, for God. God creates man to become his viceroy, his representative to rule over the rest of creation on God's behalf. In olden times the emperor's statue received the same honor and respect as the emperor himself and represented him where he could not travel in his vast domains. That is the high privilege bestowed on each human person, male and female, as the passage goes on to explain that each human being is God's own representative, own viceroy or ambassador. No mention is made of race or nationality or color. It is the fact of their being created by God that endows them with this infinite and eternal value. But note also that they are expected to rule over the rest of creation on behalf of God. So already in those early verses of the Bible we get definite adumbrations of the Kingdom of God about which the New Testament is so explicit and to which I want to refer later.

May I point out that the biblical author depicts the primal state of affairs as being such that harmony, unity, fellowship and friendliness abound? Poetically and symbolically this is done by saying that every living creature was at this stage a vegetarian. There was no bloodshed in God's creation according to his will and intention. There was no bloodshed, not even for blood sacrifices. Nature was not yet red in tooth and claw.

The second creation story speaks about the idyllic paradise of Eden in which Adam and Eve lived happily. There was abundant food. Adam named the animals to demonstrate his hegemony over all creation. Adam and Eve were as innocents abroad, communicating directly with God, who visited them as a man visits his friends, walking with them in the garden in the cool of the evening. The animals did not prey on each other. The lion gamboled with the lamb. The picture we have is of a creation at peace, abounding in harmony, unity and fellowship; that this was God's intention for the entire universe because unity means peace, prosperity, fellowship, justice, wholeness, compassion, love and joy et al., conveyed in the virtually untranslatable Hebrew word "shalom." It was a condition in which God's will was being done, in which his laws were being obeyed.

The Bible declares that things then went horribly, badly wrong because sin entered God's good creation. There is no speculation about the origin of sin. We have a phenomenological account of what followed in the train of sin. The primal unity was disrupted. Where there was unity, there was now disunity; harmony was replaced by disharmony. There was alienation and hatred and enmity. Fellowship and communion were destroyed and not just humankind was affected. The rest of creation fell with human beings. The ground brought forth thistles. There was murder and death (the story of Cain and Abel), war and strife. And the Genesis stories culminate in the shattering story of the Tower of Babel where human community and fellowship become impossible—human beings can no longer communicate with one another because God has confused their languages and people are torn apart. That is the ultimate consequence, according to the Bible, of sin, separation, alienation, apartness. It is a perverse exegesis that would hold that the story of the Tower of Babel is a justification for racial separation, a divine sanction for the diversity of nations. It is to declare that the divine punishment of sin had become the divine intention for humankind. That is a position the Bible would not support.

The entire situation at the end of the story of the Tower of Babel cried out for reconciliation, for atonement. Please note that this word atonement is also at-one-ment, meaning the at-one-ing, the reconciling of those who are separated . . . The story of the Bible could be said to be the story of God's movement, God's mission to restore the harmony, the unity, the fellowship, the communion, the community which were there at the beginning when his rule, his reign would be acknowledged once again. This is the divine movement and activity in which the SACC is involved as it prays and works for the unity of the churches and of humankind. . . .

And so God sent his Son to effect reconciliation to bring about the at-one-ment that would achieve the peace, justice, friendliness, compassion, wholeness which were his intention for his creation from the very beginning. St. Paul says, "God was in Christ reconciling the world to himself" (2 Corinthians 5:19).

Jesus, speaking about his coming crucifixion, declares, "I, if I be lifted up, will draw all men to me" (John 12:32), underlining that his chief work in the salvation of the world would be a uniting, a reconciling one. And we must recall that Christian tradition, referring to Christ's seamless robe, speaks of it as symbolizing the unity of the church and so of all humankind. And in St. John's Gospel is to be found what tradition speaks of as the high priestly prayer of our Lord, as recorded in chapter 17. The heart of that prayer is the petition that his followers will be one with a unity that reflects the unity that subsists between the Father and the Son (John 17:11 and 20–23). The unity is not for merely pragmatic reasons, that it is economical to have one church building rather than several serving the same community and locality, but because a divided church is a scandal, making it difficult for people to believe the Gospel of God's love.

The SACC is concerned for unity in all its aspects because it exists to proclaim the Good News of God's love for his world, for which he gave his only begotten Son, in obedience to the commission our Lord gave to his followers when he said:

FULL AUTHORITY IN heaven and earth has been committed to me. Go forth therefore and make all nations my disciples; baptize men everywhere in the name of the Father and the Son and the Holy Spirit and teach them to observe all that I commanded you. And be assured I am with you always, to the end of time.

It is because, as St. Paul declares, "God has reconciled us men to himself through Christ, and he has enlisted us in this service of reconciliation" (2 Corinthians 5:18–21).

We are engaged in the ministry of proclaiming the love of God for all his people through the death and resurrection of Jesus Christ our Lord and proclaiming the message of reconciliation which is another aspect of unity, of peace, of harmony, of justice, of compassion, of love, of brotherliness. That is why in its organizational structure the SACC has a Division of Mission and Evangelism, which was established to help the churches in their proclamation of the Christian Gospel through word and deed. Our concern is to win men and women for Christ so that, converted by the Holy Spirit, they would accept Jesus and acknowledge him as their Lord and Master and their Saviour.

We are concerned for justice, but that is a biblical concern. And we are also concerned and work for reconciliation. We have a division called the Division of Justice and Reconciliation to work for real peace and brotherhood in our land and throughout the world . . .

St. Paul waxes quite indignant when he thinks the unity of the Christian community has been jeopardized or undermined. In his First Letter to the Corinthians, he is supposed to be responding to questions that the Corinthian church had asked, but because of the disquieting news of factions and divisions in that church, Paul spends the first six chapters dealing with this matter of divisiveness before he deals with their other problems. That is strange conduct unless unity was of paramount importance. And he stresses that the church is the body of Christ endowed with different spiritual and other gifts (charismata), having different limbs and organs with different functions—but all designed to function for the good and the benefit of the whole. He stresses the unity, the harmony, the oneness. It is a body in which the natural distinctions of race, status, sex, culture are of no moment any longer. They have been transcended in Jesus Christ our Lord. He mentions this fact first in 1 Corinthians 12:12–13 and then again in Galatians 3:26–28.

This was what attracted the first converts when they saw this amazing spectacle of Christian koinonia. They were led to exclaim, "How these Christians love one another." St. Paul exhorts Christians to have the mind of Christ, in Philippians, in order to maintain this precious thing—this unity.

The Making of a Peaceful Revolution   *63*

In Ephesians we learn that this was God's intention (Ephesians 1:10), a return to the primordial time of the beginning; and this is what Paul says in Romans 8:19–22.

That is the divine movement in which the SACC and its member churches are caught up. It is to demonstrate in our lives that the Jesus whom we worship as Lord and Master has, as Ephesians declares, broken down the wall of partition which separated Jew from Gentile (Ephesians 2:11–22). This movement, this divine activity is for bringing together, for uniting, for reconciling, for atoning. Teilhard de Chardin, the French Jesuit paleontologist, spoke of much the same thing when he said the whole of creation was moving from a point alpha to its goal in the point omega.

The only separation the Bible knows is between believers on the one hand and unbelievers on the other. Any other kind of separation, division, disunity is of the devil. It is evil and from sin.

Do I still need to demonstrate that apartheid is evil after all that I have said about the centrality for the Bible of unity and reconciliation?

Apartheid is evil for at least three reasons:

a) The Bible declares right at the beginning that human beings are created in the image and likeness of God. I showed why this fact endows each person with a unique and infinite value, a person whose very hairs are numbered. And what makes any human being valuable therefore is not any biological characteristic. No, it is the fact that he or she is created in the image of and likeness of God. Apartheid exalts a biological quality, which is a total irrelevancy, to the status of what determines the value, the worth of a human being. Why should skin color or race be any more useful as a criterion than, say, the size of one's nose? What has the size of my nose to do with whether I am intelligent? It has no more to do with my worth as a human being than the color of my eyes.

b) Secondly, the chief work that Jesus came to perform on earth can be summed up in the word "reconciliation." I have already demonstrated that. He came to restore human community and brotherhood which sin destroyed. He came to say that God had intended us for fellowship, for *koinonia*, for togetherness, without destroying our distinctiveness, our cultural otherness. Apartheid quite deliberately denies and repudiates this central act of Jesus and says we are made for separateness, for disunity, for enmity, for alienation which we have shown to be fruits of sin. For this reason alone apartheid is totally unchristian and unbiblical, for it denies not just a peripheral matter but a central verity of the Christian faith.

Professor Jaap Durand, in his response to Professor Johan Heyns's article in *Stormkompas*, has these words to say:

THE FACT THAT the concept of the irreconcilability of people is neglected by the churches is more than just an unfortunate state of affairs. The nub of the issue is that we have here a repudiation of the essence of the church. If I read Ephesians 2 correctly, in which the Apostle Paul deals with the middle wall of partition which is broken down in Christ, then the very existence of the church is a denial of the artificial and ideological separation of people.

How is it still possible that within church circles such separation can be discussed and experienced as the will of God and in keeping with the Gospel?

It is to the credit of the Nederduitse Gereformeerde Sendingkerk in South Africa [Dutch Reformed Mission Church, established for Colored people] that at its synod session in Belhar in 1978 it reduced the problem of South African society to its theological core: reconciliation. The decision reads:

"This church declares its conviction that the policy of apartheid and/or separate development, as implemented by the authorities, is in conflict with the Gospel:

"1. because, as opposed to the Gospel of Christ's stress on the reconciliation of the human being with God and fellow humans, the forced separation of people on the grounds of race and color is based at heart on a belief in the fundamental irreconcilability of the people so separated;

"2. because the system which results from such a policy must necessarily lead, and has led, to increasing polarization between people, especially because its practical implementation has undoubtedly shown that one part of the population, namely whites, is privileged and that as a result the biblical demand of justice for all has not been met; and

"3. because the policy has undermined the human worth not only of nonprivileged sections of the population but of all who are affected."

One sometimes gets the impression that those in, for example, the Dutch Reformed Church who know about the above decision write it off too lightly as just an example of a church resolution against apartheid. But the theological implications of the resolution cannot be ignored. It asks a deeply penetrating question of the church or churches which deem that apartheid can in one way or another be theologically shored up or supported. These churches (and with them all churches) are challenged as to the genuineness of their nature as churches in South Africa.*

c) Thirdly, when moralists are uncertain about the moral quality of an act, then they will ask what the consequences of that particular act or policy are. If the consequences are evil, then the act being evaluated is declared to be evil. Apartheid treats human beings, God's children, as if they were less than this. It manipulates persons and treats them as if they were means to some end. Immanuel Kant declared that a human person is always an *end*, never a means to an end.

I said that in the Old Testament we already had foreshadowings of the teaching about the Kingdom of God—for instance, in man acting on behalf of God to rule over all creation. It was God's intention to rule as sovereign Lord. In his Kingdom he was absolute ruler and he demanded undivided loyalty to himself alone. That is why Israel, his chosen people, are constantly castigated by God's spokesmen, the

---

*Stormkompas, edited by Nico J. Smith, F. E. O'Brien Geldenhuys and Piet Meiring (Tafelberg Publishers, Cape Town, 1981). The book, whose name translates as "Storm Compass," was a collection of articles by Afrikaner theologians that questioned the Dutch Reformed Church's support for apartheid. This extract was reproduced in Afrikaans in the original evidence to the commission. Professor Johan Heyns was at the University of Pretoria and later became moderator of the NGK. Professor Jaap Durand of the Sendingkerk was at the University of the Western Cape.

prophets, for their disloyalty, which is likened to adultery since Israel is married to Yahweh, God alone. The devil and the powers of evil have usurped God's rule and God has, as it were, permitted them to set up their counter-kingdom. This world is in the power and control of the evil one; consequently, there is evil, war, disease, death, etc. God's children, many of them, are held in bondage and in shackles by the evil one and his minions. But God would intervene through his Messiah, the long-expected one, the Anointed one, and when he came he would inaugurate the Kingdom of God. It is this long-awaited one, who is referred to in the earlier quotation from Isaiah, who will be imbued with God's spirit. Christians believe that this promised Messiah has come in Jesus Christ our Lord.

We believe that God has intervened decisively in and through Jesus Christ, who is verily God himself and yet who became a real human being in that act of stupendous divine condescension called the Incarnation—God becoming man. By this act, God declared that human history is important and that all of human life is important. God declared that he is a jealous God, brooking no rival whatsoever. "I am the Lord your God and you shall have no other gods beside me." But he was and is the Lord of all life . . . When the imprisoned John the Baptist asked whether Jesus was indeed the Messiah, Jesus pointed to the things that he was doing, including material things, here and now, as signs of the Kingdom (Luke 7:18–23). All of these things were thoroughly religious and spiritual but many of them were so physical, so secular, so profane . . .

I want to underline that these are thoroughly political, thoroughly mundane things. If we are to say that religion cannot be concerned with politics, then we are really saying that there is a substantial part of human life in which God's writ does not run. If it is not God's, then whose is it? Who is in charge if not the God and Father of our Lord Jesus Christ? On the church and politics we could say much, much more. Is it not interesting just how often people and churches are accused of mixing religion with politics? Almost always it is when they condemn a particular sociopolitical dispensation as being unjust. If the South African Council of Churches were to say now that it thought apartheid was not so bad, I am as certain as anything that we would not be finding ourselves where we are today. Why is it not being political for a religious body or a religious leader to praise a sociopolitical dispensation?

I need to point out that in the Old Testament God was first experienced by the Israelites in the event of the Exodus. They were at the time just a rabble of slaves. They did not encounter God in some religious event such as a sacrifice or at worship; he revealed himself in helping them to escape from bondage, and what could be more political than helping captives to escape? And it is this political event of the Exodus which becomes the founding event of the people of God. It becomes the paradigmatic event of the Bible, so that, looking at what God did in the Exodus, they extrapolate backward and say that a God who did so-and-so must clearly be *the* God—the Lord of creation. They can extrapolate forward and say that God who can choose a people in this way must be a God who has a purpose for them. That is why we have said God has taken human history seriously, unlike the nature gods. And when God redeemed us in our Lord and Saviour Jesus Christ, it was not through a religious event. No, it was through an act of execution used against common criminals. It was through a judicial event that it would be sanctioned, not by the ecclesiastical leaders, but by the political ruler in Judea in the day.

I want to quote some strange words. I will explain afterward where they come from, M'Lord.

Rest in the Status Quo

The other extreme, however, is still more fatal to the church's effective witness to the world, and that is acquiescence in unjust conditions. Silence may never be kept about the social implications of the Gospel of Christ. There can be little doubt that the present low level of spiritual life is in no small measure due to the dilution of the eternal principles. The whole church longs and prays for a revival, but is it psychologically sound to expect enthusiastic, joyful spiritual life among those living in misery, hunger and privation? Moses and Aaron also claimed to quicken new hope and courage in the hearts of their enslaved people, but what do we read in Exodus 6, verse 8? They did not listen to Moses on account of the despondency and cruel bondage . . .

The Charge Against the Church

The strongest charge against the church is born exactly out of the conception of many that she has not grieved over the ruin of Joseph, but acquiesced in the conditions of injustice, exploitation and coercion. The Evangelical Lutheran Church in 1931 made a survey in a vast suburb of Berlin among 1,000 former members who had left the church. Not one of them recorded objections against the doctrines of the church as a reason for cessation. The great charge was that the church had no eye or ear for justice or for the oppressed. The church identified only with those on the sunny side of life . . . The church was on the side of the vested interests of ruling classes instead of rebuking or condemning their despotism and injustice. She admonished the poor and oppressed to be docile, to bear their hard burden patiently, to hope for better conditions in the hereafter, to suffer the ills of the present in order to receive the heaven of the future.

Our church in South Africa must honestly face the charges brought against her. She is too much inclined to demand support and respect of members on account of past services to the people. The city laborer wants more than this. The past leaves him cold. He wants to know what the church does for him here and now. In former years the reverence in which the church was regarded silenced her members even though they differed from her, but now the city dweller is much more critically inclined, and he is more candid in airing his grievances. One of the most hopeful signs in our cities is that the church is so close to the working classes. Today she is almost exclusively supported by the laborer, by the low-paid person. These constitute her office bearers and her best members. . . .

Now, that is not a statement by the SACC. It is a statement made by the Dutch Reformed Church, published in a book entitled *Kerk en Stad* ["Church and City"]. It was in preparation for the Volkskongres [the People's Congress] in July 1947. It is quoted from a paper that was delivered by Dominee [the Reverend] Dawid Botha, the Moderator of the Sendingkerk. The paper, "The Kingdom of God and the Churches in South Africa," was delivered at the national conference of the SACC in 1980 . . . I do not know whether those who accuse us of being political will say that that was true of the Dutch Reformed Church as well.

Our God does not permit us to dwell in a kind of spiritual ghetto, insulated from real life out there. Jesus used to go out and be alone with God in deep prayerful meditation, but he did not remain there. He refused to remain on the Mount of Transfiguration but descended to the valley beneath to be involved with healing the possessed boy. He was . . . prodigal in the giving of himself precisely and only because he was a man of prayer . . . That is our paradigm. He did not use religion as a form of escapism.

That is why he could say we must love God and love our neighbor as well, quoting from the Old Testament. These were two sides of the same coin. The one without the other was unacceptable. Love of God was authenticated and expressed in and through love of our neighbor. This is what is often referred to as the vertical dimension (relationship with God) and the horizontal dimension (relationship with neighbor) in our Christian faith. The First Letter of John is quite firm and unequivocal about this aspect of our Christianity: 1 John 3:15–18; 4:19–21; and the Epistle of James 1:27; 2:14–17.

Our Lord has shocked many religious people by his parable of the Last Judgment, for here he provides a list of things which the doing or the omission of determines whether we qualify or do not qualify for heaven. The things he mentions could not by any stretch of the imagination be called religious in the narrow sense; it is feeding the hungry, clothing the naked, visiting the sick and those who are imprisoned . . . He goes on to say that to do them to the least, the despised ones, is to do it as to himself. Here he identifies God firmly with the downtrodden, the oppressed, the marginalized ones. And he is only being true to the nature of God as revealed in the Old Testament. The Old Testament prophets, speaking on behalf of God, rejected the elaborate religious ceremonies of his people. Why? Because they dealt unjustly with the poor and the powerless (Isaiah 1:10–17 and 58:3–8; Amos 5:21–28, 5:7–12 and 2:6–8). Elijah denounces King Ahab because his wife, Jezebel, had caused the judicial murder of a nonentity, Naboth, because the king wanted Naboth's vineyard. On behalf of God, Elijah speaks up against this tyrannical act.

The prophets are deeply involved in politics because politics is the sphere where God's people demonstrate their obedience or their disobedience. The prophet Nathan rebuked King David not for a so-called religious misdemeanor but for the political act of causing the death of Bathsheba's husband.

Our religion is concerned about the here and now because that determines to a large extent the hereafter. Time in the Hebrew-Christian understanding has eternal significance and that is why human lives and human decisions are important. All life belongs to God. The Christian faith believes that God uses ordinary material things as vehicles for God's spiritual grace and divine life as in the sacraments. Our religion is incarnational through and through.

William Temple, the great Archbishop of Canterbury, referring to this quality of the Christian faith, said, "Christianity is the most materialistic of the great religions." We declare that we believe in the resurrection of the body and not in the immortality of the soul. The body, according to St. Paul, is the temple of the Holy Spirit. Christians are not dualists who believe that matter is intrinsically evil, and therefore all God's created universe, material and spiritual, counts for us. The whole of life is important: the political, the economic and the social. None of these aspects is untouched by religion as we understand it.

It is part of God's mission and purpose for his world to bring about wholeness, justice, good health, righteousness, peace, harmony and reconciliation. These are what belong to the Kingdom of God and we are his agents to work with him as his partners to bring to pass all that God wants for his universe . . . He takes the side of the poor, the weak, the oppressed, the widow, the orphan and the alien. That is a refrain you get in the book of Deuteronomy—look after these because they represent a class in society which tends to be marginalized, to be pushed to the periphery, the bottom of the pile, the end of the queue. God can't help it. He always takes sides. He is no neutral God. He takes the side of the weak and the oppressed. I am not saying so. I have shown it to be so in the Bible.

Where there is injustice, exploitation and oppression, then, the Bible and the God of the Bible are subversive of such a situation. Our God, unlike the pagan nature gods, is not God sanctifying the status quo. He is a God of surprises, uprooting the powerful and unjust to establish his Kingdom. We see it in the entire history of Israel.

I want to say what I have said before on another occasion: the Bible is the most revolutionary, the most radical book there is. If a book had to be banned by those who rule unjustly and as tyrants, then it ought to have been the Bible. Whites brought us the Bible and we are taking it seriously.

We are involved with God in his activity to set us all free from all that enslaves us, from all that makes us less than what he intended us to be. . . .

The SACC is basically law-abiding and concerned for justice, peace, reconciliation and unity. But in a real sense, because we are opposed to injustice and oppression, we cannot support a system where these are found, and to seek to change such a system even by reasonably peaceful means is to be a destabilizing factor in such a society. We want to dismantle apartheid, and the perpetrators of apartheid don't like that at all. They could hardly regard us as blue-eyed boys, because the privilege they enjoy as a result of apartheid is threatened. And so we have the total onslaught of the apartheid machinery turned against us.

We are concerned to work for a new kind of South Africa, a nonracial, truly democratic and more just society, by reasonably peaceful means. We as a council deplore all forms of violence—we have said so times without number—both the structural and legalized violence used to maintain an unjust sociopolitical dispensation and the violence of those who would overthrow the state. But we have consistently warned, too, that oppressed people will become desperate and desperate people will use desperate methods.

We have a Commission on Violence and Nonviolence and are concerned about the increasing militarization of our land. We believe conscientious objectors should be given alternative forms of national service as in most normal societies. We believe in negotiation, discussion and dialogue. That is why in 1980 we had discussions with the government to try to arrange for it to meet with the authentic leaders of all sections of South African society (for blacks it would include political prisoners and people in exile). That is why we still call for a national convention.

I myself believe in dialogue and meeting. I have spoken at all the Afrikaans university campuses . . . I have spoken to some mainly Afrikaans organizations and groups . . . That could not be the attitude of someone out for confrontation, could it? Many in the black community ask why I still waste my time talking to whites and I tell them that our mandate is biblical. Moses went to Pharaoh several times even when he knew that it was futile. The prophets addressed the kings of Israel time and time again because theirs was to deliver the message faithfully even if they were being rejected.

The national conference of the SACC in June [1982] declared apartheid a heresy and said we should have no further dialogue with the Dutch Reformed Church until it denounces apartheid as evil. But I want to tell you that we reached this point only after several efforts at holding out a hand of fellowship. In 1978, I reminded Dr. [Frans O'Brien] Geldenhuys, then the church's ecumenical officer and later its chief executive officer, that my predecessor had written on behalf of our executive committee to invite the church to send an observer to its meeting . . . He replied to say his synod had turned down our invitation. Then we said do not let it be an official observer, let it be an unofficial observer; it need not be a mutual arrangement—we do not ask to appoint or allow someone from the SACC to sit in on your meetings. He wrote back to say that even this invitation had been rejected.

But, nothing daunted, we went on: we invited them to participate in a consultation on racism in 1980. They did not even reply to my letter, except by statements in the press. The consultation was quite angry at this action. But I asked the permission of the consultation: I said I felt I was under divine constraint to write to the Dutch Reformed Church saying that they should please forgive us of the SACC and its member churches for anything we had done to hurt them in the past, but that we believed nothing substantial would happen in this country to change its unjust structures unless that powerful and mighty church were to be involved. A small delegation came to see me in what they said must be a totally confidential meeting.

So we have tried to engage them in dialogue and we have been rebuffed. What more could we do? We are sad at what has happened to them in Ottawa. We do not gloat and we continue to pray for their conversion because, and this is my pet theory, once an Afrikaner sees the light of Jesus Christ as other people see it, there is no stopping him, for there are no half-measures with him. When an Afrikaner is committed, and committed to the Gospel of Jesus Christ, then he is committed to the hilt.

We of the South African Council of Churches belong to the Church of God, the one holy Catholic and Apostolic church. What it means is that we belong to something quite tremendous. Those who are for us are many times more than those against us. We belong to this remarkable fellowship, so that we can receive a letter, as we have done, from a Lutheran pastor in Alaska assuring us that he and his congregation are praying for us. When I lost my passport for the first time [withdrawn by the government from March 1980 to January 1981], I was overwhelmed by messages of sympathy and support from all over the world, but nothing touched me more than to get from the Sunday-school children at St. James's, Madison Avenue, in New York, what the children called passports of love, which I pasted up on the walls of my office. How can anyone range himself against this international, this global fellowship?

I want to stress what I said in the preamble: the church is made up of frail, fallible human beings, so also for the SACC. In the New Testament we hear Our Lord's parable of the Kingdom as consisting of wheat and tares. That is a picture, too, of the church, which is an agent for the Kingdom. The church is the home of sinners and the school for saints. We always marvel that God can want to use such unworthy creatures as we know ourselves to be. His treasure, St. Paul tells us, is held in us, who are but earthenware vessels, so that the abounding glory should belong rightly where it belongs, not to us, but to God.

I have shown that the teaching which we proclaim, which is under scrutiny by this commission, is based squarely and truly on the Bible. But it is also in line with the teaching of the Church of God throughout the world. It is a fact of life that can be noted by anyone who has eyes to see and does want to see, who is not biased, that the South African Council of Churches enjoys the support of the overwhelming segment of the Christian community in the world. I am not aware that, for instance, the Dutch Reformed Church, which supports apartheid, enjoys even a fraction of the support we enjoy. I am not boasting; I am just stating a fact. In fact, some people criticize us precisely because we have this support, expressed in money gifts to us.

Why do we enjoy such worldwide support? It is possible to deceive some people some of the time but surely we could not be endowed with the ability to deceive such a large body of responsible and mature Christians for so long. We have operated and we continue to operate openly. We report regularly to our member churches . . . We do not operate secretly and yet there are private, secret societies in this land which are alleged—I do not know whether this is true—to exercise an enormous influence on some churches and on political leaders.* Such secret societies are not, to my knowledge, investigated. We do not receive funds clandestinely. They are recorded openly, and yet there are organizations, even religious organizations, some of which were involved in the Information scandal, which have received clandestine funding.† They were set up precisely to undermine a legitimate body such as the SACC, and those sinister organizations continue with impunity to spew forth their poisonous filth. A bank recently lost over a million rand through the malfeasance of one of its employees. The court found she had in fact been assisted by other bank officials, yet I have not heard that that bank, which deals with far more of the public's funds than the SACC could ever hope to, is being investigated by any commission. Why not, if we are?

*A reference to the Afrikaner Broederbond (the Afrikaner Brotherhood), an elite secret society dedicated to promoting Afrikaner interests. It was regarded as a secret power behind the ruling establishment, rather as Freemasonry is seen in parts of Europe.
†During the 1979 funding scandal involving the government's Department of Information, it was revealed that among the propaganda fronts it supported was a right-wing body, the Christian League of Southern Africa.

We are told that we do not enjoy the support of the churches in South Africa. That statement may be true to some extent, if we mean by South African churches the white part of the church. In our membership by and large, white Christians form only 20 percent of our constituency. The black membership, forming nearly 80 percent, can be said without fear of contradiction to represent that part of the church that supports the SACC to a very considerable extent. But even if this were not the case, our Lord has warned us that we must beware when all men speak well of us. . . .

M'Lord, you will not find any SACC staff members in their offices if you come to Khotso House in Johannesburg at eight-thirty every morning, because we are in chapel. Every Wednesday at lunchtime we have prayers for justice and reconciliation in our land and some of us have a fast on Thursdays for the same purpose . . . We have a daily Eucharist and substantial daily Bible studies as features of every national conference. Before each national conference I write to religious communities in this country and abroad, asking for their prayers for the conference, which is thus surrounded by a considerable volume of prayer. As a bishop of the church, I am under obligation to pray the Office of the church twice a day. I want to say that for me the most important, the most cardinal fact about our life is the spiritual—that encounter with God in prayer, in worship, in meditation.

I am sorry to reveal this secret part of our lives, which scripture exhorts must not be paraded before men. I have been compelled to talk about it to show that we try to be persons of prayer, people who try to wait on our Lord. We may not always hear him aright and often perhaps when we hear what he says, we do not like what he is asking us to do. But I want to assure you that we are not politicians. We are attempting to be devout Christians. Speaking for myself, I want to say that there is nothing the government can do to me that will stop me from being involved in what I believe is what God wants me to do. I do not do it because I like doing it. I do it because I am under what I believe to be the influence of God's hand. I cannot help it. When I see injustice I cannot keep quiet, for, as Jeremiah says, when I try to keep quiet God's word burns like a fire in my breast. But what is it that they can ultimately do? The most awful thing that they can do is to kill me, and death is not the worst thing that could happen to a Christian.

Our Lord has tried to weld us into a family: people of different races, who demonstrate, however feebly and fitfully, what this beautiful land can be. If only we could begin to treat people as persons created by God in his image, redeemed by Jesus Christ and sanctified by the Holy Spirit, what a wonderful land it would be. And we believe that it will happen . . .

Of course, it cannot happen without suffering and anguish. Jesus did not promise his followers a bed of roses. On the contrary, and central to it all, was the inevitability and unavoidable nature of suffering. It could be said from this that a church that does not suffer cannot be the church of Jesus Christ. I do not mean we should be masochists. Suffering will seek us out. It is part of the divine economy of salvation.

Interestingly enough, M'lord, in the Anglican calendar this week we are bidden to think of the church as the suffering community, and this is the special prayer for this week:

GOD, OUR LOVING Father, you gave your only Son to die, to suffer and to die for men. Grant that when we are found worthy to endure suffering for Christ's name, we may rejoice in our calling and be enabled to bear our part in completing his sufferings for the sake of your church.

We are not to be surprised at suffering that comes to us because of witnessing for the Kingdom of God and for the Gospel of Jesus Christ. Listen to these words of Our Lord:

IF THE WORLD hates you, it hated me first, as you know well. If you belonged to the world, the world would love its own; but because you do not belong to the world, because I have chosen you out of the world, for that reason the world hates you. Remember what I said: "A servant is not greater than his master."

The Making of a Peaceful Revolution

As they persecuted me, they will persecute you; they will follow your teaching as little as they have followed mine. It is on my account that they will treat you thus, because they do not know the one who sent me (John 15:18–21).

And in Matthew 10:17–22:

AND BE ON your guard, for men will hand you over to their courts, they will flog you in the synagogues, and you will be brought before governors and kings, for my sake, to testify before them and the heathen. But when you are arrested, do not worry about what you are to say; when the time comes, the words you need will be given you; for it is not you who will be speaking: it will be the Spirit of your Father speaking in you. Brother will betray brother to death and the father his child; children will turn against their parents and send them to their death. All will hate you for your allegiance to me; but the man who holds out to the end will be saved.

God's purposes are certain. They may remove a Tutu, they may remove the South African Council of Churches, but God's intention to establish his Kingdom of justice, of love, of compassion, will not be thwarted. We are not scared, certainly not of the government, or any other perpetrators of injustice and oppression, for victory is ours through him who loved us.

I end, M'lord and members of the commission. With all this in mind what are we to say? If God is on our side, who is against us? What can separate us from the love of Christ? Can affliction or hardship, can persecution, hunger, nakedness, peril or the sword? We are being done to death for thy sake all day long, the scripture says. We have been treated like sheep for slaughter, and yet, in spite of all, overwhelming victory is ours through him who loved us. For I am convinced that there is nothing in death or life, in the realm of spirits or superhuman powers, in the world as it is or in the world as it shall be, in the forces of the universe, in heights or depths; there is nothing in all creation that can separate us from the love of God in Christ Jesus our Lord. Thank you.

7

Not Even Invited to the Party

(1983)

A KEY element of the government's reform program was an attempt to bolster white rule by co-opting the Colored and Indian people. In the early 1980s much political debate was devoted to proposals for a new constitution which would achieve what was called power sharing with representatives of these groups. Strong opposition to power sharing led the right wing of the National Party, headed by Andries Treurnicht, to break away in March 1982 and form the Conservative Party. In July the National Party announced proposals for a constitution which would establish a racially segregated, tricameral parliament. The proposals were designed to ensure that Colored and Indian members could never outvote whites—even if members of minority parties in the white chamber agreed with them on an issue. In January 1983 the Labor Party, which organized those classified as Colored, decided at its annual congress to participate in the new constitutional dispensation.

Tutu presented his view on the constitutional proposals to an audience at the University of Cape Town in February 1983.

You ask me how I feel, how most black Africans feel, about the constitutional proposals which have set most of the country agog? Before I answer that question, as an aside it is beginning to be difficult to know how you describe the different sectors of our population. Black seems to be the all-inclusive term which many of us prefer, but what happens when you have to make distinctions forced upon us, as between Indians, so-called Coloreds and those who have been excluded? Things were certainly easier in bygone days when we were called Native with capital N; though you then had those queer creatures, Foreign Natives. Do you remember some such road sign as this: "Careful, Natives cross here," which was changed by a wag to read: "Careful, Natives very cross here." Perhaps that sums it all up. The natives of this beautiful country, the indigenous inhabitants, the sons and daughters of this black soil, are very angry.

Let me put it this way: Have you ever gone to a cocktail party where everybody seemed to know everybody else and as you stood at the door and looked around you realized that you did not know a soul? Everybody there regarded you as an intruder—some as something that the cat had brought in.

We feel like that guest, only more so, for we have not even been invited to the party. We resent being treated as if we were invisible. Mr. Chairman, you know that Africans make a proper song and dance about the ritual of greeting and get quite annoyed when you don't greet them. The point about greeting someone and asking genuinely after their well-being is that it acknowledges their humanity, their personhood. Not to greet someone is really to destroy or dehumanize them. They are not persons—for all you care, they could be trees. These proposals refuse to acknowledge our existence. We are here without being here, invisible. That is why even theologically they are iniquitous and evil and a sure recipe for national disaster.

Having spoken about not being invited, I need to say categorically that if we had been invited in the first place, we would have turned down the invitation. Why? Because these proposals are not designed to do the thing that would solve the crisis in our land—that is, to dismantle apartheid and create a new kind of society in South Africa, a nonracial, truly democratic society.

We hear that the Westminster model is to be jettisoned because it enshrines winner-take-all domination and that the new setup will ensure that no group enjoys domination. Well, here we have proposals which talk about a ratio of 4:2:1 as between whites, Coloreds and Indians. My friends, we have been told that we are slow thinkers, and I will be the first to concede that slow thinkers can't help it when they count and they find, however you look at it, four always comes out as more than two plus one. Quick thinkers might discover a different answer.

However you look at it, the proposals are designed to perpetuate the domination of one group—and that a minority of a minority. It is domination by whatever name you want to call it. Racial separation, the bane of South Africa, will continue to the extent that the parliamentarians won't ordinarily mix racially when they deliberate. They are going to be together separately. The government has succeeded splendidly in throwing all the opposition forces into disarray. The Progressive Federal Party doesn't really know quite what they want to do. Even the Afrikaner opposition is at sixes and sevens. You heard the story: "Why can't the Herstigte Nasionale Party and the Conservative Party unite?" "The HNP wants to drive the Bantu into the sea and the CP does not allow Bantu on the beaches."

The black community is torn from top to bottom. Mr. P. W. Botha can rub his hands in glee. He is riding the crest of an enormous wave. He has got the constitutional proposals accepted by his party congresses. He has sown confusion in the ranks of his opponents. And it even appears he has a hot line to heaven, because soon after the day of prayer be called for, the rains came. Even up there someone is batting for him.

And he has got the cherry on the top—the agreement of the Labor Party. They are honorable men. But I just want to say I am surprised that they are saying the things they are saying. I believed differently about them. What are they going to negotiate when the lines are drawn so clearly and so rigidly? There was a plea in the black community to the West Indian cricketers not to try and tell us cock-and-bull stories about how their coming here would help destroy apartheid. It would be better and more honest for them to come clean and say they were here for the money [offered by South African sports officials to attract international teams to break the anti-apartheid sports boycott]. People would understand and be more tolerant. I think I want to say the same thing to the Labor Party. Cut out the cock-and-bull story about how you are going to change the system from within. Be more honest and say you are in it for what you can get. People would respect at least your honesty. Man, they must know something is horribly, badly wrong when overnight they become blue-eyed boys of *Die Transvaler, Burger, Beeld* and *Vaderland* [newspapers] and the pinups of the South African Broadcasting Corporation.

I want to register, too, my deep annoyance with the United States and Great Britain. I did not expect it of Great Britain. The Reagan administration I have written off as an unmitigated disaster for us blacks. I am annoyed at the rubbish they can talk in welcoming the Labor Party decision and saying it shows reform is happening in South Africa. Poppycock! The Labor Party knows it has been co-opted to perpetuate apartheid and to be co-oppressors with the Nats [National Party] and their supporters of blacks. Freedom is certain and they are delaying the day of liberation when South Africa will be truly free.

8

Apartheid's "Final Solution"

(1984)

THE NEW constitution was approved by the white parliament in August 1983 and endorsed by two-thirds of the voters in a referendum in November. In June, Desmond Tutu was one of the leaders who convened a new black umbrella body, the National Forum Committee, initiated by adherents of black consciousness who had called for a united stand against the constitutional proposals. August saw the national launching of the nonracial United Democratic Front in response to an appeal by Allan Boesak of the Dutch Reformed Mission Church. The UDF brought together progressive nonracial organizations to oppose both the proposals and plans to foist on black communities a new system of local government. Representatives of 575 organizations attended. Desmond Tutu was one of the patrons, a position he held until becoming Bishop of Johannesburg in 1985, when he believed he should distance himself from any appearance of party partisanship.

The implementation of the new constitution in September 1984 was marked by a new wave of resistance and repression, leading to the most widespread violence since the Soweto uprising. School disturbances began early in the year and were followed by protests against the "Indian" and "Colored" elections in August. In an election boycott, only 18 percent of those eligible to vote in the Colored community took part, and 16 percent in the Indian community. In the Vaal Triangle, south of Johannesburg, violence erupted after rent increases were imposed in black townships by local councillors, who represented less than 10 percent of eligible voters and were regarded by many as collaborators. Po-

lice opened fire on demonstrators during a work boycott on September 2, three of the councillors were killed and sixty people died in the month which followed. Protests spread, leading to the biggest political strike in South Africa's history on November 5 and 6. Between September 3 and the end of 1984, at least 149 people were reported killed. Amid international controversy, troops of the South African Defense Force were deployed in the townships in October. In the same month the Norwegian Nobel Committee recognized the South Africans' struggle for democracy by awarding the 1984 Peace Prize to Desmond Tutu. The 1984 Nobel Lecture was delivered in December.

Your Majesty, members of the Royal Family, Mr. Chairman, ladies and gentlemen:

Before I left South Africa, a land I love passionately, we had an emergency meeting of the executive committee of the South African Council of Churches with the leaders of our member churches. We called the meeting because of the deepening crisis in our land, which has claimed nearly two hundred lives this year alone. We visited some of the trouble spots on the Witwatersrand. I went with others to the East Rand. We visited the home of an old lady. She told us that she looked after her grandson and the children of neighbors while their parents were at work. One day the police chased some pupils who had been boycotting classes, but they disappeared between the township houses. The police drove down the old lady's street. She was sitting at the back of the house in her kitchen, while her charges were playing in the yard in front of the house. Her daughter rushed into the house, calling out to her to come quickly. The old lady dashed out of the kitchen into the living room. Her grandson had fallen just inside the door, dead. He had been shot in the back by the police. He was six years old. A few weeks later, a white mother, trying to register her black servant for work, drove through a black township. Black rioters stoned her car and killed her baby of a few months old, the first white casualty of the current unrest in South Africa. Such deaths are two too many. These are part of the high cost of apartheid.

Every day in a squatter camp near Cape Town called KTC, the authorities have been demolishing flimsy plastic shelters which black mothers have erected because they were taking their marriage vows seriously. They have been reduced to sitting on soaking mattresses, with their household effects strewn round their feet, and whimpering babies on their laps, in the cold Cape winter rain. Every day the authorities have carried out these callous demolitions. What heinous crime have these women committed, to be hounded like criminals in this manner? All they have wanted is to be with their husbands, the fathers of their children. Everywhere else in the world they would be highly commended, but in South Africa, a land which claims to be Christian and which boasts a public holiday called Family Day, these gallant women are treated so inhumanely. Yet all they want is to have a decent and stable family life. Unfortunately, in the land of their birth it is a criminal offense for them to live happily with their husbands and the fathers of their children. Black family life is thus being undermined, not accidentally but by deliberate government policy. It is part of the price human beings, God's children, are called to pay for apartheid. An unacceptable price.

I come from a beautiful land, richly endowed by God with wonderful natural resources, wide expanses, rolling mountains, singing birds, bright shining stars out of blue skies, with radiant sunshine, golden sunshine. There is enough of the good things that come from God's bounty, there is enough for everyone, but apartheid has confirmed some in their selfishness, causing them to grasp greedily a disproportionate share, the lion's share, because of their power. They have taken 87 percent of the land, though being only about 20 percent of our population. The rest have had to make do with the remaining 13 percent. Apartheid has decreed the politics of exclusion: 73 percent of the population is excluded from any meaningful participation in the political decision-making processes of the land of their birth. The new constitution, making provision for three chambers, for whites, Coloreds and Indians, mentions blacks only once and thereafter ignores them completely. Thus this new constitution, lauded in parts of the West as a step in the right direction, entrenches racism and ethnicity. The constitutional committees are composed in the ratio of four whites to two Coloreds to one Indian—zero black . . . Hence this constitution perpetuates by law and entrenches white minority rule.

Blacks are expected to exercise their political ambitions in unviable, poverty-stricken, arid bantustan homelands, ghettos of misery, inexhaustible reservoirs of cheap black labor, bantustans into which South Africa is being balkanized. Blacks are systematically being stripped of their South African citizenship and being turned into aliens in the land of their birth.* This is apartheid's final solution, just as Nazism had its final solution for the Jews in Hitler's Aryan madness. The South African government is smart. Aliens can claim but very few rights, least of all political rights.

In pursuance of apartheid's ideological racist dream, over three million of God's children have been uprooted from their homes, which have been demolished, while they have been dumped in the bantustan homeland resettlement camps. I say dumped advisedly: only rubbish or things are dumped, not human beings. Apartheid has, however, ensured that God's children, just because they are black, should be treated as if they were things and not as of infinite value as being created in the image of God. These dumping grounds are far from where work and food can be procured easily. Children starve, suffer from the often irreversible consequences of malnutrition. This happens to them not accidentally but by deliberate government policy. They starve in a land that could be the bread basket of Africa, a land that normally is a net exporter of food.

The father leaves his family in the bantustan homeland, there eking out a miserable existence, while he, if he is lucky, goes to the so-called white man's town as a migrant, to live an unnatural life in a single-sex hostel for eleven months, being prey there to drunkenness, prostitution and worse. This migratory labor policy is declared government policy and has been condemned as a cancer in our society even by the white Dutch Reformed Church—not noted for being quick to criticize the government. This cancer, eating away at the vitals of black family life, is deliberate government policy. It is part of the cost of apartheid, exorbitant in terms of human suffering.

*Connie Mulder, Minister of Bantu Administration and Development (BAD), said in 1978: "If our policy is taken to its logical conclusion . . . there will not be one black man with South African citizenship . . . Every black man in South Africa will eventually be accommodated in some independent new state in this honorable way and there will no longer be a moral obligation on this parliament to accommodate these people politically." (South African Hansard, proceedings of the South African parliament, Cape Town, February 7, 1978, quoted by legal academic John Dugard and reproduced in *The Apartheid Handbook,* by Roger Omond [Penguin 1985].)

Apartheid has spawned discriminatory education such as Bantu education, education for serfdom, ensuring that the government spends only about one-tenth on a black child per annum for education of what it spends on a white child. It is education that is decidedly separate and unequal. It is to be wantonly wasteful of human resources, because so many of God's children are prevented, by deliberate government policy, from attaining their fullest potential. South Africa is paying a heavy price already for this iniquitous policy, because there is a desperate shortage of skilled manpower, a direct result of the shortsighted schemes of the racist regime. It is a moral universe that we inhabit, and good and right and equity matter in the universe of the God we worship. And so, in this matter, the South African government and its supporters are being properly hoisted with their own petard.

Apartheid is upheld by a phalanx of iniquitous laws, such as the Population Registration Act, which decrees that all South Africans must be classified ethnically and duly registered according to these race categories. Many times, in the same family one child has been classified white while another with a slightly darker hue has been classified Colored, with all the horrible consequences for the latter of being shut out from membership of a greatly privileged caste. There have, as a result, been several child suicides. This is too high a price to pay for racial purity, for it is doubtful whether any end, however desirable, can justify such a means. There are laws, such as the Prohibition of Mixed Marriages Act, which regard marriages between a white and a person of another race as illegal. Race becomes an impediment to a valid marriage. Two persons who have fallen in love are prevented by race from consummating their love in the marriage bond. Something beautiful is made to be sordid and ugly. The Immorality Act decrees that fornication and adultery are illegal if they happen between a white and one of another race. The police are reduced to the level of Peeping Toms to catch couples red-handed. Many whites have committed suicide rather than face the disastrous consequences that follow in the train of even just being charged under this law. The cost is too great and intolerable.

Such an evil system, totally indefensible by normally acceptable methods, relies on a whole phalanx of draconian laws such as the security legislation which is almost peculiar to South Africa. There are the laws which permit the indefinite detention of persons whom the Minister of Law and Order has decided are a threat to the security of the state. They are detained at his pleasure, in solitary confinement, without access to their family, their own doctor, or a lawyer. That is severe punishment when the evidence apparently available to the minister has not been tested in an open court—perhaps it could stand up to such rigorous scrutiny, perhaps not; we are never to know. It is a far too convenient device for a repressive regime. The minister would have to be extra special not to succumb to the temptation to circumvent the awkward process of testing his evidence in an open court; and thus he lets his power under the law be open to the abuse where he is both judge and prosecutor. Many, too many, have died mysteriously in detention. All this is too costly in terms of human lives. The minister is able, too, to place people under banning orders without being subjected to the annoyance of the checks and balances of due process. A banned person for three or five years becomes a nonperson who cannot be quoted during the period of her banning order. She cannot attend a gathering, which means more than one other person. Two persons together talking to a banned person are a gathering! She cannot attend the wedding or funeral of even her own child without special permission. She must be at home from 6 P.M. of one day to 6 A.M. of the next, on all public holidays and from 6 P.M. on Fridays until 6 A.M. on Mondays. She cannot go on holiday outside the magisterial area to which she has been confined. She cannot go to the cinema, or to a picnic. That is severe punishment, inflicted without the evidence allegedly justifying it being made available to the banned person, or having it scrutinized in a court of law. It is serious erosion and violation of basic human rights, of which blacks have precious few in the land of their birth. They do not enjoy the rights of freedom of movement and association. They do not enjoy security of tenure, the right to participate in the making of decisions that affect their lives. In short, this land, richly endowed in so many ways, is sadly lacking in justice.

Once a Zambian and a South African, it is said, were talking. The Zambian boasted about their Minister of Naval Affairs. The South African asked, "But you have no navy, no access to the sea. How then can you have a Minister of Naval Affairs?" The Zambian retorted: "Well, in South Africa you have a Minister of Justice, don't you?"

It is against this system that our people have sought to protest peacefully since 1912 at least, with the founding of the African National Congress. They have used the conventional methods of peaceful protest—petitions, demonstrations, deputations and even a passive resistance campaign. A tribute to our people's commitment to peaceful change is the fact that the only South Africans to win the Nobel Peace Prize are both black.* Our people are peace-loving to a fault. The response of the authorities has been an escalating intransigence and violence, the violence of police dogs, tear gas, detention without trial, exile, and even death. Our people protested peacefully against the pass laws in 1960 and 69 of them were killed on March 21, 1960, at Sharpeville, many shot in the back running away. Our children protested against inferior education, singing songs and displaying placards and marching peacefully. Many in 1976, on June 16 and subsequent times, were killed or imprisoned. Over 500 people died in that uprising. Many children went into exile. The whereabouts of many are unknown to their parents. At present, to protest that selfsame discriminatory education and the exclusion of blacks from the new constitutional dispensation, the sham local black government, rising unemployment, increased rents and General Sales Tax, our people have boycotted and demonstrated. They have staged a successful two-day stay-away. Over 150 people have been killed. It is far too high a price to pay. There has been little revulsion or outrage in the West at this wanton destruction of human life.

In parenthesis, can somebody please explain to me something that has puzzled me? When a priest goes missing and is subsequently found dead, the media in the West carry his story in very extensive coverage.† I am glad that the death of one person can cause so much concern. But in the selfsame week when this priest is found dead, the South African police kill 24 blacks who had been participating in a protest, 6,000 blacks are sacked for being similarly involved, and you

*The other South African peace laureate had been Chief Albert Luthuli, President-General of the African National Congress, in 1960.
†A reference to the abduction and murder of Father Jerzy Popieluszko by the Polish secret police in October 1984.

are lucky to get that much coverage. Are we being told something I do not want to believe, that we blacks are expendable and that blood is thicker than water, that when it comes to the crunch, you cannot trust whites, that they will club together against us? I don't want to believe that this is the message being conveyed to us.

Be that as it may, we see before us a land bereft of much justice, and therefore without peace and security. Unrest is endemic and will remain an unchanging feature of the South African scene until apartheid, the root cause of it all, is finally dismantled. At this time the army is being quartered on the civilian population. There is a civil war being waged. South Africans are on either side. When the ANC and the PAC were banned in 1960, they declared that they had no option but to carry out the armed struggle. We in the SACC have said that we are opposed to all forms of violence—that of a repressive and unjust system and that of those who seek to overthrow that system. However, we have added that we understand those who say that they have had to adopt what is a last resort for them. Violence is not being introduced into the South African situation de novo from outside by those who are called terrorists or freedom fighters, depending on whether you are oppressed or an oppressor. The South African situation is violent already and the primary violence is that of apartheid, the violence of forced population removals, of inferior education, of detention without trial, of the migratory labor system, etc.

There is war on the border of our country. South African faces fellow South African. South African soldiers are fighting against Namibians who oppose the illegal occupation of their country by South Africa, which has sought to extend its repressive systems of apartheid, unjust and exploitative.

There is no peace in Southern Africa. There is no peace because there is no justice. There can be no real peace and security until there be first justice enjoyed by all the inhabitants of that beautiful land. The Bible knows nothing about peace without justice, for that would be crying, "Peace, peace, where there is no peace." God's shalom, peace, involves inevitably righteousness, justice, wholeness, fullness of life, participation in decision making, goodness, laughter, joy, compassion, sharing and reconciliation.

I have spoken extensively about South Africa, first because it is the land I know best, but because it is also a microcosm of the world and an example of what is to be found in other lands in differing degree— when there is injustice, invariably peace becomes a casualty. In El Salvador, in Nicaragua and elsewhere in Latin America, there have been repressive regimes which have aroused opposition in those countries. Fellow citizens are pitted against one another, sometimes attracting the unhelpful attention and interest of outside powers, who want to extend their spheres of influence. We see this in the Middle East, in Korea, in the Philippines, in Kampuchea, in Vietnam, in Ulster, in Afghanistan, in Mozambique, in Angola, in Zimbabwe, behind the Iron Curtain.

Because there is global insecurity, nations are engaged in a mad arms race, spending billions of dollars wastefully on instruments of destruction, when millions are starving. And yet, just a fraction of what is expended so obscenely on defense budgets would make the difference in enabling God's children to fill their stomachs, be educated and given the chance to lead fulfilled and happy lives. We have the capacity to feed ourselves several times over but we are daily haunted by the spectacle of the gaunt dregs of humanity shuffling along in endless queues, with bowls to collect what the charity of the world has provided, too little too late. When will we learn, when will the people of the world get up and say, enough is enough? God created us for fellowship. God created us so that we should form the human family, existing together because we were made for one another. We are not made for an exclusive self-sufficiency but for interdependence, and we break that law of our being at our peril. When will we learn that an escalating arms race merely escalates global insecurity? We are now much closer to a nuclear holocaust than when our technology and our spending were less.

Unless we work assiduously so that all of God's children, our brothers and sisters, members of our one human family, enjoy the basic human rights, the right to a fulfilled life, the right of movement, the freedom to be fully human within a humanity measured by nothing less than the humanity of Jesus Christ himself, then we are on the road inexorably to self-destruction, we are not far from global suicide. And yet it could be so different.

When will we learn that human beings are of infinite value because they have been created in the image of God, that it is blasphemy to treat them as if they were less than this, and to do so ultimately recoils on those who do this? In dehumanizing others, they are themselves dehumanized. Perhaps oppression dehumanizes the oppressor as much as, if not more than, the oppressed. They need each other to become truly free, to become human. We can be human only in fellowship, in community, in *koinonia*, in peace.

Let us work to be peacemakers, those given a wonderful share in our Lord's ministry of reconciliation. If we want peace, so we have been told, let us work for justice. Let us beat our swords into plowshares.

God calls us to be fellow workers with him so that we can extend his kingdom of shalom, of justice, of goodness, of compassion, of caring, of sharing, of laughter, joy and reconciliation, so that the kingdoms of this world will become the Kingdom of our God and of his Christ, and he shall reign for ever and ever. Amen. Then there will be fulfillment of the wonderful vision in the Revelation of St. John the Divine (Revelation 7:9ff).

Part Three

"THERE IS NO PEACE"

The States of Emergency

9

You Don't Reform a Frankenstein

(1985)

THE PROTESTS *which began in 1984, bolstered by the organizational capacity of such groups as the UDF, turned into the most sustained revolt against apartheid since 1976. In July 1985, Prime Minister Botha declared a state of emergency for the first time since the period following the Sharpeville killings in 1960. Security forces were granted extraordinary powers of arrest, detention, censorship and control of public assembly. Nearly 8,000 people were reported to have been detained under emergency regulations between July 1985 and March 1986, when they were temporarily lifted in an attempt to retain support from conservative Western governments. The regulations also indemnified the security forces against criminal or civil court proceedings and extended powers they already had allowing them to arrest people without charges and search them without a warrant. Guerrilla activity expanded, but conflict within the black community increased, as did attacks on blacks perceived to be collaborators. Especially gruesome were "necklace" killings, in which a tire doused with gasoline was placed around an alleged collaborator's neck and set on fire.*

As repression intensified, international pressure against apartheid built up. Financial institutions, led by Chase Manhattan Bank in the United States, decided not to extend loans to South African institutions, precipitating a financial crisis. In August, the Foreign Minister, Pik Botha, suggested that P. W. Botha would announce important political reforms to a National Party congress in Natal. There was speculation about drastic change, but P. W. Botha, apparently angered by the pres-

sure, delivered an aggressive speech which dashed expectations. The value of the South African rand plummeted to an unprecedented low. Trading on the Johannesburg Stock Exchange was suspended for the first time since Sharpeville. A temporary freeze on repayments of foreign debt was imposed to protect foreign currency reserves. A group including the country's most powerful businessmen defied government disapproval of dealing with "terrorists" and flew to Zambia for discussions with the exiled leadership of the African National Congress.

Violence against people accused of collaboration reached such a pitch that in July 1985 Tutu and several fellow clergymen had to intervene to protect the life of a suspected informer who was being attacked by members of a crowd at a funeral in Duduza, east of Johannesburg. Some days later, at another funeral in Duduza, which Tutu did not attend, cameras recorded the brutal killing of Maki Skosana, a young woman suspected of being associated with a policeman. Tutu's response, at a third funeral in the same region, was given international publicity:

WE HAVE A cause that is just. We have a cause that is going to prevail. For goodness' sake, let us not spoil it by the kind of methods that we use.

And if we do this again, I must tell you that I am going to find it difficult to be able to speak up for our liberation. I will find it difficult—it is already difficult in this country to talk the truth, but if we use methods such as the ones that we saw in Duduza, then, my friends, I am going to collect my family and leave a country that I love very deeply, a country that I love passionately . . .

Later Tutu was to reject the use by the media of the term "black-on-black" violence. The phrase implied that there was a qualitative difference when blacks killed people of their own race instead of those of another, he said. He had never seen violence in Northern Ireland described as "white-on-white."

In a speech to the Political Committee of the UN General Assembly in New York in October 1985, Tutu, who had become Bishop of Johannesburg soon after winning the Nobel Prize, addressed the international community on the crisis.

In the present phase of apartheid we have been regaled with the language of reform. Of course, apartheid cannot be reformed. It must be dismantled. You don't reform a Frankenstein—you destroy it. Everybody has been agog to support change, when things have sadly remained the same. In fact, for blacks they have got worse. The pass laws are firmly in place. Last year 160,000 blacks fell afoul of the pass laws which rigidly control our right to move freely in the land of our birth. This in the year of reform, when the government claimed it was waging war against the pass book . . . It is quite remarkable that our people have remained peace-loving to a fault. A very recent Human Sciences Research Council report [in Pretoria] shows that less than 50 percent of blacks believe that violence is the only solution to apartheid . . .

I am a bishop in the church of God. I am fifty-four years old. I am a Nobel laureate. Many would say I was reasonably responsible. In the land of my birth I cannot vote. An eighteen-year-old, because he or she is white (or since August last year so-called Colored or Indian), can. Our people have sought to march peacefully. You have seen on your television screens the violence that has been unleashed against them and the brutal viciousness of the police with their whips, their rubber bullets, their guns. Over 700 people have died [in the latest violence]. Blacks have burned and killed other blacks. We have expressed our utter abhorrence of all violence, including black-on-black violence. But this is not a phenomenon peculiar to blacks. During World War II the Quisling was given short shrift. In Northern Ireland the IRA traitor is shot without compunction or is kneecapped. Those who are believed to be collaborators with apartheid are detested deeply and they are liquidated. I don't condone this. To end it we must end its cause, apartheid.

South Africa is a violent country and the primary violence, as I have shown, is the violence of apartheid. The ANC and the PAC espoused the armed struggle only after the South African government, aided and abetted by most of the West, declared them to be illegal organizations. Many Western countries received their independence only after a violent and bloody struggle. The West has lauded to the skies the resistance movement during World War II. It has hailed Dietrich Bonhoeffer [the German Protestant theologian executed in 1945 for alleged involvement in a plot to kill Hitler] as a modern-day saint. I agree. But he was executed for being involved in a plot to assassinate his head of state. And yet when it comes to black liberation, the West wakes up and suddenly finds it has become pacifist.

They say South Africa is a bulwark against Communism. But injustice and oppression are surely the best breeding grounds for Communism. The West is giving free enterprise and capitalism very bad names as the allies of that vicious system of apartheid. Many of our people reject capitalism and the free enterprise system as exploitative and for us the enemy of our enemy is our friend. Anyone who supports us against apartheid, not just with fine words but with fine matching actions, is our friend—actions like those taken by the Scandinavian countries, by France and those proposed by Canada [sanctions]. Someone once said that when you have fallen into a well and a hand is stretched out to pull you out, you don't ask for their credentials. You grab that hand joyfully. When the West fought Nazism it was deeply thankful for the support of the Soviet Union. Did that make the West Communist?

You have seen the violence meted out to our people. You have seen police hiding in boxes to lure youngsters to stone them, and when they did, the police opened fire and killed three of them.* That is what we are talking about. Peaceful resistance and protest are virtually impossible in South Africa. If you are an effective opponent of apartheid then you may be charged with high treason or you may be detained under the emergency regulations; you may be banned. A three-year-old was killed by a police rubber bullet. An eleven-year-old was assaulted by the police until he died, also only recently. Another eleven-year-old

*A reference to the "Trojan Horse" incident in Athlone, Cape Town, in October 1985. Armed security forces hid in crates on the back of a truck which had the appearance of a government-owned vehicle, then cruised down a street. When they were stoned, they emerged from the crates and opened fire, killing three, two of them youths of eleven and sixteen.

was kept in jail for nearly two months for throwing stones, kept in custody with hardened criminals before he was released. A teenager had five teeth kicked out by police recently. I saw a teenager who was tortured in detention. He is a vegetable now. He says he wishes he could die. He walks and talks like a zombie. My son was detained for fourteen days because he swore at the police. He was said to be a danger to the security of the state.

We run the gauntlet of roadblocks. I am the Bishop of Johannesburg and I am a Nobel laureate, as I said before. My wife and daughters have been stripped to be body-searched at a roadblock. Your dignity is not just rubbed in the dust. It is trodden underfoot and spat on. Our people are being killed as if they were but flies. Is that nothing to you who pass by? What must we say that we have not said? "God, give us eloquence such that the world will hear that all we want is to be recognized for what we are—human beings created in your image." Is it nothing to the world that 800 black pupils are arrested, some as young as seven, and have to spend the night in jail? Aren't you appalled and outraged? Would the West be so passive if the casualties were white rather than black? Are blacks expendable?

Our country is on the verge of a catastrophe. Only a miracle or the intervention of the West will avert Armageddon. There is still the outside chance of a reasonably peaceful resolution taking place. But the situation is desperately bad. Whites tell you that things are improving, are getting better. With respect, I don't think they are in any position to tell us that. They are not qualified. It is the victims, not the perpetrators, who must say whether things are better or not. When you are throttling me you can't really tell me that things are better, that you are not choking me quite so badly. It is I who will say, "Ah yes, the pressure has eased." When will the world listen to the victim rather than the perpetrator?

When I became Bishop of Johannesburg, I said that if apartheid was not ended within eighteen to twenty-four months, I would call for economic sanctions. But the situation at home has developed desperately badly and I am now aligning myself with the timetable of the Commonwealth, which is six months. If apartheid has not been dismantled within six months, the world should apply punitive economic sanctions.

Signs of Hope

We have an incredible land with wonderful people. White South Africans are not demons. They are ordinary people, mostly scared. Wouldn't you be if you were outnumbered five to one? If I was white I would need a lot of grace to resist a system that provided me with such substantial privileges. Hence those whites who oppose apartheid should be lauded to the skies. There are many of them and they have paid or are paying a heavy price for that opposition. People like Beyers Naudé, the women of the Black Sash, church leaders, those young whites engaged in the End Conscription Campaign, the Detainees' Parents Support Committee, trade unionists and others. There are organizations such as the United Democratic Front, which is a rainbow coalition, saying that black and white, Colored and Indian, all belong together and must work together for the same South Africa.

I was attending a funeral in Uitenhage of those killed in the unrest. There were nearly 100,000 people there. I sat next to Allan Boesak on the platform. In front of us, out of earshot, two young women held each other as they sat on the grass. That was not remarkable. I said to Allan, "This is the South Africa we are working for." As if they could hear me, those women held each other more tightly. That was not remarkable except in South Africa, because one was white and the other black.

Let us work together for the new South Africa, when all of us, black and white, will live together amicably as members of one family, God's family, the human family. It is simple. The world must apply pressure on South Africa to end the state of emergency; to declare unequivocally their intention to dismantle apartheid; to release all political prisoners and detainees; to allow exiles to return; and to talk with the authentic representatives of each sector of our society.

We must not be fobbed off with high-sounding expressions about common citizenship and a united South African universal franchise which turn out only to be a rehash of apartheid with some poor plastic surgery done on it. The run on the rand has concentrated minds wonderfully, so that private-sector leaders have gone to talk to the ANC because they were being hurt nonviolently, peacefully, where it hurt most, in their pocketbooks. I want to suggest that here is a fairly easy, but quite effective method. Let the [foreign] bank loans be renegotiated on a clear basis that credit will be extended only when the conditions I have mentioned above have been met. Otherwise, the credit must not be extended.

It is a matter of life or death. We want a legitimate government, elected freely by all South Africans, black and white, and the world has a chance of bringing this about without any further bloodshed and violence. And remember that two surveys have shown that over 70 percent of the blacks believe that sanctions of some sort should be imposed. What I propose is in fact not the stick, but a carrot. Will you help us to become free? All of us, black and white, in South Africa? Then real security, stability and prosperity will come to our subcontinent and indeed to our entire continent.

Apartheid is a threat to world peace. We owe it to future generations to end it. Let us be part of the exhilarating enterprise of liberating South Africa for all its people, black and white together. We shall be free, all of us, black and white together. And we shall remember who helped us to be free.

10

Punitive Sanctions

(1986)

APARTHEID WAS not abolished within six months, but the precise timing of an explicit call for sanctions was dictated by developments in the Anglican Church. In April 1986 an elective assembly of the Diocese of Cape Town met to choose a successor to Philip Russell, the retiring Archbishop of Cape Town and Metropolitan (spiritual head) of the church. Desmond Tutu was asked to stand as a candidate. Sanctions were an emotional and divisive issue, so he decided to make his position clear ahead of the election. He did so on April 2, 1986. April 1, he often jokes, would not have been an auspicious date.

In 1976, out of a growing concern and deepening apprehension about the mood in Soweto, one of increasing anger and bitterness and frustration, I wrote an open letter to the then Prime Minister, Mr. B. J. Vorster. In it I was warning him that unless something was done, and done urgently, to remove the causes of black anger, then I was fearful of what was likely to erupt, because black people were growing increasingly restive under the oppressive yoke of apartheid. For young people it was represented in the insensitive determination to enforce Afrikaans as a medium of instruction on them in their inferior schools in a system of education that had been designed by its author, Dr. [Hendrik] Verwoerd [Vorster's predecessor], for inferiority. My letter was dismissed contemptuously by Mr. Vorster as a propaganda ploy somehow engineered by the Progressive Federal Party. He did not even think I could as a black person have the intelligence to know the grievances of my own people, nor the ability, if I did, to compose a letter to express those grievances.

A few weeks later, on June 16, Soweto happened, and South Africa has not had real peace and stability since then.

I refer to this first effort to show that for over ten years I have attempted to alert the authorities in this land to the dangers to which their misguided and iniquitous policies were exposing our beloved country. In that 1976 letter I referred to some of the minimum conditions that would enable blacks to feel that their plight was being taken seriously. I have made many public statements urging the government to act decisively and to give blacks hope.

I have since then on many occasions intervened in delicate, volatile situations to try and help defuse them. I have with other black and white leaders gone to Turfloop and Fort Hare universities [black universities] to offer our good offices to resolve the perennial problems relating to student boycotts on those campuses. This was the action of someone who believed that problems can be solved by people sitting down together to discuss their differences. This has been a fundamental stance on my part. I have spoken to various white groups and addressed audiences at all the white university campuses, except the University of Port Elizabeth. I have been even to the University of the Orange Free State and I can tell you that that was something else. I have been to some of these universities often, more than just once. I was criticized in the black community for doing so because it was said I was just wasting time. I believed and I still believe that we must try to undo the evil consequences of apartheid and one of these is that white and black don't really know one another. So I was ready, as I still am ready, to talk especially to young whites to help them see and so help them to think, in the hope that by thinking independently they would come to reject this horrendous policy, so utterly evil, immoral and unchristian, which their fathers and mothers have tended to support, and by their rejection help to save our country from catastrophe. For I still believe our young people, black and white, will be our salvation.

In 1980, on my initiative, some of the leaders of the South African Council of Churches and of member churches went to see Mr. P. W. Botha, who was then Prime Minister, and his senior cabinet col-

"I am writing to you as one human person to another human person . . ." Balthazar Johannes Vorster, pictured through the gun port of an armored personnel carrier, ignored Desmond Tutu's warning of rising tensions in May 1976. *Richard Bell/Mayibuye collection*

June 16, 1976, was a watershed that marked the beginning of a new era of open defiance. The V sign made by these Soweto student leaders at a 1977 protest was used at that time to indicate peaceful intentions. *Mayibuye Center*

Steve Biko's coffin, marked "One Azania, One Nation," below a Black People's Convention banner. Azania is the name given to South Africa by the Pan-Africanist Congress and the black consciousness movement.
Mayibuye Center

"That suffering [caused by forced removals] is what has tipped the scales for me in calling for economic pressure on this country." A shack from a resettlement camp was erected in the foyer of Khotso House, Johannesburg, headquarters of the South African Council of Churches, to draw attention to the plight of people in remote rural areas.
Frank Black/The Star, *Johannesburg*

"God called [Steve Biko] to be the founder father of the black consciousness movement . . ." The then Bishop Tutu in front of a Black People's Convention banner at Biko's funeral. *Mayibuye*

"I will do all I can to destroy this diabolical system [of forced removals] whatever the cost to me." The three million victims of the system were often dumped amid a sea of corrugated iron toilets in poverty-stricken rural areas, and left to build their own shelter. *Mayibuye Center*

"Police opened fire, killing thirteen-year-old Hector Peterson . . ." This picture of Mbuyiselo Makhubu carrying Hector away, Hector's sister Antoinette crying alongside, has become the best-known image of the Soweto schoolchildren's revolt. The photographer, Sam Nzima, worked for *The World*, a newspaper that was banned sixteen months later.

Sam Nzima/International Defense and Aid Fund Collection at the Mayibuye Center

Colonel Theuns Swanepoel, head of the police riot squad in Johannesburg, informs clergy at their 1980 march that they are under arrest. Nicknamed "the Red Russian," Swanepoel was a feared Security Police interrogator in the 1960s. With Desmond Tutu are the Reverend Jimmy Palos and the Reverend Cecil Begbie (face obscured), both of the Methodist Church.

The Star, *Johannesburg*

Under P. W. Botha's rule the military gained prominence. Framed beneath the barrel of a gun, he and fellow ministers take the salute at a military parade in Pretoria in 1980. On Botha's right is General Magnus Malan, a former chief of the South African Defense Force who succeeded Botha as Minister of Defense.
Paul Weinberg/ SouthLight

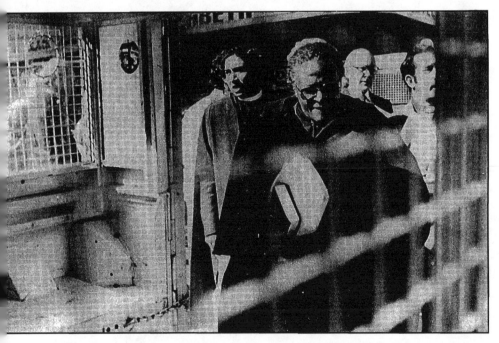

Church leaders mounted an illegal march in Johannesburg in May 1980 to protest the detention of a colleague. Desmond Tutu and other clergy prepare to climb into a police van after their arrest. They spent a night in jail awaiting their court appearance. *Mark Peters/*
The Star, *Johannesburg*

P. W. Botha "is sadly now trying to prove that he is a man of iron." As Prime Minister and then President, Botha was caricatured by satirists for wagging his index finger when emphasizing a point. The National Party's symbol at the time was a powder horn. *Mayibuye Center*

When a new constitution was introduced in 1984, giving the Colored and Indian communities the right to choose representatives for racially segregated chambers of parliament, most of those eligible to vote boycotted the polls, leaving election monitors with little to do. *Mayibuye Center*

"If we use methods such as [necklace murders] . . . then my friends I am going to collect my family and leave a country that I love very deeply . . ." Desmond Tutu, speaking at a funeral on the East Rand in 1985, condemns the killing of people accused of being police informers.
Gill de Vlieg/Mayibuye Center

Speaking to Colonel G. M. Erasmus, head of the Security Police in Johannesburg, after handing him a petition demanding the release of the Anglican Bishop Suffragan of Johannesburg, Sigisbert Ndwandwe, in April 1985. *Kevin Carter*/The Star

leagues. We were trying to make them understand that unrest would be endemic in South Africa unless its root cause was removed—and that root cause was apartheid. We declared then that we knew that politics was the art of the possible and did not want to suggest they do anything which would erode their support among their constituency. We put forward four things which, if they were done, would be a dramatic demonstration of the government's intention to effect real political change leading to political power sharing [see p. 43]. These were not wild, radical demands, and if the government had implemented them, then we would have been saved a great deal of anguish, bloodshed and the loss of property and an increase in bitterness and hatred and anger. We were criticized in the black community for going to the government. These were much the same conditions I had mentioned in my 1976 letter to Mr. Vorster. But you know what happened? These were ignored. In fact, we later discovered that the government had dealt dishonorably with us, for while we were discussing with them in good faith, all the while they were employing the Christian League as a front organization in their nefarious efforts to subvert, malign and discredit the SACC, as was to be revealed in the infamous Info scandal. Actually the government intensified its efforts to undermine the council and me personally by getting its sycophantic South African Broadcasting Corporation and other of its media lickspittle supporters to denigrate and vilify us, culminating in the Eloff commission to investigate the SACC. That ended up with the government being embarrassed . . . and the SACC and I received a global vindication by the award of the Nobel Peace Prize. The government was thoroughly hoisted with its own petard because our member churches and overseas supporters rallied to our support in an unprecedented way.

Despite all this negative response from the government, I was often in delegations to see various government ministers, trying to make them take different attitudes especially on the issues of forced population removals and education. Mr. Barend du Plessis, then minister responsible for black education, publicly thanked me for helping to defuse the situation in Atteridgeville before the funeral of . . . [Emma] Sathekge . . . [a fifteen-year-old girl run over by a police car on the grounds of a school during unrest in 1984]. He has thus far been the only government minister to my knowledge to do so. We went to Atteridgeville with the Rev. Stanley Mogoba [later Presiding Bishop of the Methodist Church] on behalf of the SACC. It was just carrying out my belief that we must try to talk ourselves out of a crisis. I offered myself as a go-between between the government and the African National Congress, long before it was fashionable to go to Lusaka [Zambia], in the hope that the authorities would seize an opportunity to start the negotiations that are inevitable if we are to save our country from disaster.

In 1984, far from heeding our calls for negotiation leading to power sharing, the government introduced a constitution which was the climax of the policies of exclusion to which blacks had been subjected since 1910. Seventy-three percent of the population was excluded from any participation in this monumental hoax, designed to hoodwink the international community: that apartheid was being reformed. Apartheid is irreformable. It must be destroyed before it destroys our country. That constitution was meant to entrench white minority rule with the co-opted help of so-called Coloreds and Indians, collaborators in their own and our oppression and exploitation. The people have rejected it unequivocally and August 1984 saw the beginning of the current wave of unrest.

Despite all this, I tried again last year to see State President [Botha, who held this title as head of government under the new constitution] to talk with him as one South African to a fellow South African, as one grandfather to another, as one Christian to another. I acted in the hope that he would act as only he could, the one white South African for whom blacks would have been ready to erect a statue as the man who would have gone down in history as having presided over the dissolution of apartheid and the emergence of a new, a more equitable, a just, a nonracial and truly democratic South Africa. He turned me down. In parenthesis I might add that I have said he needed to be commended for his courage in telling whites that there was no way in which they alone could determine the future of this country forever. Sadly he did not go far enough and so ended up pleasing neither the blacks nor his so-called right wing. To turn an English expression around, we see the sad spectacle of a man who does not have the convictions of his courage. Yet I was ready to go to Alexandra Township to help defuse the tense situation there and to go in a delegation to Cape Town to talk with the government about that situation and the situation in the country.

Nothing in South Africa, or very little, has changed without pressure from the international community. The sports policy changed only as a result of the sports boycott, which I have supported, and continue to do so as a nonviolent method to bring about change. I have called on the international community to exert pressure on the government, political, diplomatic but above all economic pressure to persuade it to go to the negotiating table with the authentic representatives of all sections of our society and I have said for blacks this would mean those in jail or in exile. I have said this umpteen times. I have been accused of advocating sanctions and I said I have not yet called for sanctions. I have said each country should surely decide for itself the nature of economic pressure it wishes to apply.

I have lost my passport on a few occasions, once for two years because I was accused of advocating sanctions, and I have consistently been attacked in the media as such an advocate. South Africans are so good at finding scapegoats and enemies instead of dealing with the problem which stares us in the face . . . I have been depicted by nearly all the white media, even so-called responsible liberal English newspapers, as that "public enemy." They have succeeded in inciting whites to a pitch of hostility where they must take the responsibility if whites do then kill such as ourselves . . .

Most Western countries have rejected economic sanctions because we are told these would hurt blacks most of all. I hope that most who use this argument would just drop it quietly and stop being so hypocritical. It is amazing how everybody has become so solicitous for blacks and become such wonderful altruists. It is remarkable that in South Africa the most vehement in their concern for blacks have been whites. Very few blacks have repudiated me for my stance. This is very odd. They are not stupid. They would know if they were going to suffer and they would reject out of hand one who wanted to bring that suffering on them. And yet in the black community my standing is very high. Even more remarkably, two recent surveys have shown that over 70 percent of blacks support sanctions of some sort. Blacks have carried out consumer boycotts; they have staged massive stay-aways to make a political statement.

Over 1,200 blacks have died since August 1984. Blacks are killed mainly by the security forces, almost as if they were flies. Children are detained. Children are killed. It is alleged fifty were shot in the back outside a court. I have heard hardly a squeak from the whites who claim they are concerned for black suffering. This is real, actual black suffering, not future possible suffering. They say the state of emergency has been lifted. On Easter Sunday I saw a Casspir [armored troop carrier] rumbling down Soweto Highway. On Easter Monday in our part of Soweto, much the most quiet part, four Casspirs and personnel carriers drove past my house. My wife said, "The border is here." [South African troops were resisting incursions by Swapo and the ANC from bordering states.] The troops are still in the townships after the Durban education conference, which took a brave decision about the children staying in school [after threats of boycotts], and we have the insensitivity of the authorities displaying their military might when they know the presence of the troops in the townships is highly provocative.

Nothing that Mr. Botha has said has made me believe that he and his government are serious about dismantling apartheid. He says we are one nation, and just as we are rejoicing, then he says we are a nation of minorities—the unadulterated and dangerous nonsense of bantustans. If we are one nation, then why should kwaNdebele [a bantustan] be going for this spurious independence, why should the people of Moutse [who resisted being incorporated into kwaNdebele] die to satisfy a racist ideology?*

We are told there will be an end to the pass laws and we say "Hurrah!" And then we hear that there will be "orderly urbanization." Since blacks have been artificially stopped from being urbanized, or-

*The 120,000 residents of the Moutse district of the Lebowa homeland in the Transvaal were transferred by the South African government to the jurisdiction of the kwaNdebele authorities in January 1986. Their leaders believed their area was given to kwaNdebele as a reward for accepting "independence" and there was strong resistance to the transfer. More than forty people were reported killed in clashes between residents and kwaNdebele vigilantes early in 1986. Later in the year kwaNdebele was forced by popular pressure to abandon "independence," and in 1988 the Supreme Court ruled the transfer unlawful.

derly urbanization will apply to them alone and so some form of influx control will have to be applied [leaving citizens of "independent" homelands still subject to restrictions].

But the giveaway is surely the public dressing-down that [Foreign Minister] Mr. Pik Botha got [from P. W. Botha for suggesting there could one day be a black President]. For once when he was speaking the truth, he is repudiated. The State President said there would be power sharing. Surely the sheer arithmetic of South Africa should indicate that there will be a black President. Even the law of averages decrees this if we have one nation . . .

Then there were the devastating resignations of Dr. van Zyl Slabbert and Dr. Alex Boraine [opposition leaders who pulled out of the white parliament in February 1986]. The media played down their significance. These two gentlemen were endorsing our long-stated views that parliament in South Africa is a mere charade. The Progressive Federal Party have always given the world the illusory impression that we have a parliamentary democracy when we really have a one-party state which is viciously oppressive and unjust and violent in putting down opposition and dissent. You are banned, detained or charged with high treason!

I have no hope of real change from this government unless they are forced. We face a catastrophe in this land and only the action of the international community by applying pressure can save us. Our children are dying. Our land is burning and bleeding and so I call the international community to apply punitive sanctions against this government to help us establish a new South Africa—nonracial, democratic, participatory and just. This is a nonviolent strategy to help us do so. There is a great deal of goodwill still in our country between the races. Let us not be so wanton in destroying it. We can live together as one people, one family, black and white together.

11

Agents of Transfiguration
(1986)

CONTRARY TO *his expectations, after announcing his support for sanctions Tutu was elected Archbishop of Cape Town. He had been the first black South African to be Dean of Johannesburg, then the first to be Bishop of Johannesburg. Now he became the first to head the church, formally called the Church of the Province of Southern Africa, and covering South Africa, Lesotho, Mozambique, Namibia, Swaziland and the island of St. Helena in the South Atlantic Ocean. On September 7, 1986, he set the tone for his archiepiscopacy when he was enthroned in St. George's Cathedral in Cape Town.*

His sermon, an edited extract of which follows, was delivered at a time when resistance was high. The government had retreated from some elements of apartheid, repealing the laws prohibiting interracial sex and marriage, desegregating many public facilities and ignoring contraventions of the Group Areas Act committed by blacks who went to live in "white" areas. Tutu himself was never prosecuted for living in Bishopscourt, the official residence of archbishops, in a Cape Town suburb. But beyond these highly circumscribed reforms, suppression was intensified. A state of emergency had been reimposed in June 1986 and was to be renewed annually until after Nelson Mandela's release from prison in 1990. Again, extraordinary powers were given to the security forces. Funerals of victims of political violence became rallying points for dissent, so restrictions were imposed on how they were conducted. In addition, tight clamps were placed on the media: journalists were banned from scenes of unrest and reporting on security force activity

*was put under government control. When newspapers left blank spaces
to indicate they had been censored, the blank spaces were prohibited.
The Detainees' Parents Support Committee estimated that 25,000 people were detained under emergency regulations between June and December 1976. The South African Institute of Race Relations reported
that almost 1,300 people died in political violence in 1986.*

Centrality of the Spiritual

I have recently been reading the book of the prophet Ezekiel. It struck
me how the prophet starts by describing that extraordinary vision of
the glory of God and then he is overwhelmed . . . The prophet falls
prostrate. But God raises him to his feet because he wants to send him
to this recalcitrant house of Israel . . . He receives the Word or is imbued with the Spirit . . . The Spirit is given, the divine is encountered,
for the sake of others. I am sure you have noted before that this seemed
to be the almost universal rhythm. Moses encounters the divine at the
burning bush and he receives his instructions to go tell Pharaoh to "let
my people go." The seventy elders receive a share in the Spirit given
to Moses to assist him in judging the people; Saul is spirit-filled so
that he can become king and the Spirit is snatched back when he
proves disobedient . . . All these and other servants of Yahweh must
have had what they believed to be an encounter with the divine when
they had a sense of being called and equipped for mission. It must
have been that personal gifts were enhanced and they became more
truly what God wanted them to be . . . but all this not just for their own
sakes but for the sake of others.

This rhythm is repeated in the New Testament. Our Lord, having
spent nearly thirty years in a hidden life preparing for his Messianic
mission, waits until he is anointed by the Holy Spirit at his baptism.
Mark says this Spirit virtually propelled Jesus into the desert to enter
the fray against the evil one. Again the Spirit is not given so that the
individual person may luxuriate in its possession. It is given to goad
him or her into action, to prepare him for the stern business of loving
God and loving neighbor, not in a nebulous fashion but in flesh-and-
blood terms, love incarnated in the harsh reality that forms the . . . or-

dinary life setting of so many of God's children. Jesus commands his disciples to wait in Jerusalem for the gift from on high before they can embark on their mission to be his witnesses in Jerusalem and unto the ends of the earth. And they would remember that it had been so with their Lord and Master. Some of them had been with him on the mountaintop to share in the sublime experience of the Transfiguration and they had wanted to remain there undisturbed by the clamor of the uncomprehending, demanding, madding crowd. Surely that is how God wanted to be worshipped and adored. But no—they did not understand yet. The Transfiguration was happening so that they could descend to the valley of human need, of faithlessness, of dangerous evil spirits. In this life we could never remain on the mountaintop. The authenticity of the transfiguration mountaintop experience would be attested by how it fitted us to be God's presence, healing, restoring, forgiving, reconciling, admonishing, comforting in the world alienated from him and yet which remained the object of his love, so much so that for it he had given his only begotten Son. It is all truly intoxicating stuff, for the God we would worship and adore is he who said:

I HAVE INDEED seen the misery of my people in Egypt. I have heard their outcry against their slave-masters. I have taken heed of their sufferings, and have come down to rescue them from the power of Egypt, and to bring them up out of that country into a fine, broad land; it is a land flowing with milk and honey . . . The outcry of the Israelites has now reached me; yes, I have seen the brutality of the Egyptians towards them. (Exodus 3:7–9)

He is this God who, choosing his people for his own, wants them to reflect his character, so that others will know what sort of a God he is by seeing what kind of people they are. They must be holy because he their God is holy. They must be compassionate because he their God was compassionate, especially when they were slaves in Egypt. This

God loved all his human creatures but he had a special concern for the weak, the hungry, the powerless. And so if his people were truly his people, then they too must reveal a like concern, so they are exhorted constantly to show compassion especially to the widow, the orphan and the alien, for they represented in most societies those who tended to be marginalized, pushed to the back of the queue; what a friend has described as the "left-behinds." We would worship a God who spurns a religiosity marked by however meticulous a concern for the elaborate minutiae of ritual and sacrifice but which lacks an impact on how the worshippers live their lives day by day. And so when the people offer him sacrifice and a cacophony of music and prayers, he rejects these in words that must have shocked the worshippers:

HEAR THE WORD of the Lord, you rulers of Sodom; attend, you people of Gomorrah, to the instruction of our God: your countless sacrifices, what are they to me? says the Lord. I am sated with whole-offerings of rams and the fat of buffaloes; I have no desire for the blood of bulls, of sheep and he-goats. Whenever you come to enter my presence—who asked you for this? No more shall you trample my courts. The offer of your gifts is useless, the reek of sacrifice is abhorrent to me. New moons and sabbaths and assemblies, sacred seasons and ceremonies, I cannot endure. I cannot tolerate your new moons and your festivals; they have become a burden to me, and I can put up with them no longer. When you lift your hands outspread in prayer, I will hide my eyes from you. Though you offer countless prayers, I will not listen. There is blood on your hands . . . (Isaiah 1:10–15)

The people thought nothing could be more religious than fasting. And yet the God we would worship would not accept it . . .

It is because he is a God who, when a nonentity—as the world computes these things—such as Naboth is done to death because the queen wanted an awkward customer out of the way so that her husband could confiscate his vineyard, well, when that happened, this God intervened in political, in judicial matters because for this God, our God, no one is a nonentity. For this God, our God, everybody is a somebody. All life belongs to him. Because of him all life is religious. There are no false dichotomies so greatly loved by those especially who are comfortable in this life. Consequently, if you say you love God whom you have not seen and hate your brother whom you have, the Bible does not use delicate language; it does not say you are guilty of a terminological inexactitude. It says bluntly you are a liar. For he who would love God must love his brother also. And so the divine judgment about our fitness for heaven will be based not on whether we went to church, whether we prayed or did other equally important religious things. No, Jesus says it will be based on whether we fed the hungry, clothed the naked, because in doing these things to those whom he called the least of his brethren we would have done them as to himself. Our God, this hidden God, is also the incarnate God, the God made flesh, our flesh. And if we take the incarnation seriously we must be concerned about where people live, how they live, whether they have justice, whether they are uprooted and dumped as rubbish in resettlement camps, whether they are detained without trial, whether they receive an inferior education, whether they have a say in the decisions that affect their lives most deeply . . .

Friends, we do this not because of our politics, but because of our religion. Blessed be God our God for being such a God. And so for us the spiritual is utterly crucial. I am only repeating what Archbishop Philip declared to the Provincial Synod last year. If we can be a church that prays, a church that meditates, a church whose members are regular at the Eucharist, a church whose members go on retreat as a matter of course, who use the other sacraments faithfully, why then we shall be an effective agent in the hands of God. I have appointed Father Francis Cull to be director for the study of spirituality to help us to grow in holiness and become truly spiritual persons. I hope that in time we could have a whole army of persons skilled as spiritual directors and retreat conductors. I know that many of our parishes have a daily Eucharist. I want to urge that this surely ought to be uniform practice in the Diocese and the Province. We have sometimes sat loosely to hallowed catholic practice. I bid you recover the biblical practice of fasting. Why can't it be standard for the Diocese and the Province to fast, say, every Friday? Jesus is reported as saying that some demons could not be exorcised except by prayer and fasting. The demons of injustice, oppression and exploitation can be exorcised only by prayer and fasting. I know that it is often not possible to have fasting communions, but that does not mean we should become overfamiliar with the things of God. Why must we not deepen our sense of awe and reverence? I must say I have often been appalled to see people smoking just before Holy Communion. I am old-fashioned enough to say I hope I won't have to see it anymore. I urge you, my sisters and brothers, to pray earnestly for our beautiful, our wonderful land as we pray for other parts of our Province. I am reiterating calls that have been made before. Could we, for instance, as we choose to fast corporately on Fridays, agree to pray especially on that day for our Republic of South Africa that injustice and oppression and unjust rule will end and that God's righteousness, love, peace and reconciliation will prevail?

The Church as Family

Our Lord came into a deeply divided and polarized society. There was the divide between the hated foreign oppressor and the citizens of the vassal state. Within Judaism there were different religious groupings, the Pharisees, the Sadducees, the Zealots. There was the divide between the Jew, the Gentile and the Samaritan. And then men were segregated from women. There were free persons and there were slaves. There were the rich, there were the poor. There were collaborators and those who worked within the hateful system. The world saw a veritable miracle unfolding before its very eyes as all sorts and conditions of women and men, rich and poor, slave and free, Jew and Gentile—all these came to belong in one fellowship, one *koinonia*, one communion. They did not regard one another just as equals. That in itself would have been a huge miracle, for a slave to be accepted as an equal by his former master. An equal you can acknowledge once and then forever thereafter ignore. No, they regarded one another not just as equals but as sisters and brothers, members of one family, God's family. Extraordinarily a once-apprehensive Ananias can actually call a former persecutor of Christians *"Brother* Saul . . ."" You don't choose your family. They are God's gift to you, as you are to them. Perhaps if we could, we might have chosen different brothers and sisters. Fortunately or unfortunately we can't. We have them as they have us. And no matter how your brother may be, you can't renounce him. He may be a murderer or worse, but he remains forever your brother. Our baptism has made us brothers and sisters. Can you imagine what would happen in this land if we accepted that theological fact about ourselves—that whether we like it or not we are members of one family? Whether I like it or not, whether he likes it or not, as I have said before, P. W. Botha is my brother and I must desire and pray for the best for him.

The wonderful thing about family is that you are not expected to agree about everything under the sun. Show me a man and wife who have never disagreed and I will show you some accomplished fibbers. But those disagreements, pray God, do not usually destroy the unity of the family. And so it should be with God's family, the church. We are not expected at all times to be unanimous or to have a consensus on every conceivable subject. As long as we are as one on the fundamentals and refuse to let go of one another. You are not expected as Anglicans to agree with your archbishop on every issue. Healthy differences of opinion can help the body to be more lively. After all, it is unity we are talking about, not uniformity. What is needed is to respect one another's points of view and not to impute unworthy motives to one another or to seek to impugn the integrity of the other. Our maturity will be judged by how well we are able to agree to disagree and yet continue to love one another, to care for one another and to cherish one another and seek the greater good of the other. As the church, we are set as a sign in the world, the first fruits of the Kingdom, to demonstrate what God intends human society to be, united in a rich diversity, to demonstrate that Christ has indeed broken down the middle wall of partition, and so we must accelerate the pace of true nonracialism, especially in our appointments.

Another characteristic of the family is its willingness to share. The early church went so far as to have its members selling their property, each refusing to claim as his exclusive property what had belonged to him before. They had all things in common. When the one part suffered the whole suffered with it and when one part prospered then the whole prospered with it. There was a mutuality in the relationship in which all gave and all received. Some gave more conspicuously in spiritual things while others gave in material gifts. Hence the collection for the saints was a deeply spiritual exercise. In a happy family you don't receive in proportion to your input. You receive in relation to your needs, the ones who make the least material contribution often being the ones who are most cared for—the young and the aged. How I pray that in our church we can learn to emulate a true family, emulate the divine generosity of our Lord Jesus Christ, who, although rich, for our sakes became poor that we through his poverty might become rich. How I pray for the day when the Anglican Church would be marked by a membership that knows that all things come from God and all belongs to him, that we have the privilege of being his stewards and that the very least we should give in thanksgiving for God's abundant bounty and limitless generosity is the tithe. Our church in many parts of this Province has always seemed to have money problems. If only we could give as those who tithe, there would be no problem. God's work suffers because we are so ungenerous, many of us. We cannot expand the work of God's Kingdom because we lack financial and people resources and yet God has blessed us abundantly. Some have said the diocese I have left had money troubles because of the views of its bishop. I want to point out that there have been many who were generous and the giving in 1985 actually went up by 17 percent in a time of recession and unemployment as well as threats of disinvestment. As a Province we have the capacity to assist other parts of our communion generously with people and money, instead of being the recipients of so much, given unstintingly by our sisters and brothers elsewhere.

Members of a family have a gentle caring and compassion for one another. How I pray that our Lord would open our eyes so that we would see the real, the true identity of each one of us, that this is not a so-called Coloured or white, or black or Indian, but a brother, a sister, and to treat each other as such. Would you let your brother live an unnatural life as a migrant worker in a single-sex hostel? Would you let his family, your relatives, eke out a miserable existence in a poverty-stricken bantustan homeland? Would you tell your brother or your sister, "No, you have no right here, because you are an alien," an alien deliberately produced by an evil and totally immoral and unchristian policy?

Would you deny your sister, your brother, a proper education, fobbing them off with something that you had designed as an inferior and cheaper commodity than that which you provided for other members of the same family? Would you refuse your brother and sister a just participation in the decision-making processes of the land of their birth, treating them always as if they were minors for whom decisions were to be made, since others always knew what was best for them?

If we could but recognize our common humanity, that we do belong together, that our destinies are bound up with one another's, that we can be free only together, that we can survive only together, that we can be human only together, then a glorious South Africa would come into being where all of us lived harmoniously together as members of one family, the human family, God's family. In truth a transfiguration would have taken place.

Transfiguration

The principle of transfiguration is at work when something so unlikely as the gray grass that covers our veld in winter, or the tree with gnarled leafless branches, bursts forth with the sap flowing so that the grass is green again and the birds sit chirping in the leafy branches and the once-dry streams gurgle with swift-flowing water—when winter gives way to spring and nature seems to have experienced its own resurrection. The principle of transfiguration is at work when mundane everyday fare, bread and wine, apparently recalcitrant matter, is lifted to a higher order of being or becomes the channel for the divine life, quite surprisingly so that this bread broken and this cup shed become now the body and blood of the victim who gave his life once for all in the all-sufficient and perfect sacrifice on the Cross availing for the forgiveness of our sins.

The principle of transfiguration says nothing, no one and no situation is "untransfigurable," that the very creation, nature, waits expectantly for its transfiguration when it will be released from its bondage and share in the glorious liberty of the children of God, when it will not be just dry inert matter but will be translucent with a divine glory. The principle of transfiguration avers that an erstwhile persecutor can become the greatest missionary of the truth he once persecuted, that one who denied his Master not once but three times could become the prince of apostles proclaiming boldly faith in a Jesus Christ when only a short while before he was cowering in abject fear behind locked doors. It is the principle of transfiguration at work when an instrument of the most painful and shameful death can become the life-giving Cross which Christians wear with pride and which is traced over them at significant moments in their life.

And so it is the principle of transfiguration at work when one so unlikely, so unfitting can be called to be the Archbishop and Metropolitan of this great church. He knows that there is much in him that would be a let and a hindrance to others and he asks for your fervent prayers that he will not impede the work of God, that he will learn ways to commend the Gospel of grace graciously and with due humility.

God calls on us to be his fellow workers. He wants to enlist our support to be his agents of transfiguration, of transformation. There is much evil afoot in the world, in this land. Many years ago there used to be signs that read: "Natives and dogs not allowed." They spoke eloquently about the attitude of some whites toward blacks. We were thought to be human but not quite as human as white people, for we lacked what seemed indispensable to that humanity, a particular skin color. That attitude made possible some gross ill-treatment meted out to black people by their white compatriots. Have things changed? Yes and no. I am sad to say that I believe that the fundamental attitude that "blacks are human, but . . ." has not changed. I do not intend to shock you. I wish I were totally wrong. We do not express it with the same crudity, but it remains all the same. But let me give you some instances. At the present time one of our bishops is not here. He is in detention—his second detention. His first ended when we declared that we were going to march to the jail in which he was being held. He was quickly brought to court and after three court appearances had charges withdrawn. Sometime during his second detention he and other black ministers held with him were released. A few yards away from their place of detention they were accosted by white policemen, laughing and feeling very pleased with themselves, who said they were re-detaining them. They were taken into custody and they were stripped, he to his underpants and the others quite naked. The reason, it was said, was to search them for dangerous weapons. Where would they have got these unless detainees are supplied with weapons in detention? Was it not in order to humiliate them, to humiliate this bishop of the Church of God and his fellow ministers of the Gospel? Would this have happened had they been white? Yes, perhaps—François Bill, the moderator of the Evangelical Presbyterian Church, while in detention was brought in shackles and leg irons to meet someone from the Swiss Legation. Perhaps he was thought to be beyond the pale because he is moderator of a church which is almost exclusively black. You have heard the allegations of torture by Father Smangaliso Mkhatshwa [secretary-general of the Southern African Catholic Bishops' Conference], in a country that has a constitution that calls on the name of God.

Why can it happen that when twenty or so white children die in a bus accident, the papers cover this awful disaster extensively and the bus driver is actually brought to court . . . or when a very few whites are killed, say, by a land mine, that too is covered extensively, and yet just this past week over twenty people were killed by the police in Soweto and there is not too much fuss? I am glad that the PFP have called for a judicial inquiry—but I think I have made my point. Any death is one death too many and yet it does seem some are more equal than others in life and in death. Can you imagine the outcry there would have been had it been a white four-year-old killed by a police rubber bullet as happened recently, or had it been a white eleven-year-old kept in solitary confinement for five months? Would white women have been treated as the women of KTC camp [near Cape Town] in 1983, who in the middle of winter had their flimsy plastic shelters regularly demolished by the authorities as they sat with whimpering babies on their laps in the rain, with their pathetic household effects gathered around their feet? Would white pensioners have been dismissed as "superfluous appendages" as a former cabinet minister declared our fathers and mothers who could no longer work? And what about the juveniles who were recently sentenced very severely to long stretches in jail? Would that have happened had they been white? I have been told that in Soweto in some schools the troops lie on the floor and let girl pupils file past them while looking up the girls' tunics. We will get ritual denials but the fact of the matter is that in the townships the police and the soldiers are hated. They are not regarded as protectors. They are placed in an invidious position because they are perceived as defending the indefensible and that is tragic for the fabric of society. Why do it to us?

Have you been to Alexandra Township, a stone's throw away from one of the most affluent parts of Johannesburg; Alexandra Township with its dusty ill-lit streets with unemptied night-soil buckets sometimes lining those streets—and people laugh and love and marry and children play in Alexandra Township? Why do it to us? Mercifully many in affluent Sandton are concerned about Alexandra Township and do something. Yes, there are wonderful people in this land. Black Sash ladies working themselves to the bone to help blacks; young whites with the End Conscription Campaign ready to pay a heavy price not to be part of a Defense Force they perceive as helping to uphold an unjust dispensation; wonderful people who bring succor and help to suffering people in Crossroads and elsewhere.

We have a wonderful country with truly magnificent people if only we could be allowed to be human together. We are all dehumanized by injustice and oppression, so that a man can actually say he is left cold by the death of a fellow human being. We have a wonderful country. Many whites are fearful that blacks, come liberation, would treat them as they have treated us. And yet our people are not like that. A young former colleague after 230 days in solitary confinement and nearly a year in preventive detention said on his release, "Let us not be consumed by bitterness." He is one of the twenty-two appearing in the Delmas treason trial and one of my richest memories of today is a card signed by those twenty-two, which they gave to their advocate, George Bizos, to bring here. Another former detainee—someone who is now a priest in this diocese—told me that as he was being tortured he thought: "By the way, these are God's children and they are behaving like animals. They need us to help them recover the humanity they have lost." Most would have said that Kenya after Mau Mau would be a white man's graveyard. But what is the reality? President Daniel arap Moi told me that the staunchest Kenyans and certainly among the best Kenyan farmers are Afrikaners from South Africa who remained in Kenya. We were led to expect the worst in Zimbabwe, but the much-maligned Robert Mugabe spoke about reconciliation, rehabilitation and reconstruction and included whites in his first cabinet. Whatever the South African media may tell you as they concentrate on the un-unique teething troubles of a new nation, the truth is that in Zimbabwe the races are coexisting very happily and harmoniously together. After all, Mr. Ian Smith is still a member of parliament. Isn't that remarkable? The whites who fled to South Africa are returning to their home.

We Africans speak about a concept difficult to render in English. We speak of *ubuntu* or *botho.* You know when it is there and it is obvious when it is absent. It has to do with what it means to be truly human, it refers to gentleness, to compassion, to hospitality, to openness to others, to vulnerability, to be available for others and to know that you are bound up with them in the bundle of life, for a person is only a person through other persons. And so we search for this ultimate attribute and reject ethnicity and other such qualities as irrelevancies. A person is a person because he recognizes others as persons. At the height of racial tension in South Africa 20,000 people attended the funeral of a Molly Blackburn [a white human rights activist] and over 90 percent of these were black, because Molly looked on you and saw a human being of infinite worth, because you had been created in the image of God. She did not see you as black first, but as a human being. Why can't we be human together in South Africa?

Conclusion

Friends, like you I abhor all violence. I condemn the violence of an unjust system such as apartheid and that of those who want to overthrow it. But it is absolutely important for South African whites to know that the ANC and the PAC were nonviolent for most of their history . . . It is important when talking about violence to note that the primary violence in this country is the violence of apartheid. The miracle of our land is that it has not gone up in flames. Would white people still be talking about nonviolent change, as some of us do, if what they have done to us and they continue to do to us had been done to them?

I am not sure the government wants real change, which would mean an entirely new dispensation with a new disposition of political power and a greater sharing of the good things so abundant in South Africa— land, wealth and other resources. In this they are not different from politicians everywhere who want to gain power and hold on to it for as long as possible. I am amazed that there are many white people who actually want the kind of change I have referred to. God be praised for those whites. I have often commended the State President for his courage, but he has always stopped just disastrously short of providing the solution we all want. It is no good looking for scapegoats either in the form of the total onslaught from outside, or Communism and agitators, or those such as your archbishop who are picked on as bringing on us our present sad state of affairs. Supposing you did liquidate Tutu, what have you solved? No, let us acknowledge that all our problems, all the violence we are experiencing (necklacing, etc., which we condemn roundly and repeatedly) ultimately stem from apartheid. And it can never be the perpetrators of apartheid who can say apartheid is changing. The world will believe that this is so when we, the victims of this vicious evil, declare that it is indeed changing. If white people are so impressed with all the changes, would they swap places with blacks even for one day? We have appealed to the government and to white South Africans to recognize us as human beings with inalienable rights, just like whites.

I do not want sanctions. I know that those who advocate sanctions don't want them either. I have told the State President as much. I said if you were to lift the state of emergency, remove the troops from our townships, release political prisoners and all detainees, unban our political organizations and then sit down with the authentic representatives of every section of our community to negotiate a new constitution for one undivided South Africa, then for what it is worth I would say to the world: "Put your sanctions plans on hold." I mean that. Please spare us your newfound altruism. Where were you when Sophiatown, District Six, Pageview and many other black communities were destroyed? Where was your concern when blacks received an inferior education, were cheap labor, when black family life was deliberately being destroyed by the migratory labor system? Why did you not utter a squeak—most of you—about real, actual suffering? The onus must be on those who say "no" to sanctions; you must provide us with a viable nonviolent strategy to force the dismantling of apartheid. Remember that the government has rejected gentle persuasion. The ball is still in the court of the government and the white community. We want to live amicably with you. We want one united South Africa where everyone matters because each of us is created in God's image.

We shall be free, all of us, black and white, for it is God's intention. He enlists us to help him to transfigure all the ugliness of this world into the beauty of his kingdom. We shall be free, all of us, because the death and resurrection of Jesus Christ our Lord assures us that life has overcome death, light has overcome darkness, love has overcome hate, righteousness has overcome injustice and oppression, goodness has overcome evil, and that compassion and caring, laughter and joy, sharing and peace, reconciliation and forgiveness have overcome their awful counterparts in God's Kingdom where God is all in all.

O DEPTH OF wealth, wisdom and knowledge in God! How unsearchable his judgments, how untraceable his ways! Who knows the mind of the Lord? Who has been his counselor? Who has ever made a gift to him, to receive a gift in return? Source, Guide and Goal of all that is—to him be the glory forever! Amen. (Romans 11:33–36)

"In the beginning God . . . in the end, God."

Perhaps Even to Die
(1987)

AS OUTLINED in the Nobel Lecture in 1984, Tutu understood the views of those who had taken up arms to overthrow apartheid but did not endorse them. However, not being a universal pacifist—one who eschews the use of force in all situations—he believed there could come a time when the use of force as a last resort was legitimate under Christian theology. His most frequently quoted examples were the use of violence against Adolf Hitler and Idi Amin.

In June 1987 controversy blew up over the issue. It had its roots in a question asked at a news conference in Mozambique's capital, Maputo, on June 15 which took place at the beginning of an official visit to the Anglican diocese of Lebombo. At the time, Mozambique, despite the signing of a nonaggression pact with the South African government in 1984, was regarded by many white South Africans virtually as "enemy territory," a Marxist country which was providing facilities for the ANC.

QUESTION: Archbishop, then it has not reached the stage, as far as you are concerned, where black South Africans will give up and turn solely to violence as part of their liberation struggle? You have often said in the past that day may come. Most anti-government groups have said that June 16 should be observed with dignity. You're still going along with that at this stage?

ANSWER: Oh, absolutely. Yes. I would say that I will tell you the day I believe we must tell the world that now we have reached a point where we must use violence to overthrow an unjust system. I do not believe we are there yet. And the onus really lies with the international community. They now see stark naked the viciousness of apartheid when you can have the Minister of Foreign Affairs in South Africa trying to justify the detention of children by claiming that all of those children were detained because they were involved in criminal offenses. We say that we know that he cannot be speaking the truth because if that was true all they need to do is to take those children to court and the court would have found them guilty. I mean, how can he say that when he claims that South Africa has one of the best legal systems? What we keep trying to say to the world is that we have an evil system, apartheid, which can survive only because it defends itself with equally evil methods. I will announce the day I believe we have reached the end of the tether.

The remark confirmed a previously expressed standpoint and was either not reported or not given prominence by most journalists. But the Associated Press news agency led its report with the news that the archbishop planned to announce the day black South Africans could turn to violence. Right-wing South African newspapers gave the issue front-page coverage and government sources told them charges were being considered. The South African police seized television videotapes of the news conference and, before being ordered by the Supreme Court to return them, told a judge that an offense of high treason or terrorism was suspected. Contact with colleagues and family in South Africa indicated that a furor was brewing in the white community. On the eve of his return to Johannesburg, Tutu told his personal assistant at the time, Matt Esau, where his will could be found.

The extracts which follow are from a sermon delivered in the Church of St. Stephen and St. Lawrence, Maputo, on the morning of June 29, the day on which the church commemorated the feast of St. Peter and St. Paul.

Before his ascension, our Lord said to his apostles, "I want you to be witnesses to me, starting in Jerusalem through to Samaria and up to the uttermost parts of the earth." Now we say that our church is apostolic. It means first of all that it is a church that follows the teachings of the apostles, to follow the example of the apostles, that also it is a church that is sent because an apostle is the one who is sent. When you are a witness, you are either a trustworthy witness or you are one without credibility. When you go to a court you will find that, for instance, the accused person needs to have good witnesses to support his case and the prosecutor will try to prove that this person or that person is not a trustworthy witness. Then the court will not believe what the witness attests to.

Now, we are supposed to be witnesses to the love of God. If you say to someone with your mouth, "I love you," and then, when the person is still smiling because you say you love them, you knock them on the head, your words and your actions don't tally. Then people will say you are a hypocrite, someone who is playacting. And so also with our faith. Many people have said, "Oh, I don't go to church anymore. Have you seen how churchgoers behave? Have you seen how they quarrel? Have you seen how they backbite other people? Have you seen how jealous they are? When they see somebody with a beautiful thing they don't like saying, 'Oh, you really are lovely!' They want to find something wrong to say. Instead of saying, 'Oh, we are so glad that you have a beautiful dress,' they say, 'Aha, aha, just look at her stockings. They've got potatoes, big holes.' "

Those people are saying something that is true. We expect Christians to be people of a certain kind, not by what they say through their mouths but by the kind of people they are. We expect them to reflect the character of Jesus Christ. We expect Christians to be gentle, not always quarreling and scratching. We expect Christians to be humble as Jesus was humble, as he said in the Gospel. We expect Christians to be peace-loving and people who work for peace. We expect Christians to be loving. We expect Christians to be those who try to create peace among those who are quarreling. We expect Christians to be people who are caring. We expect Christians to be people filled with love. We expect Christians to be people who forgive as Jesus forgave even those who were nailing him to the Cross. But we expect Christians also to be those who stand up for the truth, we expect Christians to be those who stand up for justice, we expect Christians to be those who stand on the side of the poor and the hungry and the homeless and the naked, and when that happens then Christians will be trustworthy, believable witnesses.

Now, the word for "witness" in the Greek language is the word from which we have got the English word "martyr." So a martyr is a Christian who witnesses to the faith, witnesses to the faith until death. And that is what Paul and Peter gave. And it may happen that you and I and all of us, that we may be called to witness for Jesus Christ, witness at great cost, witness even when we are made to suffer because we are Christians and perhaps even to die for the faith. Because martyrs keep happening in the church, even today.

And we pray that God will strengthen us, that when the time of trial comes we can be faithful witnesses to our Lord and that God will give us his blessing so that we can be true witnesses to our Lord and Saviour Jesus Christ. And we thank God for you.

Tutu was given an enthusiastic farewell at Maputo's airport, but the warmth ended at the door of the South African Airways aircraft. He was stared at by white businessmen and officials in almost complete silence. He was greeted at home by a large crowd of supporters and journalists at the airport. Staff were to take him to Johannesburg in a rented car. Shortly before the car pulled away, a bystander caught sight of the front on-side tire. It was worn down to the canvas lining, with pieces of wire from the steel belt inside protruding where the tread should have been. The car was changed. Later a senior executive of the car-rental company denied emphatically that any of his staff could have sabotaged the vehicle. He said they must have overlooked the state of the tire but did not explain how this could have happened during the repeated checks it must have gone through while the tread was being worn away. Charges of treason or terrorism against Tutu never materialized.

You Give Yourself a Left Hook

(1987)

IN SEPTEMBER and October 1987, long-festering conflict in the province of Natal flared into violence of new proportions in the townships of the provincial capital, Pietermaritzburg. It was rooted partly in tensions arising from a protracted strike at a rubber company but it also reflected rivalry between the United Democratic Front and the Congress of South African Trade Unions on the one hand (representing forces largely sympathetic to the ANC) and the Inkatha movement led by Chief Mangosuthu Buthelezi, Chief Minister of the kwaZulu homeland, on the other.

Inkatha Yenkululeko Yesizwe, or the Inkatha national cultural liberation movement, was founded in 1975, and Buthelezi had early consultations with the ANC in exile. He rejected government pressure to join the ranks of homelands which took "independence" and kept up steady pressure for Nelson Mandela's release but nevertheless came to be isolated, first by black consciousness leaders and then by the UDF and ANC leadership over his participation in homeland government.

Thirty-nine people died in the Pietermaritzburg area in September and by late October another thirty-eight had died. Church leaders convened an urgent meeting in Johannesburg on October 28 and decided to hold a peace service.

These extracts are from a sermon delivered at the Lay Ecumenical Center at Edendale, Pietermaritzburg, on November 1, 1987. The audience responded frequently, applauding and laughing.

I would want first of all to thank all those who have been involved in trying to bring about peace in a situation of great distress. There have been very many who have been concerned, who have tried to be ambassadors of Christ, to be instruments of justice and peace, and on behalf of many who would want to have said so on their own behalf: I thank you all.

We do not come here as those seeking to be peace negotiators . . . We come as those who are constrained by the Gospel of our Lord Jesus Christ to be peacemakers to those who are at daggers drawn. So I want also to thank those who have worked so hard within a short space of time to arrange this particular service. For it was only on Wednesday last that some of us, as the chairman has indicated, met and said, "Let us be the Church of God." We don't have anything that we can offer the world except spiritual resources. We ought not to be ashamed that we are going to pray, that we have been praying. We have nothing else to give and we ought to be proud that we can put the world in touch with the greatest resource of all, God. We thank you, too, the people of God, who have responded at short notice. For God will ask us, "What did you do, what did you do when the situation got out of hand?" And you'll say, "Aaah, I didn't know what to do." And yet God told us that we are his fellow workers. Doesn't St. Paul say an extraordinary thing about those who are believers—you are fellow workers with God! We are fellow workers with God to change evil, to change darkness, to change oppression, to change chaos into their opposites, their glorious opposites. So we are in touch with an invincible power . . .

We come saying, we appeal on behalf of God and on behalf of our Lord and Saviour Jesus Christ, to those who are involved in this carnage, who are involved in bloodletting: please follow us, just give our fathers and our mothers who lived in an unnatural, abnormal society, please just give our mothers and our fathers, our children, our wives, our husbands, just give us a chance! How can it be that we are struck by the [apartheid] system on this side, we are being hit on the one hand, and on the other hand we are also attacking ourselves.

And so we come saying, for goodness' sake, for goodness' sake, please stop! Please stop!

Van der Merwe [the stock butt of South African jokes] had lost his job and was feeling rather depressed. So his friends said, "What is the matter, Van der Merwe?" Van der Merwe said to Van Rooyen, "I have lost my job." And so Van Rooyen said, "Why don't you go and join the police force?" And then Van der Merwe said, "No, man, they will give me an exam and I will fail." So his friend Van Rooyen said, "No, man, I will fix things up for you. I will talk to the sergeant and you will be all right." So they called Van der Merwe for the exam and the sergeant said, "Van der Merwe, think! I'm going to ask you three questions. What has one sole, eight eyes and one tongue?" And Van der Merwe scratched his head and said, "No, I don't know." So the sergeant said, "Hey, it's one takkie, one tennis shoe. Now think. What has got two tongues, sixteen eyes and two soles?" Van der Merwe scratched his head and scratched his head, and he couldn't answer. The sergeant said, "Hey, it's two takkies." Then the sergeant said, "This is your last chance. This is the third and the last question. What is this animal that's seen in the forest. It walks like this [imitating a baboon] and goes 'Hoooo.' " Van der Merwe said, "Ha, you think you've got me—it's three takkies."

Now, my friends, we might say that Van der Merwe there and some of those are not bright, but what are we doing? Hey? What are we doing? What are we doing? You have been told times without number that the enemy that stands in the way of our liberation is the system of apartheid, and we have said, many of us, times without number, we are tired of this system. This system is destined to fail. I want to ask again: Do we want to be free? Now wait, wait, wait. Just think about that answer. Do we want to be free? You must be careful what you say. There are only two answers—give only one of them. You either say, "No, we don't want to be free," or you say, "Yes, we want to be free!" ["*Yebo, yebo*" ("Yes, yes" in Zulu).]

DO YOU WANT TO BE FREE? ["*Yebo*"] . . . You want to fight, and each time you hit him, you give yourself a left hook! How can you ever hope to destroy your opponent? Because your opponent just stands there and says, "Ha, ha, ha!" Your opponent is laughing at you. Why, why are we doing things that actually make people say, "We were right when we said they are slow thinkers." Huh? God wants us to be free and the trouble with God, you see, is that he never forces his gifts on us. He wants us to be free, he wants to give us freedom, and we say, "God, not yet! We have not suffered enough." We are saying to God, "We still want to suffer and so let the system go on a little longer." When God says, "Hey, I want to lead you out of bondage, I want to take you out of Egypt, I want you to cross the Red Sea, I want to lead you into the Promised Land," we say, "*Aikona* [no], no, God, wait."

We are saying to God, "Not yet, not yet, no, we are still enjoying—" Enjoying what? Enjoying what? Enjoying being part of the oppressive system? Enjoying living in matchbox houses? Enjoying receiving inadequate pay? . . .

Do you know, friends, that there is nobody I know overseas who will ever say, "I support apartheid" . . . We who are opposed to apartheid can go anywhere in the world and we will find friends, who say, "Bishop Tutu, go and tell the people in South Africa that we support them." . . . But almost always they will say, as the South African government wants them to say, "But why are you doing this? Why are you doing this kind of thing?" . . . Many of us who go abroad trying to get more support for our struggle are getting tired of having to explain why there are thirty deaths in Pietermaritzburg. Why? And we try to find [reasons] and there are reasons we can give. But it's not good enough for them.

Please help us. Freedom is coming. Freedom is coming, there is no doubt about that. Freedom is coming and there's no doubt about that. But let us not delay it. Let us not delay it. Just hear what our Lord Jesus Christ said. Our Lord said, "Every kingdom divided against itself is laid waste and no city or house divided against itself will stand." Let us not leave a house divided against itself, for we will fall and our fall will be so great that the enemies of our freedom will be the ones who are entertained.

My sisters and brothers, my sons and daughters, let us accept the gift of God, let us accept the freedom that God wants to give us, so that you and I, all of us, black and white, will hold hands as we stride forth into this new South Africa where black and white will know that they are members of one family, God's family, the human family. If God be for us, who can be against us?

The week after the service, a group of church leaders, including the archbishop, held separate meetings with Inkatha and UDF delegations in Durban. The two organizations agreed on the wording of a joint peace appeal, but the call was not issued until January 1988, by which time the efforts of November had lost momentum. Over succeeding years many others, including trade unions, business groups, Pietermaritzburg civic leaders, local church leaders and political parties, engaged in one failed initiative after another to bring peace to Natal.

14

You Will Bite the Dust!

(1988)

IN 1988 the conflict between church and state intensified. On February 24, in an act that recalled the repression of 1960 and 1977, the government outlawed the operations of seventeen anti-apartheid organizations, including the United Democratic Front and the Azanian People's Organization (Azapo), and restricted trade unions from engaging in political activities. The authorities viewed the UDF, the nation's largest nonracial anti-apartheid group at the time, as an ANC surrogate. Azapo was the main voice of black consciousness. The government also restricted eighteen leaders, including Dr. Simon Gqubule, a former President of the Methodist Church.

Church leaders decided to protest by converging on Cape Town on February 29 and marching on the parliament buildings in defiance of the law. As the marchers, numbering about 150, left St. George's Cathedral in rows with arms linked, they encountered a contingent of police who ordered them to disperse. When they knelt on the pavement outside the cathedral and began to sing, police moved in to arrest the leaders and take them to waiting vehicles. Once the leadership had been removed, police aimed powerful jets of water from a truck-mounted water cannon to break up the rest, then carried out a mass arrest. The marchers were released some hours later. James Robbins, BBC correspondent in South Africa, reported: "South Africa entered a new era of protest today. The church has unmistakably taken over the front line of anti-apartheid protest."

Church leaders in Cape Town continued their resistance to the re-

strictions by joining educators, sports administrators and women's lead-
ers to form an informal Committee for the Defense of Democracy and
calling for a protest rally at the University of the Western Cape on
March 13. On March 12 the committee was banned from "carrying on
or performing any activities or acts whatsoever" and the local police
commissioner prohibited the rally. Archbishop Tutu, Allan Boesak, now
moderator of the Dutch Reformed Mission Church, and Archbishop
Stephen Naidoo of the Catholic Church responded by organizing an in-
terfaith service in St. George's Cathedral to replace the banned rally.
The following extracts are from the most strongly worded parts of the
archbishop's address.

We are gathered today to pray for our country facing a deepening crisis, to reflect on what is taking place and our role as believers—as
Christians, as Muslims, as Jews, whatever. What would be our role in
this crisis? In the enveloping darkness as the lights of freedom are ex-
tinguished one by one, despite all the evidence to the contrary, we
have come here to say that evil, and injustice, and oppression, and exploitation—embodied in the very essence, the very nature, of
apartheid—cannot prevail.

In the Bible, we are told to speak to spiritual things. St. John says,
"The light shineth in the darkness, and the darkness did not over-
whelm the light." We come to sustain our hope that this is so. Humanly
speaking, as we look around at our situation, that situation appears
hopeless. But we must assert, and assert confidently, that this is God's
world, that God is in charge.

We must say to our rulers, especially unjust rulers such as those in
this land, "You may be powerful, indeed very powerful. But you are not
God. You are ordinary mortals! God—the God whom we worship—
can't be mocked. You have already lost! You have already lost! Let us
say to you nicely: You have already lost, we are inviting you to come
and join the winning side. Come! Come and join the winning side.
Your cause is unjust. You are defending what is fundamentally indefensible, because it is evil. It is evil without question. It is immoral. It
is immoral without question. It is unchristian. Therefore, you will bite
the dust! And you will bite the dust comprehensively!"

Now, in this land we have prostituted language, making words mean something other than their original meaning . . . The Minister of Law and Order, in restricting the activities of a new committee, said he was doing so for the sake of "public safety." Now, you've got to be careful in this country. Do you remember Pavlov and his dog? Pavlov carried out experiments. He showed a dog meat, and the dog salivated when he saw the meat. Next he showed the dog meat and rang a bell. The dog salivated. He showed him meat, and then he rang a bell, and the dog again salivated. He showed him meat, and rang the bell, and the dog once again salivated. Then he took away the meat and simply rang the bell. The dog salivated. He called this a conditioned reflex.

Now, in this country, we have what are called conditioned reflexes. When the government uses certain words, they know that many people will react in the kind of way that they have conditioned people to react. So they say "public safety." Do you know what "public safety" means? Public safety means you can walk safely in public. The police exist to ensure that you can walk. Ha-ha! What happens in this country? People say we want to protest peacefully against pass laws. The police ought to be around to see that those people have "public safety." But what do the police do? They shoot the people protesting peacefully. The protesters don't even have stones! . . . We have never shot anyone. Has Allan Boesak ever shot anybody? Has the rector of the University of the Western Cape [Professor Jakes Gerwel, a member of the banned committee] thrown a stone at anybody? This committee has not done anything to undermine "public safety" . . . This committee did not throw stones through office windows. We didn't throw stones through the windows of Allan Boesak's office [last week]. We didn't throw stones at the home of Allan Boesak . . . "Public safety" indeed. The greatest threat to "public safety" in South Africa is this government.

Then they say, "It is also to maintain public order." Now we must say it clearly: All of us are law-abiding. We obey the laws because we know that any society, in order to survive, needs the structure of good law. If we all drove on any side of the road, chaos would result . . . We obey traffic laws which say you must travel on the left-hand side of the road. And rulers, according to public order, cannot be arbitrary in the exercise of their power. For their power is not absolute. Their power is regulated. Law must, as far as possible, embody morality. South Africa is the only country in which it is a crime for a woman to sleep with her husband if her husband happens to be a migrant worker and she has not received permission to be where he is. That is the law. And to break that law is to do something that is illegal. But that law is fundamentally immoral; to obey it is to be guilty of immorality. So, my friends, you must learn the difference between morality and legality. When something is legal, almost all of the people in the country think that it is also morally right. But it is not always so . . .

Justice is blindfolded because justice must be evenhanded. Ha-ha! Evenhanded! The conservative Afrikaners walk in uniforms. And they look like Nazis. They've got a thing on their uniforms that looks like a swastika. And they shout anti-black slogans. They march against you. They march to the Union Buildings [in Pretoria, the seat of the executive branch of government there], and when they get there, do you think they get water-cannoned? I don't. The policemen there shake hands with them. The only things we had in our hands [during the march to parliament] were our Bibles. (You know, this government is not quite as stupid as we think. We know how explosive the Bible is.) Didn't we say long ago that apartheid is as evil as Nazism? We said that long ago. And they said, "That Tutu character and all those others, they like to exaggerate. They are melodramatic." Now you see that they can take action against people who are dressed like priests! We had nothing. We just linked our hands and we tried to pray. In fact, at the police station we said, "We would like to pray." A policeman replied, "This is a police station. You don't pray here."

Another word they like to use is "revolution." Revolution! They think we run away from revolution, but the people in this country do not think revolution is necessarily a bad thing. Revolution means a radical change. If it is revolution to say I work for a South Africa that is nonracial; if it is revolution to say I am working for a South Africa that is truly democratic; if it is revolution to say I am working for a South Africa where black and white and yellow and green can walk together arm in arm, then, friends, I am for that!

I am willing to say to Mr. Adriaan Vlok [Minister of Law and Order] that I am going to continue saying the things that I have said and am saying today. Mr. Vlok, you have got all the laws that you can use if you want to use them. But I am not going to be told by you what the

Gospel of our Lord and Saviour Jesus Christ must be. If preaching the Gospel of Jesus Christ is going to lead me into any kind of trouble with you and your sort, tough luck! Tough luck! . . .

On one occasion . . . I said to a . . . judge: "I support the ANC and I support every organization that seeks a new kind of South Africa." I said, "I don't support the methods that they are using but I stick to them. They are my brothers; they are my sisters; they are my friends; they are my fathers; they are my mothers. How can I repudiate them?" The government once asked me to repudiate the ANC. I said, "Okay. Will you asking me that question repudiate your forefathers? For, according to the laws of this country, they too would be guilty of terrorism. For they fought for their freedom." Why must it be okay when they fight for their freedom and when we do, it's not good? . . .

I finish, my friends, by saying: If they want to take on the Church of God, I warn them. Read a little bit of history and see what happened to those who tried to take on the Church of God. Don't read all of history. Just read your own history. I just warn them that even if they were to remove this, that or the other person, the Church of God will stay. Our Lord and Saviour said, "Even the gates of hell will not prevail against the Church of God."

And so we say: Freedom is coming! Freedom is coming, because that is God's will for us. Freedom is coming, because God did not make us doormats on which people can wipe their dirty boots. Freedom is coming, because God has created us for freedom. Freedom is coming. And we can all walk hand in hand, black and white, together, proudly, holding our heads high in a new South Africa. A free South Africa. A South Africa where people count because they are created in the image of God. A free South Africa where all of God's people will share equally the good things that God has given us.

Freedom is coming, and we want it also for you, Mr. Vlok. We want you to be able to sleep at night and not wonder what we are up to. We want you to sleep, Mr. Vlok, and not wonder, "Where is the UDF? Where is Boesak now? What is he doing?" Freedom is coming even for you, Mr. P. W. Botha. We want you to be free. We want you to be here with us. We want you to put away the Casspirs . . . Freedom is coming for all of us. There can be no doubt about it, because if God be for us, who can be against us? Amen, and amen.

The Making of a Peaceful Revolution

15

Your Policies Are Unbiblical, Unchristian, Immoral and Evil

(1988)

BEFORE THE *church leaders' march, Tutu had written to President Botha appealing for commutation of the death sentences imposed on a group known as "the Sharpeville Six." The six, found by a court to have been in a group which killed a town councillor in Sharpeville in the Vaal Triangle during the September 1984 protests, were convicted of murder in a controversial application of the "common purpose" doctrine in South African law. On March 15, responding to news that the six were scheduled to be hanged three days later, the archbishop followed up his letter by appealing for an urgent meeting with Botha. At the same time he made telephone calls to U.S. Secretary of State George Shultz, Chancellor Helmut Kohl of West Germany and the British Prime Minister, Margaret Thatcher, asking them to put pressure on Botha to exercise clemency.*

The archbishop was granted an interview in the President's Cape Town office on March 16. He told a journalist later that after an amicable discussion of the issue at hand, Botha resorted to "bluster and scolding" over the illegal march. "I could have kept quiet," Tutu said. "I decided I might never get this chance again. Our people have not had an opportunity of telling him [their feelings], so I told him to his face. I said, 'One thing you've got to know is that I'm not a small boy. You're not going to talk to me like that. You are not my headmaster.' Actually we did behave like little boys, really. It was a shame—accu-

sation, counter-accusation sort of thing, finger-wagging at each other. I thought, well, he's certainly never heard this from a black person in this way. He hardly ever gets it from his colleagues. They are dead scared of him . . . I don't know whether that is how Jesus would have handled it. But at that moment, I didn't actually quite mind how Jesus would have handled it. I was going to handle it my way. I hope that is how he would have handled it, because it was on behalf of people who have been hurt by these guys."

At the end of the meeting, Botha handed over a written reply to the petition the church leaders had tried to deliver on their march. In the letter the President asked whether the church leaders were "acting on behalf of the kingdom of God, or the kingdom promised by the ANC and the SACP [South African Communist Party]." The archbishop responded on April 8.

The State President
Mr. P. W. Botha
Tuynhuys
Cape Town

Dear Mr. State President:

Thank you for your letter dated March 16, 1988. I must confess I am surprised that a letter marked "Personal" should have been distributed to members of parliament and to the media without the concurrence of its recipient. I thought that there were conventions governing such things.

Since you are a fair-minded person, I am sure you will ensure that my reply will receive the same publicity accorded your letter to me. Certainly I am sure you will ask SABC-TV to give it equally prominent coverage.

I am distressed that during the interview with you, which I had requested for the sole purpose of appealing to you to exercise your prerogative to commute the death sentences of the so-called Sharpeville Six and which you then used as an occasion for haranguing me about the church leaders and our petition, you appeared to sit loosely to facts.

You had already been reported in an interview with the *Wash-*

ington Times as alleging that our petition was drawn up after the march. I tried to correct this erroneous view. But you then proceeded to accuse me of having preached under a flag depicting the hammer and sickle. I denied this accusation. You did not withdraw your extraordinary accusations, but claimed that you had photographs to prove your charge. I challenged you to produce this photographic evidence, which I knew was nonexistent because I have never been so photographed as you had alleged. I refer to this matter because of the questions in your letter about atheistic Marxism.

I want to state quite categorically that I stand by all that I have done and said in the past concerning the application of the Gospel of Jesus Christ to the situation of injustice and oppression and exploitation which are of the very essence of apartheid, a policy which your government has carried out with ruthless efficiency. My position in this matter is not one of which I am ashamed or for which I would ever want to apologize. I know that I stand in the mainline Christian tradition. I want you to know that I have never listened to Radio Freedom [an ANC station] nor do I have the opportunity to read *Sechaba* [an ANC publication]. My theological position derives from the Bible and from the teaching of the church. The Bible and the church predate Marxism and the ANC by several centuries.

May I give you a few illustrations? The Bible teaches that what invests each person with infinite value is not this or that arbitrarily chosen biological attribute, but the fact that each person is created in the image of God (Genesis 1:26). Apartheid, the policy of your government, claims that what makes a person qualify for privilege and political power is that biological irrelevance, the color of a person's skin and his ethnic antecedents. Apartheid says those are what make a person matter. That is clearly at variance with the teaching of the Bible and the teaching of our Lord and Saviour Jesus Christ. Hence the church's criticism that your apartheid policies are not only unjust and oppressive. They are positively unbiblical, unchristian, immoral and evil.

Apartheid has said that ultimately people are intended for separation. You have carried out policies enshrined in the Population Registration Act, the Group Areas Act, segregated education, health, etc. The Bible teaches quite unequivocally that people are created for fellowship, for togetherness, not for alienation, apartness, enmity and division (Genesis 2:18; Genesis 11:1–9; 1 Corinthians 12:12–13; Romans 12:3–5; Galatians 3:28; Acts 17:26).

The experience of the United States and the findings of its highest court were that it is in fact impossible to carry out a policy of "separate but equal." The policies of apartheid do not even pretend to seek to embody "separate but equal." Quite unabashedly they are intended to be separate and unequal. Just note the grossly unfair distribution of land between black and white or the unequal government expenditure on black and white education. I could multiply the examples. Apartheid, the policy of your government, is thus shown yet again to be unbiblical, unchristian, immoral and evil in its very nature.

I could show that apartheid teaches the fundamental irreconcilability of people because they belong to different races. This is at variance with the central teaching of the Christian faith about the reconciling work of our Lord and Saviour Jesus Christ. "God was in Christ reconciling the world to himself" declares St. Paul (2 Corinthians 5:9), summing up teaching contained in other parts of the New Testament (John 12:32; Ephesians 1:10; Ephesians 2:14; etc.). I could show that in dealing with human beings as if they were less than those who are created in the image of God and by inflicting untold and unnecessary suffering on them, as through your vicious policies of forced population removals, you have contravened basic ethical tenets. I could provide further evidence that your apartheid policies are unbiblical, unchristian, immoral and evil. It is for these and other reasons that our church and other churches have declared apartheid a heresy. I am quite ready to debate this issue with a theologian from your church whom you might care to nominate.

I have not deviated from the teaching of our church on this matter at any point. I enclose copies of the statements issued by my fellow bishops and others showing that they believe I stand in the teaching and tradition of our church. I want to submit respectfully that it is more likely that they would be better judges of the orthodoxy of my position than the State President and his advisers, theological and otherwise.

What we are doing is no innovation when we bring the Word of God as we understand it to bear on the situation in which we are involved. The prophets of old when they declared "Thus saith the Lord . . ." to the rulers and the powerful of their day were our forerunners. They spoke about the need for religion to show its authenticity by how it affected the everyday life of the people and especially by how the rich, the powerful, the privileged and the rulers dealt with the less privileged, the poor, the hungry, the oppressed, the widow, the orphan and the alien.

Isaiah said God rejected all religious observances however punctilious and elaborate. He urged worshippers to

PUT AWAY THE evil of your deeds, away out of my sight. Cease to do evil and learn to do right, pursue justice and champion the oppressed; give the orphan his rights, plead the widow's cause. (Isaiah 1:16–17)

Elsewhere he claimed that God was not pleased with their religious fasts. God declared through the prophet:

IS NOT THIS what I require of you as a fast:
to loose the fetters of injustice,
to untie the knots of the yoke,
to snap every yoke
and set free those who have been crushed?
Is it not sharing your food with the hungry,
taking the homeless poor into your house,
clothing the naked when you meet them
and never evading a duty to your kinsfolk? (Isaiah 58:6–7)

Elijah confronted the king about his injustice to Naboth, a nonentity as far as the king was concerned but who was championed by God (1 Kings 21); Nathan was not afraid to convict David of his sinfulness (2 Samuel 12). This kind of involvement of religion with politics and the habit of religious leaders to speak to the sociopolitical and economic situation can be attested to as standard practice in the Bible, which provides our mandate and paradigm.

Our marching orders come from Christ himself and not from any human being. Our mandate is provided by the Bible and the teaching of the church, not by any political group or ideology, Marxist or otherwise.

Our Lord himself adopted as a description of his program that which was outlined by Isaiah:

THE SPIRIT OF the Lord God is upon me
because the Lord has anointed me;
he has sent me to bring good news to the humble,
to bind up the broken-hearted,
to proclaim liberty to captives
and release to those in prison;
to proclaim a year of the Lord's favor
and a day of the vengeance of our God. (Isaiah 61:1–2)

This is found in his first sermon as recorded by St. Luke (Luke 4:16–21). He stood in the prophetic tradition when he taught what criteria would be used to judge the nations—it would be not through observance of narrowly defined religious duties but by whether they had fed the hungry, clothed the naked, visited the sick and imprisoned, etc. (Matthew 25:31–46).

It was impossible to love God whom one had not seen if one hated the brother that one had seen, testified another part of the New Testament (1 John 4:20–21).

The followers of Jesus are constrained by the imperatives of his Gospel to be concerned for those he has called the least of his brethren. The NGK [the white Dutch Reformed Church] recognized this when it was in the forefront of the struggle for justice for the poor whites, as evidenced by the words of Dr. C. D. Brink in a paper delivered at the Volkskongres in 1947:

THE AIM OF the church is to bring about social justice. Justice must be done to the poor and the oppressed, and if the present system does not serve this purpose, the public conscience must be roused to demand another. If the church does not exert itself for justice in society, and together with the help she can offer also be prepared to serve as champion for the cause of the poor, others will do it. The poor have their right today: I do not ask for your charity, but I ask to be given an opportunity to live a life of human dignity.

We are law-abiding. Good laws make human society possible. When laws are unjust then Christian tradition teaches that they do not oblige obedience. Our Lord broke not just man's law but what was considered more serious, he broke God's law in order to meet human need—as when he broke the law of the Sabbath observance (John 5:8–14). He paid due regard to the secular ruler in the person of Pontius Pilate but subsequently engaged in a defiance of that secular authority when he refused to answer his questions (Mark 15:3–5).

It is a hallowed tradition of direct nonviolent action such as we engaged in when we tried to process to parliament. We were mindful, too, of what the apostles said to the Jewish Sanhedrin, that obedience to God takes precedence over obedience to human beings (Acts 4:19, 5:29).

We accept wholeheartedly St. Paul's teaching in Romans 13— that we should submit ourselves to earthly rulers. Their authority, however, is not absolute. They themselves also stand under God's judgment as his servants. They are meant to instill fear only in those who do wrong, holding no terror for those who do right (Romans 7:3–4). The ruler is God's servant to do the subjects good (Romans 7:4). The ruler rules for the benefit of the ruled. That comes not out of a political manifesto but from the Holy Scriptures. The corollary is that you must not submit yourself to a ruler who subverts your good. That is why we admire those who oppose unjust regimes—e.g., totalitarian Communist governments. The Bible teaches that governments can become beasts in the symbolic language of the Book of Revelation (Revelation 13). Not too many governments nor their apologists who use Romans 13 with glee are quite so enthusiastic about its full implications nor of Revelation 13.

I am sure you could not have been serious when you quoted a passage allegedly from Radio Freedom in which you underline certain words such as "church," "liberation struggle," "justice," and because our petition uses similar words you want to suggest that there must be a sinister connection between us and the ANC. If a Communist were to say, "Water makes you wet," would you say, "No, water does not make you wet," for fear that people would accuse you of being a Communist? I would have thought our discussion was at a slightly higher level.

I told you in my interview that I support the ANC in its objectives to establish a nonracial, democratic South Africa; but I do not support its methods. That is a statement I have made in the Supreme Court in Pretoria and on other occasions. My views have never been clandestine. You appointed the Eloff commission to investigate the SACC when I was still its General Secretary. Your Security Police investigated my personal life and looked into my bank accounts and tried to discredit me in their evidence before the commission. They were unable to find anything of which to accuse me. Not even Craig Williamson [a Security Police spy] could produce evidence that I held different views to those I had expressed in public. You know I went to Lusaka twice last year. I tried to persuade the ANC to suspend the armed struggle; that is a matter of public record.*

I am committed to work for a nonracial, just and democratic South Africa. I reject atheistic Marxism as I reject apartheid, which I find equally abhorrent and evil. Transfer of power to the people of South Africa means exactly that.† The latest apartheid constitution cannot by any stretch of imagination be described as democratic when it excludes 73 percent of the people of South Africa from any meaningful participation in the political decision-making process. I long for and have dedicated myself to work for a South Africa where all South Africans are South Africans, citizens in an undivided South Africa, not one that is balkanized into unviable bantustan homelands. When you are a citizen you share through the exercise of your vote in the political decision-making process either directly or through duly elected representatives.

Since 1976 I have appealed to the government to heed our cri de coeur. I have said nobody in their right senses expected these real changes to happen overnight. You yourself can bear me out that when a SACC leaders' delegation met you and your cabinet colleagues in 1980, I again said that if you did something dramatic then I would be among the first to say to our people, "Hold it. Give them a chance, now they are talking real change." Then I said, "Declare your commitment to a common citizenship for all South Africans in an undivided South Africa; abolish the pass laws; stop immediately all forced population removals and establish a uniform education policy." That was eight years ago. How much time has been wasted and how many lives have been lost trying to beautify

*Tutu held his first official talks with the ANC as archbishop on March 21 and 22, 1987. He visited the exiled leadership in Lusaka, Zambia, and proposed that the ANC renounce violence in order to put pressure on the South African government to enter into talks with it. He returned to Lusaka for the World Conference on Religion and Peace in September 1987.
†Botha had asked in his letter of March 16: "Does the phrase: 'the transfer of power to all the people of our country' as used in your petition have the same meaning as the same phrase used by the ANC and the SACP, that is for the ultimate creation of a Marxist regime in South Africa?"

apartheid through cosmetic improvements when the pillars of a vicious system still remain firmly in place.

I would say if you were to lift the state of emergency, unban all our political organizations, release all detainees and political prisoners and permit exiles to return and then say you would be ready to sit down with the authentic representatives and leaders of every section of our society to negotiate the dismantling of apartheid and drawing up of a new constitution, I would say to our people, "Please give him a chance. He is talking real change." Your apartheid policies are leading our beautiful land to disaster. We love South Africa passionately. Our black fathers fought against the Nazis for it, many Afrikaners being pro-Nazi at the time refused to support the war effort, and many who wore the uniform of the Union Defense Force used to be turned away from NGK church services.

We long for the day when black and white will live amicably and harmoniously together in the new South Africa.

Kindly confirm whether you include me in the paragraph in your letter to the Reverend Frank Chikane [General Secretary of the SACC] which reads: "You love and praise the ANC/SACP with its Marxist and atheistic ideology, land mines, bombs and necklaces perpetrating the most horrendous atrocities imaginable; and you embrace and participate in their call for violence, hatred, sanctions, insurrection and revolution . . ." because as supporting evidence you then quote what I said in St. Paul's Cathedral, London.*

I want to state the obvious—that I am a Christian religious leader—by definition that surely means I reject Communism and Marxism as atheistic and materialistic. I try to work for the extension of the Kingdom of God which will ultimately have rulers such as the ones described in Isaiah 11:1–9 and in Psalm 72:1–4 and 12–14:

---

*Chikane had written to Botha criticizing his response to the church leaders' march. It was not clear from Botha's reply to Chikane whether he included the archbishop in his allegation that church leaders had participated in a call for violence. The Anglican Church wanted the matter clarified, since it was considering suing Botha for defamation. Botha never replied to this letter.

O God, endow the king with thy own justice,
and give thy righteousness to a king's son,
that he may judge thy people rightly
and deal out justice to the poor and suffering.
May the hills and mountains afford the people
peace and prosperity in righteousness.
He shall give judgment for the suffering
and help those of the people that are needy;
he shall crush the oppressor.

For he shall rescue the needy from their rich oppressors,
the distressed who have no protector.
May he have pity on the needy and the poor,
deliver the poor from death;
may he redeem them from oppression and violence
and may their blood be precious in his eyes.

I work for God's Kingdom. For whose Kingdom with your apartheid policy do you work? I pray for you, as I do for your Ministerial colleagues, every day by name.

God bless you.

Yours sincerely
† Desmond Cape Town

In May, the churches of the SACC resolved to launch a campaign of nonviolent direct action against apartheid under the banner "Standing for the Truth." The government responded by stepping up harassment: government-supporting black politicians with no discernible constituencies recruited people from unemployment lines for anti-Tutu protests at airports; pamphlets and bumper stickers, often lewd, were circulated; and shortly after 1 A.M. on August 31, a bomb wrecked Khotso House, headquarters of the SACC in Johannesburg. In October the government attempted to legitimize its policies by securing a high black turnout for elections to segregated municipal councils. The churches made an illegal appeal for a boycott of the elections and the archbishop repeated it from the pulpit of St. George's Cathedral. Police confiscated a tape recording and said they were investigating charges.

Early in 1989 church leaders played a role in resolving a crisis over a hunger strike by about 300 political prisoners. The detainees were in jail indefinitely under emergency regulations with not even the prospect of a trial under the draconian security laws. Some had been held for more than thirty months. By taking their lives into their hands, the hunger strikers scored a crucial victory: the release of hundreds of talented leaders prepared the way for a successful campaign of defiance later in 1989.

16

All That Has Changed Is the Complexion of the Oppressor

(1989)

DESPITE THE *hectic pace of ministry, the archbishop had to find time to fulfill his outside commitments: to the All Africa Conference of Churches (AACC), of which he had become president in 1987; to the Anglican Communion; and to the wider international community, which expected a Nobel peace laureate to campaign on issues beyond apartheid. Churches in other parts of Africa were particularly eager to see him—the prominence he gained in the fight against apartheid gave him access to heads of state and the credibility to speak out against human rights abuses throughout the continent.*

At the end of a visit to Zaire in February 1989, about 15,000 people gathered for a service on the grounds of the national legislature in Kinshasa, the capital. Scores of armed troops were present. The service was initially booked for a stadium which would have accommodated more people, but the AACC was told the government wanted the service to be held in the same place as a service during a papal visit. Some church sources were more skeptical and suggested the change was made to prevent student demonstrations against the government of President Mobutu Sese Seko. The following were extracts from the sermon.

Africa is still being exploited by neocolonialism. Africa is groaning under the heavy debt burden. Africa is still afflicted by poverty, ignorance and disease. Africa is still in bondage because of the iniquity and injustice of racism and apartheid. Africa groans because of the devastation of natural disasters such as drought and floods.

But Africa groans, too, because of man-made disasters. Africa is being devastated by civil wars, as in Angola, in Mozambique, in Ethiopia, Eritrea, in Uganda and the Sudan. Africa has the unenviable distinction of producing the world's greatest number of refugees. Of course, many of these are refugees from natural disasters . . . But sadly, my brothers and sisters, the majority of these refugees are refugees from injustice and oppression in their motherlands.

For we must confess, sadly and humbly, that Africa has one of the worst records of violations of human rights. Africa has a spate of military dictatorships. In many places, all that has changed for the people who suffer is the complexion of the oppressor. In colonial times the oppressor was of a different complexion. Sadly, today the complexion of the oppressor is the same as the complexion of the oppressed.

The God we worship is the same yesterday, today and forever. That God knows, that God hears, that God sees, and that God will come down to deliver his people. There is no doubt about that. The God we worship is not a God who is neutral. Our God is a God who takes sides. Our God is a God who takes the side of the poor, of the oppressed, of the downtrodden, and that is where the Church of God must be found. The Church of God must be found on the side of the downtrodden. The Church of God must be the voice of the voiceless ones. The Church of God must be with the poor, the homeless, the naked and the hungry.

God has certain expectations of rulers. The ruler who rules according to God's way is this one: "May he judge thy people with righteousness, and thy poor with justice! May he defend the cause of the poor of the people . . . For he delivers the needy when he calls, the poor and him who has no helper. He has pity on the weak and the needy, and saves the lives of the needy. From oppression and violence he redeems their life; and precious is their blood in his sight." [Psalm 72:2, 4 and 12–14.]

So we say to all unjust rulers everywhere: "Beware! Watch it! Look out in South Africa. Look out wherever you may be, unjust ruler." We have no doubt that we shall be free. The blood of Jesus Christ bought us so that we would be free to enjoy the glorious liberty of the children of God.

17
You Are Not God!
(1989)

IN MARCH 1989, Archbishop Tutu visited Anglicans in Nicaragua and Panama with three other Anglican leaders: the Most Reverend Edmond L. Browning, Presiding Bishop of the Episcopal Church in the United States; the Most Reverend Orland Lindsay, Primate of the West Indies; and the Most Reverend Michael Peers, Primate of Canada.

Panama was preparing for elections under the military leader and de facto head of government, General Manuel Noriega. In a meeting with Noriega the archbishops raised the issues of political detainees, allowing independent observers at the elections and freedom of the press.

Tyranny was one of the subjects of a sermon on the night of March 20, delivered to 3,000 people in the Civic Center of Panama City. The Episcopal News Service reported: "Tutu, throughout his sermon, assured the audience that he was talking only about South Africa. However, the audience made it obvious that they knew he was talking about far more than a country thousands of miles away."

In the book Exodus, chapter 3, from verse 7, we hear these words: "And the Lord God said, 'I have seen the miserable state of my people in Egypt. I have heard their appeal to be free of their slave-drivers. And I know their sufferings. And I have come down to deliver them.'"

What a wonderful God this one is, the living God, the God who sees, the God who hears, the God who knows and the God who acts. When God sees his children in bondage and suffering, God does not fold God's hands and look on. Our God sees the sufferings of his people. God hears the cries of his suffering people. And God knows, and then God decides to come down and deliver God's people.

In the Bible, we keep being told of those who were not gods, the idols that were worshipped by those who did not worship God. And at one point, the prophet Isaiah pokes fun at these "no-gods." Isaiah says, "You really must be funny. You cut down a tree. With part of the tree, you make a fire and you sit by the fire and warm yourselves and you say, 'Ah, I am warm.' And you cook on this fire and then with part of the same wood you make your god. And you bow down before this god, and you worship it and you pray to it. And you say to this thing, 'Save me because you are my god.' How utterly ridiculous!"

And the prophet goes on and says, "Look at these gods that they have made for themselves. They have to be carried. They can't move from here to there. And you say this is a god? Our God carries his people on eagle's wings." Our God is the living God, the God who sees, the God who hears, the God who knows, the God who comes down to deliver.

Well, God came down and God delivered the children of Israel from bondage in Egypt. But you say, "Uh-uh! That happened long ago. It happened in the Old Testament times." And then in the Epistle to the Hebrews, in chapter 13, verse 8, we hear these words: "Jesus Christ, who is God, is the same yesterday, today and forever."

And so when God looked down on us, enslaved in a new bondage to sin, God saw, God heard, God knew and God came down in Jesus Christ to deliver us. And this week is the week when we commemorate the events of our deliverance. God saw us in a new Egypt and God heard the cry of his people. God saw the suffering of his people. God saw anew, and God came to set us free. God, in Christ, came to save us. We were like those who had been kidnapped and Jesus Christ paid the ransom to set us free.

The Epistle of St. Peter says we were not bought by perishable things like gold and silver. We were bought with the precious blood of Jesus Christ. God loved us then, God loves us now, God will continue to love us for ever and ever. God loves you. God loves you. God loves you. God loves you as if you were the only person on earth.

God, looking on us here, does not see us as a mass. God knows us each by name. God says, "Your name is engraved on the palms of my hands." Your name! As God lifts God's palms, God sees you engraved on the palms of his hands. When God created us out of dust, God breathed the breath of God into our nostrils. And we are those precious things that God carries gently. God carries each one of us as if we were fragile. And if God dropped us, then we would be smashed into smithereens. You are precious to God. God cares for you.

Where we come from in South Africa, the majority of the people there, 80 percent of the population, are oppressed and downtrodden by a small minority. This minority controls all political power . . . This small minority controls economic power. People do the same work and some get higher wages than others on the basis of the color of their skin. Of course this is changing, but there are certain jobs that are reserved for white people, there are jobs that black people may not do because they are black.

Now just tell me, what does the color of a person's skin tell you about that person? Does the color of a person's skin tell you whether that person is intelligent? Does it tell you that that person is loving? Supposing we said that the thing that determines privilege is the size of your nose? Now, I have a large nose—supposing we said people with large noses are the privileged people? And they say now, "Ah, you want to go to a toilet; that toilet is reserved only for large noses." If you have a small nose you are going to be in trouble. That university, you enter only if you have a large nose like mine. If you have a small nose then you must apply to the Minister of Small Nose Affairs for permission to attend the university for large noses.

Now, it is quite clear that that is ridiculous! And yet people at home have been made to suffer because of something they couldn't do anything about. That small minority at home controls the movement of people. Twenty percent of the population have 87 percent of the land. Eighty percent of the people have 13 percent of the land. That small minority decides that it is going to spend eight times per annum on the education of one white child what it spends on one black child, so blacks have an inferior education. Group areas determine where one race lives and usually the blacks live in the slum areas, in the ghettos.

Those who oppose the government of that country, South Africa, those who oppose its injustice and its oppression are dealt with very severely. Sometimes they are banished from their homes in a kind of internal exile. Sometimes they are banned, which means they are restricted, like being put under house arrest. Sometimes they are detained without trial. I am wearing a red ribbon here tonight. The churches in our country have asked us to wear red ribbons in solidarity with people in detention without trial. Some have been in detention without trial for as long as three years. They have never been brought to court. They have not been found guilty of any crime. The police decide you are a security risk and you disappear and they don't know where you go. They often may not be able to visit you. Sometimes people get assassinated because they are opponents of the government and the police somehow are unable to find their murderers. It is a very strange coincidence—the enemies of apartheid can be killed and the police are not able to find who killed them. The headquarters of the opponents of apartheid are firebombed or petrol-bombed. Nobody seems to be able to find the culprits. To oppose apartheid becomes increasingly criminalized—some who have opposed apartheid have been found guilty of treason.

Television and the radio in South Africa are state propaganda instruments. The opponents of the government are vilified on television and over the radio and they don't get a chance to reply. The press is severely restricted. Some newspapers are closed. I'm talking about South Africa.

Often and often our people are filled with despair and they wonder, what have we done to deserve all this suffering? It is important for the Church of God to tell the people of God, "Hey, hey, hey! Our God sees. Our God hears. Our God knows and our God will come down and deliver us." And we say it. We say it—in South Africa—we say to them, "Hey, hey, hey! We are going to be free. We are not asking for permission from the rulers of our land. We know we are going to be free." And we say to our oppressors, we say to them, "Do you know what? We are being nice to you. We are inviting you to join the winning side. Come and join the winning side, because you have already lost."

Because this is what the Bible says about the good ruler: "God, give your own justice to the king, your own righteousness to the Royal Son." Why? "So that he may rule your people rightly and your people with justice, that he will defend the poorest, he will save the children of those in need. The good ruler will crush their oppressors. The good ruler will free the poor man who calls to him and those who need help. He will have pity on the poor and the feeble and save the lives of those in need."

I'm reading from the Bible. I am not reading from the manifesto of a political party. The good ruler will redeem the lives of the needy from exploitation and outrage because their lives are precious in his sight. If you are a ruler and you are not this kind of ruler, you are in trouble. You are in real trouble with God. You are in real trouble. We try to tell oppressors everywhere, "You are not God! You are just an ordinary human being. Maybe you have got a lot of power now. Aha, but watch it! Watch it! Watch it!"

You know, Hitler thought he had a lot of power. Where is Hitler today? Mussolini thought he had a lot of power. Where is he today? Franco thought he had a lot of power. Somoza [Anastasio Somoza Debayle, who was overthrown as ruler of Nicaragua in 1979; here Tutu pauses while the audience, laughing, waits to hear who the next leader on the list will be]. Uh, I'm going to Africa. I must cross the sea and go to Africa. Idi Amin thought he had a lot of power. Where is he today? We could go on and on like that. And we say: This is God's world and God is in charge in his world.

Therefore, we can stand upright with our heads held high. We don't apologize for our existence. God did not make a mistake in creating us. Our God hears. Our God cares. Our God knows and our God will come down to deliver his people. Our God will come to deliver his people, here, everywhere, in South Africa, today, maybe not today. Tomorrow? Maybe not tomorrow. But what can separate us from the love of God? Absolutely nothing can separate us from the love of God in our Lord and Saviour Jesus Christ.

If God be for us, who can be against us!

The Making of a Peaceful Revolution

Part Four

"WE ARE UNSTOPPABLE"

The Defiance Campaign and the Release of Nelson Mandela

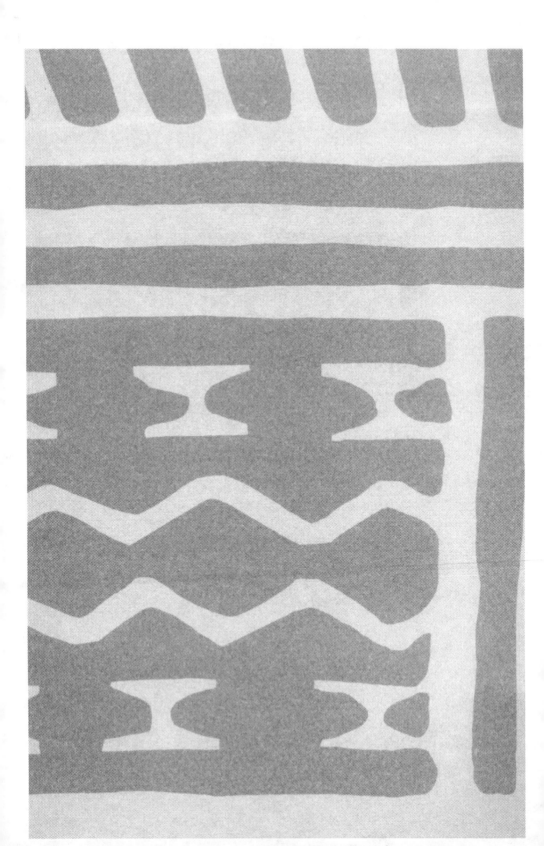

They Have Power but No Authority
(1989)

L E A D E R S   O F the heavily restricted United Democratic Front reorganized themselves into a loosely structured leadership coalition which came to be called the Mass Democratic Movement. In August 1989 the MDM launched a campaign of defiance to challenge a general election for the tricameral parliament in September. Nine national church leaders pronounced the Defiance Campaign compatible with the Standing for the Truth Campaign. In Cape Town their declaration led to six weeks of confrontation involving unlawful marches, church services in place of prohibited meetings, repeated arrests and interventions between police and protesters. This defense of church participation in the campaign was given in an interview with a Nationalist newspaper.

When a political organization or grouping is involved in a campaign which I believe is consistent with the demands of the Gospel, then I will support it. At the present time part of our concern is to work for the establishment of the Kingdom of God . . . That Kingdom expresses itself in concrete ways, in the political, social and economic dispensations, and there are certain standards in that Kingdom of how people are meant to live together. Injustice is unacceptable in the Kingdom, it is contrary to the will of God, oppression is contrary to the will of God.

Much of what should be happening through parliamentary processes has to be done through extraparliamentary groups. For that reason I support the Mass Democratic Movement and any others who say that they work for a new dispensation and I support the methods that they employ, because I am committed to nonviolence. The Defiance Campaign, the disobedience to unjust laws and obedience to God, have very many biblical parallels.

On August 2 the political leaders whose activities had been restricted upon their release from prison after the February hunger strike announced that they would defy the restriction orders. On August 5 young activists defied police bans on the display of ANC flags at the funeral of two members of Umkhonto we Sizwe (Spear of the Nation), its military wing. Police armed with shotguns and automatic rifles stormed a crowded churchyard in an attempt to seize flags and clergy stepped in to prevent clashes. At the cemetery police removed flags from the coffins and began to chase young mourners carrying flags as they arrived. A half brick and a stone were thrown but Tutu and marshals formed a line between police and young people, urging the youngsters back.

On the night of August 6, twenty community leaders addressed a crowd of about 2,000 in the African Methodist Episcopal church in Hazendal, Cape Town, in open defiance of orders confining them to their homes from early evening and prohibiting them from attending or addressing large gatherings. Church leaders were present to support them.

I just want you to know, my friends, that I stand here to speak from this Holy Book. It is important for you to recognize that what I am going to be saying is not based on any ideology, political or otherwise. It is based on this Holy Book . . .

God took an incredible risk in creating us human beings. God created us freely, for freedom. God, who alone has the perfect right to be a totalitarian, has such a respect, such a reverence for our freedom that God is prepared for us to go freely to hell [rather] than force us to go to heaven . . . We stand here to say that our freedom does not come from any human being, our freedom comes from God. This is what we mean when we say it is an inalienable right . . . To be a human being you must be free to say yes or no. You must be free to love or to hate. That is why . . . nobody, not even the state, has the right to restrict the freedom of people arbitrarily. That is why there is a thing called the rule of law. When [the South African government] pass laws which they know abrogate the rule of law, they say, "No, we will apply those laws compassionately, we will show restraint." Tell us another. If a human being has absolute power, he or she needs to be a saint not to want to use that power absolutely . . . We see it in this country: those who speak for justice, for peace, for democracy in this country, those are the ones who become criminals.

This book [the Bible] says when a ruler gives you unjust laws, disobey. You are not disobeying the ruler, you are obeying God. It is a choice that we have. And the church says, an unjust law does not oblige obedience . . .

My sisters and brothers, I stand here, humbled by you, really humbled by you, to say I commit myself to supporting you to the fullest possible extent that I can; to say to you, we are following the example of Jesus Christ. For when Pontius Pilate asked him a number of questions, Jesus answered and then in the end he said, "Ah, nonsense, man, I keep answering and he doesn't really want to hear." So when Pontius Pilate asked him a question, Jesus just stood in the dock and refused to answer. Jesus disobeyed the ruler. So we have a good example. We are following all these religious people, who when they were told, "Don't speak about Jesus Christ," said, "We will obey God rather than man."

I told Mr. Vlok [Minister of Law and Order, earlier in the year], "You know you have lost." I said it nice and quietly, I didn't shout like now. I said, "You know you have lost, you know it from your own history. You believed you were being oppressed by the British, you fought against the British and in the end you became free. The lesson you must learn from your own history is that when people decide to be free, nothing, just nothing, absolutely nothing can stop them . . ."

On August 8 scores of church leaders, academics and Anglican clergy held an illegal placard protest outside St. George's Cathedral to support restrictees facing prosecution. On August 17, after police had begun arresting and charging the restrictees, Archbishop Tutu, Dean Colin Jones of the cathedral and Professor Charles Villa-Vicencio of the Department of Religious Studies of the University of Cape Town led about 150 marchers from the cathedral toward the offices of the Security Police.

Within two city blocks they were stopped by a contingent of police-women, who tried to persuade the marchers to disperse. The marchers refused and knelt on the pavement. After a standoff lasting most of the lunch hour they were allowed to return to the cathedral. The use of policewomen and the reluctance to arrest the marchers were in sharp contrast to the frequent use of tear gas and whips by heavily armed riot police in black townships.

On Saturday, August 19, hundreds of demonstrators flocked to whites-only Western Cape beaches in defiance of the law. They first went to the Strand, east of Cape Town, where signs were displayed on the seafront reading: "Beach and Sea. Whites Only." Those in cars reached the town after passing through roadblocks set up by the security forces. But soldiers and police at a roadblock on the main coastal highway turned away buses full of township protesters. Armed South African police sealed off the beaches, using barbed wire at one point. At the main beach policemen with dogs guarded the surf line but Tutu went onto the beach. The apartheid signs were temporarily covered by notices saying: DANGER—NO ENTRY—SAP DOG TRAINING. As protesters left the beach, they were warned by police that if they did not disperse, force—including the use of live ammunition—could be used against them. Police arrested photographers and television cameramen and confiscated film showing the police presence. People began to go home and Tutu left for another beach where protesters turned back from the Strand were reported to have gone. After he left, dogs were set on people who remained. During the protest a youngster was hit on the head by a rubber bullet fired by police and was rendered a paraplegic.

At Bloubergstrand, north of Cape Town, police with whips and batons had been driving protesters from a whites-only beach as Tutu arrived. A confrontation threatened as hundreds of young people faced a small police contingent across a beachfront road and white bystanders hurled insults at the multiracial crowd of demonstrators. The archbishop, who was later credited by newspapers with defusing an explosive situation, told journalists shortly afterward what had transpired.

When we arrived here we were thrilled to see so many democrats who wanted to exercise the right to God's beaches. We arrived as people were running away from the police. I went up to the officer in charge and I said could they stop beating people up and we would try to get them back onto the buses. He agreed and we called our friends together. Some had obviously been provoked and tended to respond angrily. We just said to them, "Remember, this campaign is to be characterized by discipline and dignity. You have proved your point that these beaches belong to God and they are therefore for all of us. Now, let us return to the buses in a dignified and disciplined way." Then we sang the national anthem, "Nkosi Sikelel' iAfrika" [God Bless Africa], and the people dispersed. It was a very large crowd, and it was very impressive how they behaved. There was a fair amount of provocation from some of the white people here, and we said to our people, "Don't allow them to drag you to their level."

When you get a government, which claims to have an apartheid that is dead, deploying soldiers with guns and police with quirts [whips] and arms to stop people who are having a picnic—incredible, man! They have admitted that they have no power, they have lost, they have no moral authority at all. We showed it even here. The people have said that they've had enough of apartheid and they are going to disobey the laws of apartheid. I am not organizing campaigns but I doubt that this is just going to be one thing. I will be involved as long as I have a little breath in me left.

The police have shown they really do not know how to handle peaceful demonstrations. We were thrilled and thought they had learned their lesson when we were accosted by beautiful policewomen on Thursday. But they are behaving almost like the Chinese [who crushed the Tiananmen Square protest in June 1989]. Can you imagine the amount of money they must have spent in deploying those soldiers and the police? They should have been home with their children, man! At the Strand, a police officer said, "We are going to use violence including firearms." Firearms! I mean, we had nothing. Oh, no, no, we had sandwiches and things, you know.

On the following day St. George's Cathedral was again the site of a service called to replace a banned meeting. Police had prohibited a "People's Rally" at the University of the Western Cape. Announcing the service, the archbishop noted that events of recent weeks had shown that when people were allowed to organize and meet freely, there was peace.

The Making of a Peaceful Revolution   *173*

It was only when the right of peaceful assembly was denied that there was confrontation.

An enthusiastic crowd of about 4,000 saw representatives of the UDF and other organizations defy restriction orders, declare themselves unbanned, unfurl their banners and take them outside to be displayed on the street. Before the service police had set up roadblocks on a highway to town and stopped busloads of people from getting to the service. In response Dean Jones obtained a court order interdicting police from stopping or harassing people going to or from the service. Police kept a low profile and the service passed peacefully. This address was delivered during the service.

We said, "You have banned the People's Rally. Then I, the Archbishop of Cape Town, call a service." You know, of course, don't you, that this country claims to be a Christian country. In its constitution, it appeals to the name of God and so I say, "Ah well, we can have a church service, man, in this country we can have a church service." We don't hide, we tell them it is a service that is being held because they banned our rally. This is a Christian country, remember. On the N2 [highway], there is a roadblock. What is the roadblock for? To stop people in South Africa, in a Christian country, from coming to church.

I have just been told that people were coming in buses from Paarl, when a helicopter hovered over a bus and the police surrounded the bus, so the people of Paarl who wanted to come here will not be able to come. Actually, I am wondering whether the police in a way are not doing us a service, because if all the people who wanted to come did come, we wouldn't have space for them here. So we can say to the police, *"Dankie"* [Thank you].

But I ask this question, in all seriousness. Does the white South African government think that black people are human? Really human? That black people can feel pain? That black people can love, can laugh? That black people are people created in the image of God? I don't think so . . .

I stand here on behalf of all of our people in this land, I stand here on behalf of God, and I say to you, my friends, that we have a God who has made it quite clear that apartheid, injustice, oppression, exploitation are out. So I want us to say together, "To apartheid, no!" Right, we all say, "To apartheid, no! To injustice, no! To oppression, no! To racism, no! To the abrogation of the rule of law. No!" We say, "Yes to justice!" Yes! We say, "Yes to freedom!" Yes! We say, "Yes to goodness!" Yes! We say, "Yes to friendship!" Yes!

Why doesn't the South African government and its police come here now and look at the people of South Africa, and look at them . . . Hey, man, you are beautiful. This is how our country is going to be. This is how our country will be: Technicolor, a rainbow, a country where black and white hold together . . .

I want us, all of us, to stand and keep a moment of silence, as we think of those who are still in detention, as we think of those who are tortured, as we think of those whose noses are rubbed in the dust, as we think of those who are treated like dirt in the land of their birth. Thank you.

On August 23 a message was telephoned to the archbishop's office to say that teachers and schoolchildren in the township of Guguletu, Cape Town, intended to march to the local police station to demand the release of detained teachers and students. Fearing a bloodbath, Tutu, Jones, Jakes Gerwel, vice-chancellor of the University of the Western Cape, and Franklin Sonn, principal of the Peninsula Technikon, hurried to a Guguletu school. As teachers did not always support the political demands of pupils, the archbishop praised both groups for their unity, but he urged them not to march. After some negotiation with police outside a school, the students moved into St. Mary's Anglican Church nearby. This is what they were told.

We are involved in a noble struggle. We are involved in a moral struggle. We are involved in a struggle that will succeed. We have no doubt that we are going to be free. Because we know that we are going to be free, we can afford to be disciplined, we can afford to be dignified, and we need to underline the fact of this struggle being a nonviolent struggle. Therefore I ask you, when we finish here, I ask you to disperse peacefully, quietly, in a disciplined way.

As the leaders came out of the church ahead of most of the students, police fired tear gas in their direction, scattering people in all directions.

The Making of a Peaceful Revolution   *175*

The leaders emerged coughing from a cloud of tear gas to remonstrate with the police unit responsible.

When there was a confrontation with the police, young people often erected burning barricades on township streets. Some also resorted to stone throwing—at times directed at motorists traveling at speed on highways—which caused the deaths of at least four people during the Defiance Campaign. These tactics were addressed in sermons on August 27. One was delivered at an ecumenical service organized by the Western Province Council of Churches at St. George's Anglican Church, Silvertown, Cape Town.

You have no option but to be involved in the struggle and I call on you to be involved in the struggle for this new South Africa. I call on you to know that it is God's struggle. You say: But you will get into trouble. Of course! Who ever saw powerful people give up their power without doing anything? The powerful will get angry. So what, what is new? Tell me something else. I invite you to come into this exhilarating enterprise, God's enterprise, to change this country, to transfigure this country, to make this country what it is going to become, a land where all, black, white, green, whatever, will be able to hold hands together because they are then living as those whom God has created in his image, as brothers and sisters, as members of one family.

You must know that there are going to be casualties . . . Our children will die, people will be detained and all kinds of strange things, but let the violence come from the system. Let the violence come from the system. Our cause is too noble to be undermined by ignoble methods. I call on you young people especially. I know that you are frustrated many, many, many times. You try to be nonviolent and even a nonviolent procession provokes violence. But that is precisely to show you they [the government] have nothing else. They have no moral authority. They have power but they have no authority. They can beat you up with quirts and people will still go back and then we come, carrying nothing, and we say to our people, "Hold it, get into your buses." And our people go and they get into the buses. We have no power but God gives us a moral authority.

So let us not spoil a good thing. Those stonings, those burning barricades, those burnings—uh-uh. I call on you. So we have now chosen a way, a glorious way, the way of Jesus Christ. It doesn't mean when you are nonviolent, they will not be violent to you. Jesus Christ was totally nonviolent, and look at where he ended up. They strung him up on a Cross and then, when they thought they had done their worst, Easter happened. Jesus Christ rose from the dead. We know, we know we are going to be free . . .

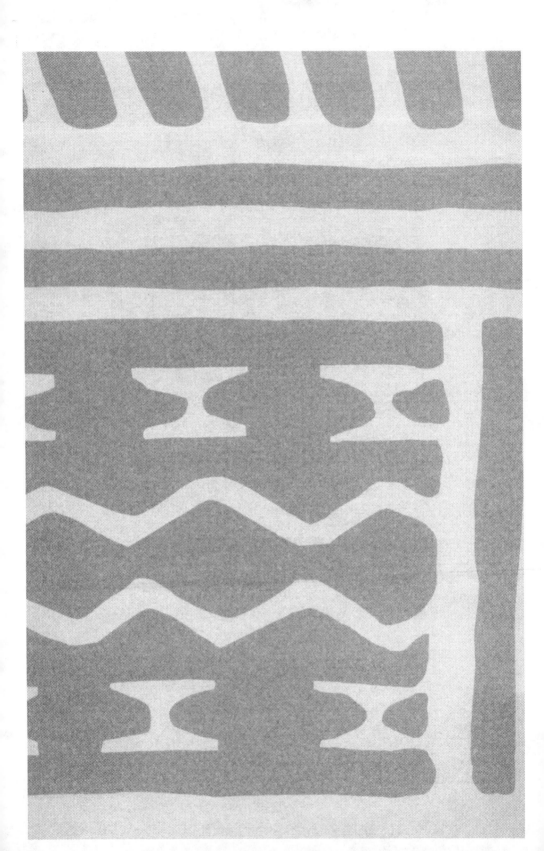

Straighten Up Your Shoulders!
(1989)

THE DEFIANCE *Campaign in Cape Town came to a climax in the week before September 6, election day. On August 30 about 170 women, including Leah Tutu, the archbishop's wife, were arrested as they tried to march to the British Embassy from the Metropolitan Methodist Church. They wanted to hand over a letter, addressed to Margaret Thatcher as a "wife and mother," protesting against death sentences and detentions. Two special courts were convened in the Cape Town Magistrate's Court and the marchers were arraigned in groups of fifteen to twenty in hearings lasting until after midnight.*

The next day leaders in the churches, the trade unions, the UDF, educational institutions and a wide range of other pro-democracy organizations held what they called "an emergency, ad hoc summit" at Bishopscourt, the archbishop's office. They gave their backing to a national call for two days of protest on September 5 and 6.

On September 1 Leah Tutu was arrested again—in the company of her husband and about thirty other leaders as they tried to make their way from the cathedral to Security Police offices to hold a placard demonstration. Participants in the Standing for the Truth Campaign had been brutally beaten outside the offices earlier in the day and leading Cape Town personalities were trying to continue the protest.

On Saturday, September 2, the Mass Democratic Movement planned marches to parliament from three different points in the Cape Town city center. Tutu had reservations about participating: the marches he had taken part in tended to be relatively small protests dominated by clergy and he was concerned at the tendency of the police—as displayed in February 1988—to treat him with kid gloves and then to deal violently with those who followed him. As a result, he did not take part but remained on standby in case trouble developed.

Police broke up the marches after arresting dozens of journalists, photographers and camera crews. At St. George's Cathedral the leaders were arrested. Then the police, in the words of a Dutch Reformed minister, Johan Retief, "bunched the group together and started to hit the remaining people with batons and whips. Many people were hurt in this process and about 200 were arrested and driven away."

At the Metropolitan Methodist Church police used other tactics. A friend of Retief, Pieter Schoombee, told the editor: "A police truck with a water cannon mounted on top entered Greenmarket Square [in front of the church] and stopped about twenty meters from the front row of the marchers. The police began firing water containing purple dye at the marchers, almost flattening them on the road. The truck also fired at people on the pavement and the walls of the church, breaking church windows. It moved down Burg Street, and as it came abreast of the building which houses the headquarters of the Cape National Party, a young marcher climbed up on it and redirected the water cannon at the facade of the building. He shoved a policeman who tried to stop him away with his foot and managed to color the front facade of the building with purple dye. He then jumped off the truck. This was met with loud cheers from the crowd. Shortly afterward tear gas was fired from the police vehicle at the back of the column into the drenched crowd on Burg Street. Later I saw truckloads of people being taken away by the police." The incident gave rise to graffiti declaring: "The purple shall govern."

The archbishop was summoned to the cathedral, where hundreds of marchers who had escaped arrest had gathered. The building was surrounded by police, but Tutu and Dean Jones negotiated with them to allow the congregation to disperse after an impromptu service. This address was delivered to the shocked marchers and their supporters.

Just show me your hands, what are you carrying in your hands? Show me! Show me, show me . . . Your hands are empty, you've got nothing! Why are they so scared of empty hands? Why are they so scared of empty hands? Why is apartheid so that they have got to deploy all those trucks and those men and some women, not too many women this time? It is important for you to know that all moral right is on your side. Yes, you may be clobbered, as some of you have been clobbered, yes, you may cry, you may get beaten. But didn't we say, or were they only slogans, didn't we say that some are still going to be arrested? Some are still going to be detained. Some are still going to run the gauntlet of tear gas. Some are even going to die. Did you think it was figures of speech? When we said that in a struggle there are casualties, did you think it was figures of speech? It is not figures of speech. This is for real, this is for real. And we have committed ourselves, we have committed ourselves to this struggle until freedom is won.

But we shouldn't behave like those who think this prize is just a cheap little prize. The prize for which we are striving is freedom, is freedom for all of us, freedom for those people standing outside [the police], freedom for them! Because, you see, when we are free, when we are free, they will be here, they will be here, joining with us celebrating that freedom, and not standing outside there stopping us from becoming free. Actually, no, you see, if we were free they would be at home watching rugby and it would be a match which they would not be ashamed of. Because we would not be stopping the world and saying, "Don't come and play rugby in our country until our country is free." Because our country would be free.

I keep saying, "Mr. Vlok, Mr. de Klerk [Acting State President], just come here and look at what South Africa will become, what South Africa is going to become. Just look at all these beautiful people. Do you really think that these are terrorists? Do you really think that these are violent people? Why do you use violence?" They . . . won't answer me. But I will answer on their behalf: "We use violence against them because there is nothing else we can use." Apartheid is in and of itself violent. Apartheid is in and of itself evil, totally and completely. There is no way in which it can use nice methods. It has, ipso facto, to use methods that are consistent with its nature.

So, my friends, do not sit there as if you have drunk an unexpected dose of castor oil. Don't sit there looking glum. Yes, I think you must feel a little sad. What were we trying to do? We were just trying to walk around our city. We wanted to walk around and look at our parliament, our parliament building, and they don't want us to do that in our country. No, man, these guys, no, man, really. So I say to you, you've got to straighten up your shoulders. Come on, straighten up your shoulders and say, "We shall be free!" Come on, stand! Stand, stand! Stand upright! Here we go: "We shall be free!" Now we say, "All of us together, black and white, in a free South Africa." Do you really mean that? Let those people [the police] hear. Do you really mean that we will be free? ["Yes!"] Sit down. Now that is not just play-play, okay?

As we go out, some of us are going to try and stand around there. We have negotiated with the police, for what it is worth. We have negotiated with them that you will not be molested if you go out singly, if you go out singly. Please don't give them any excuse.

The address also dealt with the difference between the way the police treated leaders and their followers.

I am very conscious of the fact that I am a protected species. That is a dilemma, that when I say perhaps we ought to take a particular action, on the whole this protected species will be treated differently from others of you. That worries me, that worries me. I hope that you will understand that I need to be particularly sensitive to what I do do. I can say let us march and the chances are I could march for a few yards and they would pick me up . . . remove [me] from the scene, and then deal brutally with the other people. I need to be careful of how I involve you, my sisters and brothers. And so you are aware that we have particular problems.

But I am going to be here. I am going to be here and I am going to stand around and watch that as far as possible with the Dean, and Bishop Charles [Albertyn] and Lionel Louw [chairman of the Western Province Council of Churches] and others that the police do keep their undertaking . . .

Say to yourselves, in your heart, "God loves me." In your heart: "God loves me, God loves me . . . I am of infinite value to God. God created me for freedom." In your heart: "God created me for freedom, God created me for freedom and my freedom is inalienable, my freedom is inalienable. My freedom is God-given, my freedom is God-given! I don't go around and say, Baas [Boss], please give me my freedom. God loves me, I am of infinite value because God loves me and God created me for freedom, and my freedom is inalienable, God-given." Right!

Now straighten up your shoulders, come, straighten up your shoulders like people who are born for freedom! Lovely, lovely, lovely!

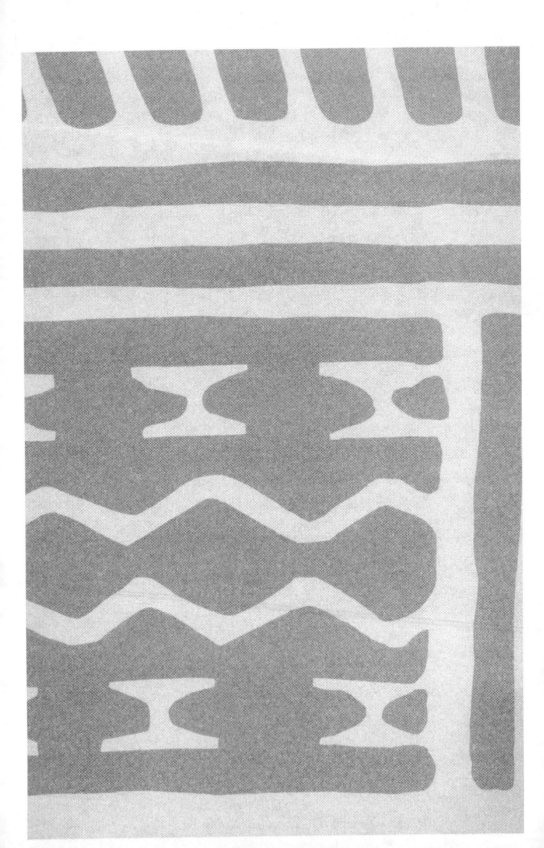

20
We Are the Rainbow People!
(1989)

ON THE night of September 4, Beyers Naudé, the dissident Afrikaner church leader, was scheduled to preach at a service at a Methodist church in Buitenkant Street, central Cape Town. The police banned the service. They went to St. George's Cathedral and, carrying weapons, entered the building with the intention of removing anyone they could find. They stopped a concert by a visiting university choir— apparently thinking it might be a cover for a replacement for the banned service. They later relented, but Dean Jones decided that since the police had desecrated the cathedral he would not allow it to reopen until it had been reconsecrated.

At the Methodist church, police pulled a Casspir armored vehicle up against the church doors, trapping people inside. When the archbishop, the dean, Beyers Naudé, Lionel Louw and others challenged the blockading of a church, they were arrested and held in nearby police cells for about ninety minutes. Only after they were released, when they heard that the Supreme Court had set aside the banning of the service, were they able to free those trapped in the church.

Bystanders complained that police had been beating people indiscriminately on the city streets during the evening. Early the next morning the archbishop reconsecrated the cathedral.

The growing police violence culminated on election day, when more than twenty people were killed in Cape Town's townships. In the country as a whole, more than two million workers stayed away from work.

On the evening of September 7, Tutu was told that reports were circulating that the previous day's death toll was much higher than so far revealed. He broke down weeping and went to his chapel. He spent the evening alone and slept badly. The following morning he told Matt Esau, his personal assistant at the time, that he wanted to call for a protest march the following Monday. But Esau appealed for more time for planning, and the date was set for Wednesday, September 13. A memorial service for those who had died was held in St. George's Cathedral on September 8. Before the service the archbishop consulted with Allan Boesak on his proposal. The outcome was a joint announcement of a march at the end of the service. Some days later Bishopscourt staff heard that some community leaders, while accepting the decision, had raised questions about Tutu's mandate.

The brutality of the police's Cape Town riot squad during the Defiance Campaign rallied support for the march. On election day a police lieutenant, Gregory Rockman—classified as Colored—had given an interview to the South African Press Association denouncing the behavior of the riot squad in the townships as being comparable to that of "wild dogs." His action contributed to anger across a wide spectrum of both black and white Capetonians. The new mayor of Cape Town, Gordon Oliver—elected by white voters—unexpectedly came to the memorial service directly after his installation. Asked by a journalist whether he would join the march, which would be illegal, he had no hesitation in saying that he would.

Boesak and Tutu held discussions with diplomats from twelve countries—including the ambassadors of Britain, the United States, France, the Federal Republic of Germany, Australia and Canada—and asked them to condemn police excesses and to monitor the march. They also met a delegation of the white Dutch Reformed Church at its request. The DRC wanted to organize a joint approach to the government seeking recognition of the right to peaceful protest. In turn, other church leaders unsuccessfully asked the DRC to join their action.

The mounting domestic and international pressure posed a major challenge to President de Klerk in the opening days of his administration. De Klerk had replaced P. W. Botha, initially as party leader after Botha suffered a stroke, then as head of government after a leadership clash. The night before the march, telephone calls from two cabinet *ministers indicated that De Klerk was about to back down and allow it. This was confirmed by newspapers the following morning.*

No one knew what support there would be, but by the time Tutu arrived at the cathedral it was packed and thousands of people filled the surrounding streets. In a spectacle not seen in South Africa since the banning of the ANC and the PAC nearly thirty years before, a crowd estimated by most newspapers at 30,000 moved triumphantly through the city to the City Hall. Some crammed into the building to hear speeches, among them the following remarks, which were received with cheers and laughter.

I'm just an old man after all these fiery speeches. I think actually we maybe ought to go home. But I want to say to you: today is the day in which we the people have scored a great victory for justice and for peace. And it is important that that is registered . . .

In England . . . Hyde Park [in London] has got . . . something called Speakers' Corner, where you can go and say anything. A policeman stands next to you, not to arrest you, he stands there to protect you from the people who may get annoyed at what you are saying. On one occasion there was a West Indian who got up on his soapbox and said, "There is nothing wrong with England," and he kept quiet for a little bit, "except for the English." We can say, "There is nothing wrong with South Africa except for the perpetrators of apartheid." No, no, no. We believe they can change. So let us not say "except for the perpetrators of apartheid."

There is nothing wrong with this beautiful country except for apartheid! There is nothing wrong with this beautiful country except for injustice! There is nothing wrong with this country except for the violence of apartheid!

And so we say to Mr. de Klerk, "Hallo!" Let's say to Mr. de Klerk, "You wanted us to show you that we can be dignified. You wanted us to show you that we are disciplined. You wanted us to show you that we are determined. You wanted us to show you that we are peaceful. Right! Mr. de Klerk, please come here! We are inviting you, Mr. de Klerk, we invite you, Mr. Vlok, we invite all the cabinet. We say, come, come here, and can you see the people of this country? Come and see what this country is going to become."

This country is a rainbow country! This country is Technicolor. You can come and see the new South Africa!

The Making of a Peaceful Revolution   *187*

I'm not going to speak for long. This is rather unusual for me. But before I tell you one or two things that we want to tell Mr. de Klerk as well, I believe there are a few people that we really must give very, very warm ovations to. We've done a little bit of that but I think we ought to show that we recognize goodness when we see it, and I want you to give, in his absence, Lieutenant Rockman a big clap. Do you think that is a big cheer? It must be heard outside . . . There are very many others that I would want us to give a big cheer to. You gave Allan [Boesak] a big cheer but not very many people remember that Allan became the youngest president of the World Alliance of Reformed Churches, which was a remarkable achievement. But as if that were not enough, Allan did something that nobody else could do. He is the first person to be reelected to that position . . . We must give Allan a loud cheer, man, a humdinger! Then I think the last persons I would like us to give a very warm cheer to: the people of Cape Town, yourselves. You have been remarkable!

We want to say to Mr. de Klerk, "We have already won. Mr. de Klerk, we have already won. Mr. de Klerk, if you know really what is good for you, join us! Join us! Join us! Join us! Join us in the struggle for this new South Africa . . . Join us in this new South Africa . . ."

I want you to do something to finish. Really. I told you I was not going to be long. I want us to stand—Capetonians, South Africans, black, white, whatever, and hold hands and know that nothing can stop us. We are unstoppable! Unstoppable!

Outside the City Hall, on Cape Town's Grand Parade, a far bigger crowd than could be accommodated inside was gathered. The main points of the address inside were repeated, followed by this exhortation, which was met with cheers.

Let's just keep quiet. "Mr. de Klerk, did you hear a pin drop?" They tried to make us one color: purple. We say we are the rainbow people! We are the new people of the new South Africa!

Afterward a journalist from the anti-apartheid Afrikaans newspaper Vrye Weekblad *asked about the event. One of the answers dealt with the issue of Tutu's mandate.*

QUESTION: Looking back on the march, what strikes you as the most successful part?

ANSWER: The fact that people of all races, given the opportunity, want to be together. Wasn't that, in fact, the most incredible thing, which we have seen so many times, but I think the general public has not. And the dignity, again which we have seen, the general public has not . . . I have to say I am still overwhelmed by the response. I had thought that we would probably get about 1,000 people, because it was during the week and there was the whole business of whether the police might not actually again do what they had done on that Saturday. Then to have that massive turnout and of course there were also the onlookers on the balconies, on the sides, many of them applauding . . . I think that it touched a very responsive chord in very many people.

God was very good because it could have gone so badly wrong—just one person maybe hitting somebody. We're glad and it's a tremendous credit to the people. We have a saying in our languages that "a leader is a leader through people" . . . All you could say we did was to think up that it was important for Cape Town to be given the opportunity to express outrage. God gave us that particular inspiration and I think a lot of people did want to do something. Often people do not know quite what to do and this gave them the opportunity and people turned out in those tremendous numbers.

QUESTION: When you decided to call for a march, was it on the spur of the moment or how did it actually come about?

ANSWER: I was sitting preparing my address for . . . the memorial service in the cathedral. I was sitting there writing when, well, you assume that you are trying to be in touch with God, and that God was saying that is what you should do.

21

We Have Seen Some Extraordinary Things

(1990)

AFTER THE Cape Town march, the government was compelled to relax its prohibition on public protest, and huge marches swept the country, with church leaders in the front ranks. Within weeks, President de Klerk gave further indications of his change in style. Early in October, he agreed to a request by the archbishop for a meeting with church leaders. Before the meeting De Klerk announced the release of a PAC officeholder and the "Rivonia trialists," top ANC leaders who were arrested in Rivonia, Johannesburg, in 1963.

Allan Boesak and SACC General Secretary Frank Chikane agreed to join the discussions with the President and his minister responsible for constitutional negotiations, Gerrit Viljoen. Tutu summarized the meeting in the following words: "We come away impressed that we were listened to, yes, but . . . while there is a commitment on the part of the State President to move toward the negotiation mode, we were not able to get the kind of specifics that would satisfy the constituencies from which we come."

On February 2, 1990, De Klerk, opening a new session of parliament, announced a range of measures, including the unbanning of the African National Congress, the Pan Africanist Congress and the South African Communist Party, and the imminent release of Nelson Mandela. These steps met some of the demands which had been made at the October meeting and which had been put forward by political groups, *trade unions, church and other organizations over many years. The archbishop telephoned the President to congratulate him and commented on the speech in the course of fourteen international media interviews and a news conference during the day.*

I have to say [that De Klerk] has amazed me and in many ways I could not believe my ears . . . I found it exhilarating, quite astounding that we seem to be at the dawn of the new South Africa for which so many people have striven . . . It is not all that I hoped for but it is a very considerable part of it. Our people are not intransigent, crazy or anything of that kind. They are going to say, many of them, that we have made a very important breakthrough . . . It is clear that . . . [the government has] taken account of the pressures that the people have exerted . . . the pressures of international opinion, sanctions, and the pressures of our people. When I say "our people," I say black and white people who have been struggling for a new dispensation . . . Extraordinary things can happen once people sit down and look each other in the eyes and are no longer ogres to one another. I myself believe that given a measure of goodwill, and some trust . . . we would see movement very rapidly.

Tutu was at home in Soweto when it was announced on Saturday, February 10, that Nelson Mandela was to be freed the following day. Before flying to Cape Town the archbishop was interviewed by an American television reporter.

QUESTION: What does Mandela's release mean for you personally?

ANSWER: We are all just exuberant. We've been praying and working and campaigning for this release and we are on cloud nine because I am quite certain myself that now negotiations are going to get underway, and he is going to be a very crucial factor in making them come to a successful conclusion.

QUESTION: What does the release mean for the black South African community and South Africa in general?

ANSWER: It is saying to us, God hears . . . God acts, God is really involved. We've been praying so long and it seemed like our prayers were just going into a void. Now [what we prayed for] is happening and we are getting hope that we are going to be free, all the people in this land, not just black people, the white people are not free either. We are all going to be free together, black and white.

QUESTION: Why is the person of Mandela particularly important?

ANSWER: He has articulated the aspirations of blacks in a particularly eloquent manner and been prepared to pay the price of his commitment. Twenty-seven years in jail is no plaything. And he has remained, even on the testimony of people who would have been his enemies, a gracious person. The State President said he's a "courteous gentleman."

QUESTION: Today, and presumably tomorrow and the next few days, is a stage for celebrations. What's the next step after the celebrations?

ANSWER: Of course, you've got to come down to terra firma and get down to the actual business of making a go of negotiations and having this new constitution and new possibilities of a nonracial, nonsexist democratic South Africa underway.

QUESTION: Are there any potential dangers in the process?

ANSWER: Of course. You might have intransigence on one side or the other. You've got the right wing already making ominous noises. There may also be people on the left wing who feel that there is too much compromise. There's a danger, yes. There's a danger, too, that people may not go into it wanting to succeed and willing themselves to succeed. But my own feeling is, let's get these [talks] underway, because when people sit down and talk to each other, they begin to discover each other . . .

QUESTION: What kind of time frame do you envisage for negotiations?

ANSWER: I'm hoping that by the end of this year we would have got something more than just an outline, where we would be beginning to talk about a constituent assembly and the actual process of enfranchising, empowering, the many who have been disenfranchised, who were without power.

QUESTION: Is the end of that a black government?

ANSWER: No, the end of that is a majority government, truly democratic, chosen by all the people of South Africa.

Crisis faced those organizing a reception for Mandela on Cape Town's Grand Parade—the point at which the September 13 march had ended. The short notice of his release resulted in inadequate provision for crowd control. People from all over the Cape Town area poured into the city center and were kept waiting for hours in the hot sun. At one stage a large group stormed its way into the neighboring City Hall and refused to leave. Tutu persuaded them to follow him through the building, through a back exit and away from the city center to a church in District Six on the outskirts of the city center. About 3,000 people from the Parade followed them to the area—still empty of buildings after the forced removal of the community in the 1960s. The archbishop, Muslim leaders and others assured the crowd they would bring Mandela to see them, but when he did not arrive most returned to the Parade. The clergy were left to deal with the angry remnants of the group which had occupied the City Hall. In the furious argument which followed, some youths threatened to kill Tutu. He finally led them back to the Parade. Later a liquor store was looted and police opened fire on alleged looters on the edge of the crowd. But calm returned by the time Nelson Mandela emerged from the City Hall to give his first speech in nearly three decades.

A service of thanksgiving for the changes in South Africa, held in St. George's Cathedral on March 6, offered an opportunity for reflection.

They tell the story of a man who was driving his car over a mountain road. The car came to grief and fell over a cliff. The man was thrown out of the car and clutched on to a very flimsy twig. Then, discovering that he was still alive, he called out, "Help, is there anyone up there?" A voice from heaven said, "Yes, my son. Do you trust me?" And he said, "Yes." "Let go of the twig and I will catch you at the bottom." And he looked down and saw the several feet that he would have to fall. A little silence. Then: "Help, is there anyone else up there?"

Sometimes after all that has happened in our country, we might have been forgiven for wondering whether God was around, whether God saw, whether God heard, whether God was aware of the suffering, the injustice and the oppression. People detained, jailed, tortured. People exiled, people killed. All of this, it seemed, did not touch God. God seemed to be indifferent or God was weak . . .

These words, which we sometimes quoted, of the Lord saying to his people, "I have witnessed the misery of my people in Egypt, and have heard them crying out because of their oppressors. I know what they are suffering and have come down to rescue them"—those words seemed such a mockery. Remember last September, remember that we had sectional elections, and people were killed protesting against those sectional elections? Do you remember how we tried to walk on God's beaches and we were stopped by police and soldiers carrying guns, tear gas, quirts; people who were ready, as they told us in the Strand, to use live ammunition to stop God's children from walking on God's beaches, even though dogs could walk on those beaches? And human beings, because they were black, were not allowed to walk on those beaches?

Do you remember the funerals that we have had? The funeral . . . when, because coffins were draped with ANC flags, the police rushed into the churchyard, and the tension with police holding their guns ready because they were trying to take ANC flags away from people?

This cathedral here will tell stories in the future. It will tell stories of how police and soldiers desecrated this holy place, this cathedral will speak of rallies that we have had when our organizations decided to unban themselves. This cathedral will speak of the start of that great march, in September, a march that started in Cape Town and was copied in the rest of South Africa. People marched in Johannesburg, in Durban, in Ceres, in all kinds of places . . .

The Making of a Peaceful Revolution

You remember how we used to say here: This is God's world. God is in charge, we said. Maybe sometimes it was like whistling in the dark to keep up our courage. Then . . . you remember how I used to say [unjust rulers] will bite the dust? I kept repeating that, and well, maybe it didn't seem as if it was true. Ha, look at what is happening now! In Eastern Europe, haven't they been toppling as if they were just dolls, puppets! They are biting the dust comprehensively . . .

We have seen some extraordinary things, haven't we? We have seen a State President say things we didn't believe. Even now you keep pinching yourself to see what has happened. People were killed because they were carrying ANC flags, now you switch on SABC-TV and there is an ANC flag. So far as I can make out . . . the sky seems still to be in place. They unbanned the ANC. We said to them long ago, let these people speak for themselves, and if they say things that will condemn them, let them condemn themselves out of their mouths. But let them speak for themselves and let the people choose. And so what do you get? Thabo [Mbeki, foreign affairs spokesman for the ANC] appears on television and he speaks with Mr. [Pik] Botha [the government's Foreign Minister], and Mr. Botha ends up saying, "Brother."

Nelson is released, and they said, "Oh no, it's really that everything about him is really a myth. He ought to be kept in jail because if he comes out people are going to be disillusioned." Disillusioned! He truly is one of the greatest people around, his generosity of spirit. How, after twenty-seven years, he can come out of jail and be so totally, totally unbitter, so ready to acknowledge the good that is in others, even others who made him suffer as much as he has suffered? It is not only he. You talk to people like Walter Sisulu [one of Mandela's earliest political associates, secretary general of the ANC, and a Rivonia trialist] and almost all of them. The incredible thing is how they care about this land and all of its people, black and white.

. . . We kept saying ethnicity is totally unacceptable to our people and then you have a couple like Professor [Jack] Simon [a former University of Cape Town academic] returning from exile and you have Ray Alexander [a trade unionist] and they receive rapturous welcomes. And most of those people who welcome them are black, because people have said it is not the color of your skin that determines where we place you, because you could be black and be one who supports the system. You could be white and be committed to our struggle.

So we have come here to say thank you, God, that you are in fact a God who . . . comes down to deliver your people. We thank you, God, that you have been on the side of those who have been oppressed. We thank God, too, for our overseas partners and friends who have supported and continue to support our struggle with their prayers, with their pressure, with their sanctions. We say to them: Keep it up. Thank you, international community . . .

Let us also acknowledge that Mr. de Klerk has been courageous and we have commended him for his courage. But you know . . . we have really only got back to 1960 . . . when our organizations were still legal. But we want to thank the people, you, the people, as well. For you have been incredible in your commitment to the struggle. You have been beaten, you have been tear-gassed, you have been arrested . . . All of you, your names are written in letters of gold in the history of this country, because when this country is free, all of us are going to be free . . .

Have you seen now how many white people who used to be a little scared are now walking with slightly straighter shoulders? There is a new pride in being South African, because the things that we kept saying are becoming true . . .

And so, friends, we have come to give thanks [for] the beginning of the end of apartheid, the dawn of a new South Africa. We come to give thanks to God for the possibilities about which we have been dreaming that we seem to be realizing. God bless you and God protect you.

Why I Believe This Is Happening
(1990)

The end of the Cold War helped precipitate the changes in South Africa, cadets at the U.S. Military Academy at West Point, New York, were told on May 9, a week after the first full-scale talks between the ANC and the South African government. About 3,000 students and members of the public heard the lecture, primarily intended for cadets studying world history.

We live in extraordinary times. Freedom is breaking out everywhere: in Eastern Europe; Namibia is independent; Nelson Mandela is free . . . People marched in . . . South Africa and people marched in Berlin and the Berlin Wall was breached. People marched here, there and everywhere, and freedom started breaking out even in unlikely places. Why? Why was it happening? Why now?

Well, in relation to South Africa I can say here are some of the reasons why I believe this is happening, that you can have something totally, totally inconceivable, almost the unthinkable, to have Mr. Nelson Mandela and his team on one side of the table and on the other side Mr. F. W. de Klerk, the State President of South Africa, and his team actually sitting across from each other and talking as if they were human beings . . . and ending up discovering that, yes, they are human beings, that even if you looked as hard as you liked, none of those in the room—so Thabo Mbeki of the ANC said—none in the room had horns. And try as hard as you did to see, none of them was sitting uncomfortably because they were sitting on a tail . . .

Some of what is happening at home was due to the fact that the government tried repression. It thought that it would knock the stuffing out of our people, and our people said, "Not on your life. We are made for something totally different. We are made freely for freedom and you are not God. You may have incredible power but do know that the precedents that you have are not comforting. Those who have been dictators and tyrants before you, who thought that they had power, are the flotsam and jetsam of history." Unfortunately, of course, we learn from history that we don't learn from history. The South African government had tried repression, if you like, from 1948, when they came to power. But for us actually it started in 1652 when Jan van Riebeeck [commander of the Dutch expedition whose members were the first European settlers in South Africa] stepped on the shores of our country. We have waited since then to become free. When the Defiance Campaign happened our people said, "Uh-uh, you can detain us, you can ban us, you can arrest us, you can tear-gas us, you can turn your dogs on us, you can shoot us, you can kill some of us, but in the end you have already had it, because ultimately freedom will out." You cannot hold people down forever, because people are made for something more glorious. That is what dictators and tyrants everywhere keep having to contend with, that God created us for freedom and human beings tend toward freedom like plants tend toward the light and toward water. No matter how long you succeed in oppressing a people, ultimately, ultimately you will come a cropper. You will bite the dust and do so ignominiously . . .

The second reason we have got where we are is because the world has heeded our pleas and applied economic pressure on the South African government. Namibia is free and independent today because South Africa could no longer afford fighting in Angola and we want to say thank you to those who have so responded to our appeal. Money or the lack of it helps to concentrate the mind pretty sharply.

Third is the quite undoubted impact of the ending of the Cold War. It has had extraordinary repercussions around the world. In South Africa the government used to talk about what they called the total Communist onslaught. Then when the Russians and this country began talking peace they could no longer at home with any hope of credibility speak about their fears of a Communism that was saying: We are no longer interested in expansion, we are interested in peace. That has been important. That has had important repercussions right around the world. It's been important that there has been a Gorbachev rather than a Stalin at the head of the Kremlin. His perestroika and glasnost has made it possible for what has been called the velvet revolution to happen in Czechoslovakia, where people have no longer had to fear the rumble of Soviet tanks that would come to blow out the lamp of freedom.

I would want to add that we have been fortunate that at this present time in South Africa the State President is Mr. de Klerk rather than his predecessor, Mr. Botha. I want to pay a very warm tribute to him, as I did after his speech on February 2. I telephoned him to congratulate him to say what we had heard was unbelievable. But Nelson Mandela is also a key factor. Somehow a rapport has taken place between Mr. Mandela and Mr. de Klerk and you hear when they refer to each other the warmth, the respect that each has for the other. Those are the individuals who have a critical importance for what is taking place at home.

For me, much the most important fact is that this is a moral universe, that God is a God who cares about right and wrong. God cares about justice and injustice. God is in charge. That is what has upheld the morale of our people, to know that in the end good will prevail. Of course, sometimes you have to hold on to this article of faith by the skin of your teeth, but it is there. When you look at the whole kaleidoscope of history you see that there is a nemesis. Sometimes you wish, of course, to say to God, "God, we know that you are in charge but why don't you make it slightly more obvious."

There is no doubt at all in the end that we are going to be free. We are going to be free because the cause which we uphold is a cause for justice. We are not seeking to dominate anybody. We are looking for a freedom that is going to be shared by all South Africans, black and white together. We say we are looking for a new South Africa, a new South Africa where the color of a person's skin, a person's race, that those are total irrelevancies, that each person is going to count because they are created in the image of God . . . We say to white people: Shed your fears, shed your apprehensions, shed your anxieties, throw in your lot with those who are on the winning side. We say: Come, join us, for when we are free, then all will be free. Until we are all free none is going to be free.

On Easter Monday, 1986, personnel carriers drove past the Tutu home in Soweto. Leah Tutu remarked: "The border is here." A lone woman protests as soldiers pass her area of Soweto. *Paul Weinberg/SouthLight*

Tutu repeatedly negotiated to prevent clashes between security forces and protestors during the successive states of emergency in the late 1980s.
*Dale Yudelman/*The Star, *Johannesburg*

Desmond Tutu blessing the city of Cape Town after his enthronement as Archbishop at St. George's Cathedral in 1986.

Dave Hartman/SouthLight

A security-force posse on township patrol in Duduza, east of Johannesburg, 1985. After a heated confrontation with members of the force in P. W. Botha's office in 1988, Desmond Tutu said he did not know whether Jesus would have handled the meeting in the same way: "I hope that is how he would have handled it, because it was on behalf of people who have been hurt by these guys." *Paul Weinberg/SouthLight*

BEACH AND SEA. WHITES ONLY. During a protest against beach apartheid at the Strand, east of Cape Town, in 1989, policemen with dogs guarded the surfline. Later, after photographers were arrested under emergency regulations for being present at the scene of police action, protesters were warned by a police officer that if they did not disperse, force—including live ammunition—could be used against them. *Eric Miller / SouthLight*

Under arrest while trying to march to Security Police offices in Cape Town for a placard demonstration. Flanking Tutu are (left) Franklin Sonn, principal of the Peninsula Technikon, and (right) Jakes Gerwel, vice-chancellor of the University of the Western Cape. Behind Tutu and Gerwel are (left) Lionel Louw, then head of the Western Province Council of Churches, and (right) Colin Jones, Anglican Dean of Cape Town. *Eric Miller / SouthLight*

Desmond Tutu and, behind him, Jakes Gerwel, vice-chancellor of the University of the Western Cape, being teargassed along with pupils outside St. Mary's Anglican Church, Guguletu, in 1989. Police launched tear-gas canisters despite the fact that students had been dispersing peacefully at Tutu's request.
Rachid Lombard

The Rainbow People of God. On September 13, 1989, a thirty-thousand-strong crowd demonstrated in Cape Town against police violence and overwhelmed the government's ban on peaceful protest. *Mayibuye Center*

"We are all just exuberant . . . We are on cloud nine . . ." Desmond Tutu and
fellow Anglican bishops meeting Nelson Mandela at St. Paul's Church in Jabavu,
Soweto, soon after his release. On Mandela's left is Michael Nuttall, Bishop of Natal,
who as Dean of the Anglican Church in Southern Africa calls himself "Number
Two to Tutu."
The other bishops are, from left, Geoff Davies (Umzimvubu), Geoff Quinlan
(Suffragan Bishop, Cape Town), and Richard Kraft (Pretoria, face partly obscured).
John Allen

"Something totally
inconceivable, almost
the unthinkable . . ."
F. W. de Klerk and
Nelson Mandela outside
the venue of the first
talks between delegations
of the government and the
African National
Congress in Cape Town,
May 1990.
Eric Miller/SouthLight

"If there is to be reconciliation, we who are the ambassadors of Christ . . . must be Christ's instruments of peace." Preaching the opening sermon at the Rustenburg Conference of Churches in November 1990.
Brett Eloff/SouthLight

"It seems as if the culture of violence is taking root in our society . . . What has gone wrong, that we have seemed to have lost our reverence for life . . ." A man being beaten to death in Soweto. *Greg Marinovich/SouthLight*

"We are not animals. We are human beings who have feelings." Visiting the injured at Boipatong after the June 1992 massacre. Frank Chikane, General Secretary of the South African Council of Churches, is beyond Tutu, center, and Michael Nuttall, Bishop of Natal, beyond Chikane.

George Mashinini /The Star, *Johannesburg*

"In spite of being surrounded by crowds of angry people who brandished *pangas,* knives and other self-made weapons, Tutu did not flinch in his call for peace . . ." *(City Press).* In Kagiso, west of Johannesburg, in August 1990.

Roger Bosch /SouthLight

Desmond Tutu voting for the first time in the Uluntu (People's) Center, a community facility in the township of Guguletu, Cape Town. Polling opened in the first democratic election on April 27, 1994. *Eric Miller*

Nearly five years after addressing "the Rainbow People of God" from a Cape Town City Hall balcony after a watershed march for peace, Desmond Tutu returned to the same place to introduce Nelson Mandela at his first public appearance after being elected President of South Africa.
Leon Müller, The Argus

23

I Am Not a Politician

(1990)

DURING THE *interviews on February 2, Tutu had told journalists that he expected the church's role to change after the lifting of restrictions on political parties. Early signs came at a meeting of the Anglican Church's Synod of Bishops two weeks after Mandela's release: the bishops resolved to ban licensed clergy from belonging to political parties and urged the liberation movements to at least suspend their armed struggle against the government.*

The archbishop's view of his new role was articulated in more detail in this extract from an interview with a Danish journalist.

QUESTION: What about you personally? Are you pulling out of politics?

ANSWER: I have said that I am going to adopt a lower profile. We had to fulfill a role and I kept saying that I was an interim leader, because our real leaders were either in jail or in exile. Now that we are normalizing the political process in this country, and our leaders are out, I will not have to be as prominent, doing things which in a normal country you would not be doing. But that does not mean we will not still be wanting to be vigilant and seeking to be prophetic, to say whether something is right or wrong.

QUESTION: But isn't this the moment when you would need all good people to work for changes, and you, too?

ANSWER: Of course, but I am not going to be providing a program, a manifesto which will be lined up side by side with, say, the manifesto of the ANC or any other grouping. I am not in competition with Nelson Mandela, Walter Sisulu, or any of those, no.

Of course, we are all going to be seeking to do all we can to facilitate the coming of the new society. We've been doing that. Already in October . . . Allan Boesak, Frank Chikane and I were the first church leaders who asked to see Mr. de Klerk in order to try and help bring about conditions, or we told him the conditions we thought were necessary for the negotiation process to take place.

QUESTION: But why not stay active in politics?

ANSWER: I am not a politician.

RESPONSE: Yes, you are.

ANSWER: No, I am a pastor, I am a pastor.

QUESTION: But you are also a politician?

ANSWER: Uh-uh, no I am not. I am a church person who believes that religion does not just deal with a certain compartment of life. Religion has a relevance for the whole of life and we have to say whether a particular policy is consistent with the policy of Jesus Christ or not, and if you want to say that that is political, then I will be a politician in those terms. But it won't be as one who is involved in party politics.

QUESTION: But still in the continued struggle for another society . . .

ANSWER: Oh yes, there's no question about that, and I would hope that Christians would be inspired by their faith to become good citizens, they would be inspired to become good politicians. It is the role of laypeople to become deeply involved in how things are run in their country. But . . . not for a church leader in the same kind of way. My role, the role of church leaders, is to be able to say: "Thus saith the Lord."

With things coming back to normal, we are in a way [where we were] in 1960, when the ANC and the PAC were banned. [Once we have normal political activity] church leaders will step aside and leave the center of the political stage to politicians.

QUESTION: And that's the way it should be?

ANSWER: That is how it should be. And they must be there, vigilant, ensuring that whoever is the government tries to govern according to ideals and standards that would be acceptable to our Lord and Saviour Jesus Christ.

However, the ban on party membership was unpopular with many young priests who had been in the forefront of political activity. A passionate defense of the policy was given in response to a challenge at a meeting of the Anglican Students' Federation in Imbali, Pietermaritzburg.

This does not mean that you should not have your preferences among the various options available. [It] does not mean when the time comes when you can vote that you shouldn't vote . . . [Nor does it] mean political neutrality . . . You are aware of the commitment of our church to work for justice, for a new dispensation. There is absolutely no question about that.

But this is a decision that was taken out of very real pastoral concern. It is quite simple. If . . . you are ANC . . . [in Natal] and Bishop Michael [Nuttall] sends you to an area that is known to be Inkatha, there is no way in which you are going to be able to carry out your ministry . . . Just two weeks ago I was enthroning the new bishop of the Diocese of South Eastern Transvaal, and when we were singing the national anthem, you had some servers with a clenched fist [indicating ANC allegiance] and some with the open palm [indicating PAC membership] . . .

With all the goodwill in the world, there is no way in which people who belong to a party that is opposite to the one to which you have declared yourself to belong are going to be able to accept openly, readily your ministration. Imagine when you have someone who says he is Inkatha and they want to come to confession, and they come for confession to a priest they know is ANC.

We are engaging as churches in the process of seeking to be facilitators in the process of negotiation. Right now in [Natal] we have been trying to bring together two groups. We are not playing marbles. People are dying because of the differences between these two groups. It is not an academic question. In order to be able to have any kind of credibility to both sides, you have to be seen to have a particular kind of impartiality. Because there is actually no one else, I don't think, able to bring those two groups together . . .

I've been General Secretary of the SACC, and I want to tell you the kind of clobbering I have had because they said the SACC was one that favored the ANC. We were looking after political prisoners and their families. When one political prisoner—who belonged to PAC and after whom the SACC had looked in equal measure to other people—when I went to see this man to celebrate his release, I came away with an earful. Only recently, a few weeks ago, we were having conversations with different organizations, including Azapo and PAC. And again they're saying there is no question at all about the bias of the SACC . . .

We are not stopping you who are unordained from joining [except for one party] . . . We could not say it was consistent with our position as a church for you to belong to the SACP [the South African Communist Party], a body that says specifically that one of its tenets is atheism . . . You would have to know that it was obvious that that is not an option that is open to you at all.

Part Five

A KIND OF ROLLER-COASTER RIDE

The Violence of Transition

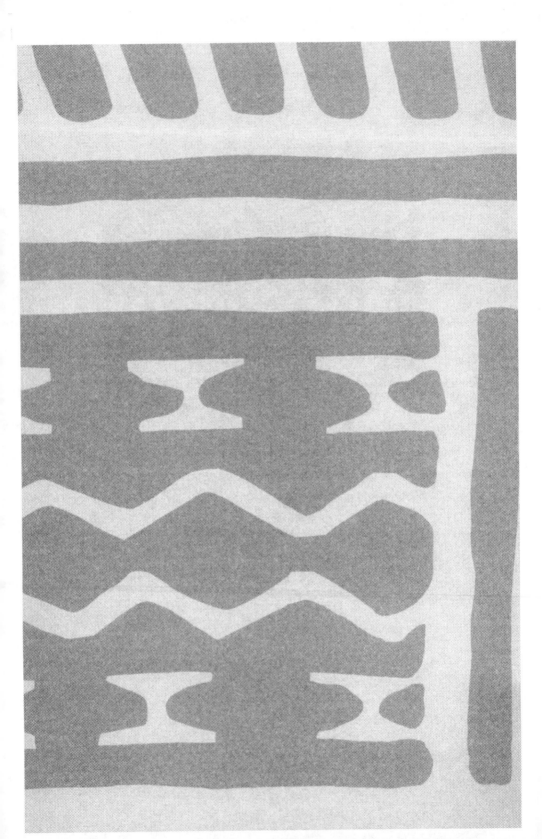

24
The Nadir of Despair
(1990)

THE VIOLENCE *in Natal which had led the church leaders to intervene in 1987 continued during 1988 and 1989 despite further attempts at reconciliation. In March 1990 fighting reached a new intensity, in what came to be called the Seven Days' War, in the Edendale Valley of Pietermaritzburg. The violence began after an Inkatha rally in Durban. Some reports said militant youths set off the clashes by stoning buses carrying Inkatha members home from the rally, but organizations allied to the ANC said Inkatha launched unprovoked attacks in townships perceived as being dominated by the ANC. Scores of people were killed and thousands fled their homes, many seeking sanctuary in churches. With the liberation movements unbanned, a new role opened for church leaders. They embarked on a round of shuttle diplomacy between political leaders in an attempt to promote peace, visiting in turn Mangosuthu Buthelezi, head of Inkatha, soon to be launched as a political party and renamed the Inkatha Freedom Party, Nelson Mandela and F. W. de Klerk. By the time they met De Klerk on April 11, it was estimated that 120 people had died in the Pietermaritzburg area. About 14,000 had been driven from their homes and were living in churches and other temporary shelters.*

The conflict in Natal spread northward later in the year when the "township war" erupted in the Transvaal, shortly after the ANC suspended its armed struggle against apartheid. The violence began with clashes between migrant workers living in hostels, on the one hand, and people living in shack settlements or established townships, on the other, but its root causes were manifold and included political rivalry between Inkatha and the ANC and intense competition for resources among the most disadvantaged groups of society.

An estimated 800 people died in August and September 1990, propelling church leaders into desperate efforts to end the carnage. Tutu cut short a visit to Canada and joined leaders of other churches and Anglican bishops in ministering in the townships of Thokoza and Katlehong on the East Rand, in Soweto, in Kagiso on the West Rand and in Sebokeng in the Vaal Triangle. They made pastoral visits to individual families and to refugees in halls and addressed crowds of people in the streets. A cross section of church leaders met De Klerk late in August and two weeks later an Anglican delegation was back in his office.

Upon his return from Canada, the archbishop's ministry began with visits in church delegations to townships on the Witwatersrand on August 23 and 24. A reporter from the Johannesburg-based City Press newspaper, Elias Maluleke, described the scenes in these extracts from his report. SACC General Secretary Frank Chikane was a member of the delegations.

Some residents welcomed the delegation warmly and sang praises to Tutu, while others turned the "peace mission" into a rowdy affair as they vented their anger and frustration. At one stage Tutu and Chikane were shouted down by a rowdy crowd in Kagiso which chanted: "No more peace, we want arms!" . . .

In spite of being surrounded by crowds of angry people who brandished pangas [machetes], knives and other self-made weapons, Tutu did not flinch in his call for peace and urged residents to stop the . . . violence for the sake of their liberation.

"By fighting and engaging in violent acts we give others the excuse to say we are not yet ready to govern ourselves," Tutu said. He said the church was not in a position to condone violence of any nature.

"We have engaged the government and forced them to the negotiating table through peaceful means. Our liberation is near, but these violent acts make other people laugh at us and we cannot continue this way. Let us negotiate a new nonracial South Africa and not destroy the prospect of peace with violence," said Tutu.

The causes of the violence were enumerated in a series of speeches and interviews during the conflict. The potential alienation of migrant workers from township people had been seen in the 1976 Soweto uprising. Apartheid forced the workers to leave their families behind in rural areas and live in appalling conditions in overcrowded hostels. This comment was made to a foreign journalist.

I think we are seeing in part the consequences of the iniquitous migratory labor system. It is making people live in those dehumanizing conditions of the hostels, isolating them from the community in the kind of way that they have, that has certainly exacerbated the kind of problems we have.

The violence was often described in the local and international press as "tribal" because the membership of the Inkatha Freedom Party (IFP) was largely Zulu and some ANC leaders were of Xhosa descent. Church and other community leaders strongly denied this, noting that Inkatha-ANC conflict in Natal involved Zulu speakers on both sides. The issue was dealt with in an impassioned address to a mass funeral in Jabulani Stadium, Soweto, on August 27.

In Soweto here, we have lived and continued to live harmoniously together . . . If we quarrel, it is not because you are a Zulu. I quarrel maybe because your suit is too nice, it is nicer than mine and so I am jealous. But we have never quarreled because of tribalism. It is a lie! It is a lie!

Everywhere we have been as church leaders—we have gone to Thokoza, Katlehong, Soweto, Kagiso—you ask the people, "What has happened?" And they say, "The police have killed us. The police have killed us." We want to say to Mr. de Klerk when we meet him, "The evidence is overwhelming that the police have not been impartial and we ask you, the police must not only be impartial, they must be seen to be impartial, they must be experienced as being impartial." We say we need a new police force, a police force that will be acceptable to the people . . .

But now I want to finish. My dear brothers and sisters, my dear children, why is it that we blacks can be bribed to kill one another? What is wrong with us? Don't we have a pride? Don't we have a pride that God has created us? Are we ashamed of being black? [Response: "No."] Are we ashamed of being black? ["No."] Say, I am proud I am black. ["I am proud I am black."] I am proud I am black. ["I am proud I am black."] And therefore we will strive for freedom. ["We will strive for freedom."] We will all be free! ["We will all be free!"] We are not going to fight amongst each other. ["We are not going to fight amongst each other."] We want peace! ["We want peace!"] We want harmony! ["We want harmony!"] We want togetherness! ["We want togetherness!"]

When you have a hand and you have only the separate fingers, it is easy for people to break the fingers. But when you put the fingers together it is difficult to break them. Let us come together and be one, let us be people of peace, let us be people of harmony.

Friends, you know when the new South Africa comes we are going to need doctors, nurses, teachers, engineers, pilots, we are going to need all these experts. We want our children and everybody to go to school, to be educated. That is our freedom, that is our freedom, that is our freedom. And we will all be free, all of us, black and white, Zulu, Tswana, all of us will be free, together. Say, we will be free. ["We will be free."] All of us. ["All of us."] Black and white. ["Black and white."] We want peace! ["We want peace!"] We want harmony! ["We want harmony!"] We want love! ["We want love!"]

The Citizen *and* Die Transvaler, *two pro-government newspapers, reported the next day that Tutu had told black South Africans to "take . . . [the struggle] into white areas." They also quoted him as saying, "We ask Mr. de Klerk not to play games with us. We are fighters." Both papers retracted and apologized for their reports a day later. The* Citizen *said it had wrongly attributed the statements of another speaker.* Die Transvaler *said its report was based on* The Citizen's *article. The owners of the newspapers later paid R25,000 in damages for publishing these and another defamatory news report.*

On August 28 national and Witwatersrand church leaders held talks with De Klerk. Between September 3 and 5 a reported total of thirty-six people died in violence in Sebokeng. News about the killings came one morning during a synod of Anglican bishops in Lesotho. The archbishop

broke down upon hearing of the death toll and the synod took the un-
precedented step of suspending its meeting to make a corporate pastoral
visit to Sebokeng on September 6. This is an edited text of a sermon
preached in St. Michael and All Angels Church, Sebokeng.

We may not be able to do anything. But we want to walk with you. We want to cry with you. We want to stand here with you as you are shattered by this particular experience. I was here only in March, when much the same kind of things had taken place here [police had opened fire on protesters, killing eleven] . . . We want to ask, "What have we done? What have we done?" I am sure the people in this area, Sebokeng, Sharpeville, ask themselves, "Hey, man, what has happened? Have they bewitched us?" I mean, Sharpeville in 1960 and then all these other occurrences. Then, well, okay, it happens in March, and you think, no, it won't happen again. And immediately after the publication of the Goldstone report [in which Judge Richard Goldstone criticized the authorities], we would have thought they would say, "No, we must be very careful about what is likely to take place in Sebokeng, around the hostels."

With Bishop Duncan [Buchanan, Anglican Bishop of Johannesburg] and Bishop [H. B.] Senatle [of the African Methodist Episcopal Church] and other church leaders, we went to see the State President and said to him, "We are very concerned at the fact that almost everyone we speak to says, 'We have been shot at by the police. The police cause a lot of our suffering.' " And we said, "We ask you, Mr. State President, please cordon off the hostels, please disarm both sides. ["Yes."] Disarm both sides so that we can really have peace."

We said it is not true that people fight because this one is a Zulu, that one is a Xhosa, that one is a Mosotho. We say that is not true, for we have lived for many, many, many years happily together . . . Tribalism has been used by many governments in this country to divide our people. ["Yes."] They've tried to divide us, they've given schools, they say, "This school is for Xhosas, this school is for Zulus, this school is for Tswanas, and so forth." And we have said, "Nonsense! We are all black, we are all African, and we are proud of it. We don't say God made a mistake in creating us black . . ."

Now, my brothers and sisters, my dear children, let us not allow the enemy to divide us. The enemy is doing everything to divide us. We must not allow the enemy to come between us! Let us not allow the enemy to fill us with hatred! We are hurt, yes, we are hurt. But we have come here to try to pour oil on your hurt. Know that your hurts are our hurts. You are not suffering alone. Your hurts are our hurts. White bishops, black bishops, weep. They weep when they hear of the things that have happened to their children. Your pain is our pain. But we come here to say, "Children of God, let us show that we are the children of God by not being filled with hatred. Let us not be filled with a desire to revenge." You know, they say in the Old Testament that there is a law that says, "An eye for an eye." Okay? ["Yes."] Now, Martin Luther King said something wonderful. He said, "Can you imagine? If we believed in that law of an eye for an eye, very soon all the people will be blind" . . .

We must not allow that to happen. Our freedom is here. Our freedom is here, we are about to touch it and there are people who are jealous, who say no, they don't want us to be free. Don't allow them to take away our prize. Don't allow it. Hold on to one another! Hold on to one another! Say, "We worship a God whom we know is a God who leads his people out of bondage into the promised land." That is the God we worship. We worship a God who will lead us out of the bondage of apartheid, the bondage of division, lead us into the promised land where black and white and all of us will be just one family, God's family.

And we who are Christians have a great privilege; we have the great privilege of saying to people: Yes, weep, weep, weep for all that has happened, but don't allow hatred. Hatred is like an acid. Once it gets into you . . . it burns away the skin. Hatred and revenge are like an acid that will eat you, and one day you will discover you are just empty. And so we come here, saying we have no doubt we are going to be free, all of us. Let us say, "We are going to be free."

After the service the bishops visited and prayed with young people on the streets of the most volatile part of the township—an area known as "Beirut." While Tutu was addressing them, a Casspir armored vehicle arrived, heightening tension. Some youths carried petrol bombs and Tutu saw a stone being thrown. However, bishops clad in bright magenta and red cassocks placed themselves between the Casspir and the

crowd and the vehicle moved off. Scared youths tried to prevent the bish-
ops from leaving, fearing they would be attacked without the protective
presence of the church. The bishops went on to tour and pray at migrant
workers' hostels, where many had been killed and injured by security
forces, and to say prayers for victims in the hospital.

Journalists raised the tribal question again after the Sebokeng service.

QUESTION: Do you see any signs or have any fears that the violence that is now going on could in part become ethnic?

ANSWER: Well, violence spawns further violence and people will look for the slightest excuse. If the easiest way of identifying people you want to fight against or whom you think are fighting against you is their tribe, then that could be so. But most of our organizations are organizations that have tried to bring people together . . .

QUESTION: We realize people are using the ethnic factor as something to divide people. But that said, is it there, is it a potential problem?

ANSWER: It could be. It could be a potential problem, yes. But I think we have a wonderful base of nontribalism in the urban areas . . . Our organizations, the Pan Africanist Congress, the African National Congress and all these other organizations, have had people who belong to the different tribes.

QUESTION: What would the danger be if this did degenerate into an ethnic sort of thing?

ANSWER: Well, you are going to get the horrible things that we have seen perhaps in a Beirut situation, some of the things that have sometimes happened in places like Uganda . . . We say God forbid, because the potential for tearing apart a fragile community . . . that has been bombarded by apartheid is very great.

QUESTION: We've been here in the township, we've heard the kids who say, "Kill the Zulus," "The Xhosas, they're cowards," "They tremble because we're coming." What do you make of that?

ANSWER: *Ja*, I would think that you can get some of that kind of element, I don't doubt that you could. But when they listen to those they claim to be their leaders, usually they try and do as they are told, to some extent. They are obviously very frustrated. When you look at the squalor here, just a small spark is enough because people's frustrations are up to here. And the remarkable thing is that this kind of violence has not happened earlier.

A new meeting with De Klerk—this time involving only Anglicans—was arranged after the bishops had been in Sebokeng. The Anglican delegation told him in Pretoria on September 10 they suspected that a "Third Force" comprising right-wingers was deliberately fomenting violence to create a climate conducive to a right-wing coup. The basis of the suspicion was outlined in explanations to reporters.

When we went to Sebokeng Hospital and spoke to some of the people who had been injured in hand-grenade blasts—so-called unsophisticated people who had no reason to lie or make up stories—they said that they had seen people wearing balaclavas who had blackened their faces but had forgotten to blacken their hands . . . You can't put it beyond the possibilities that there are those fairly high up in the hierarchy of the security establishment who would not be averse to the kind of thing that is happening . . .

The description to John Carlin of The Independent, *London, was more graphic.*

We have no doubt ourselves about the sincerity of Mr. de Klerk and his commitment to a new South Africa but it has become more and more evident that there are elements in the security establishment who are hell-bent on subverting and derailing the whole negotiation process . . . They want to ensure that negotiations don't happen because I think they believe that they are being sold down the river. And they are quite dangerous . . . Unless the government acts expeditiously to root out this element we are for the birds.

*The violence—and the report of a commission of inquiry into govern-
ment "hit squads" headed by Judge Louis Harms—was the subject of
comment in parts of the Charge to the opening service of a synod of the
Diocese of Cape Town on October 17.*

We have experienced a euphoria at the speed of events but we have
also touched the nadir of despair at the mindless violence that has
taken place in Natal and the Transvaal. Why, oh, why, has it been mis-
leadingly called black-on-black violence? Why don't the media describe the vicious bloodletting for instance in Northern Ireland as
white-on-white violence? Or that in Eastern Europe?

We believe much of the violence is being stoked by a sinister Third
Force . . . We believe that there are good soldiers and good policemen
and -women but our country has no culture of tolerance. When someone disagrees with you then they are ipso facto your enemy and there
is one thing you do with an enemy—liquidate him. We know now that
people fairly high up in the security establishment ordered the as-
sassinations of those perceived to be enemies. We have been regaled
with accounts of the quaintly named Civil Cooperation Bureau (CCB)
and their lesser exploits of finding pregnant baboons to use their fetuses to decorate Bishopscourt and Bishop's House in Johannesburg.* These are people taught to kill because someone held a view-
point unacceptable to them.

I asked Mr. de Klerk, when these things came to light at the beginning of the Harms commission sittings, at the very least to suspend General [Magnus] Malan, not because he ordered these and
other nefarious activities, but because he bore the political responsibility as Minister of Defense. Mr. de Klerk responded by saying we
should wait for the Harms commission report. I hope he will publish
it and act expeditiously against people who carried out crimes osten-
sibly for patriotic reasons. When they killed people they were com-
mitting murder and should be brought to book. And what about General Malan and all those other top brass who seem to be implicated?

*The CCB, a branch of the South African Defense Force, had been operating death
squads but had also attempted to harass prominent individuals. In the case of the
archbishop, they left baboon fetuses at his home in Cape Town and his former home
in Johannesburg.

It has been alleged that a General Webb placed R10,000 [US $3,800 at 1990 exchange rates] on my head. If it is true, I am upset that they should have thought I was so cheap.* Now that the Harms commission has reported, I want to call for General Malan to be fired from the cabinet. It is difficult to imagine how the commission will be able to give him a clean bill of health after its failure to call him to give evidence. If we say General Malan must go, we do not suggest that he is guilty. It would be obeying a convention observed in democratic countries that a cabinet minister must resign when his underlings are found guilty of a serious misdemeanor. This convention is one that keeps politicians on their toes and is effective to curb abuse of power. The new South Africa cannot afford yesterday's men with dubious morals and yesterday's attitudes . . .

The new South Africa needs a defense force and a police force that enjoy the confidence of the people. The South African police will need a great deal of rehabilitating. For too long they had the unenviable job of enforcing heartless legislation and many of them did so heartlessly, becoming heartless in the process. As a small boy I was present on occasions when my school principal father was humiliated in pass raids. Many black children have witnessed their parents humiliated in night raids for passes and a plethora of permits and those are searing experiences. As an African I find it difficult even now to consider a policeman in South Africa as a friend. Even today, though I am an archbishop, too many white constables, particularly at airports, treat me in the only way they have grown accustomed to by long years of enforcing demeaning laws, and that is with gross discourtesy. Let me add that others have been nice . . .

Mr. Vlok and General Malan's successor must purge the security establishment of those right-wing elements that have not yet crossed the Rubicon in attitudes that are necessary for the new South Africa. I want to be as proud of the South African Defense Force as I once was when my uncle wore the uniform of the Union Defense Force as a member of what was then called the Native Corps in World War II. We

*Hendrik Marinus Thiart, an ex-policeman with a criminal record, told lawyers presenting evidence to the Harms commission that the head of the CCB offered him R20,000 [US $7,600] to kill the archbishop and SACC General Secretary Frank Chikane. General Eddie Webb was reported to have denied the charge.

want to help to have police who are a real peacekeeping force, guardians of the rule of law, thoroughly depoliticized.

Why don't the government form a special force with members from the police and the liberation movements to uphold law and order, especially in the unrest areas, and also to build up much-needed mutual trust so necessary for the negotiation process? Why don't we have a permanent judicial commission to investigate allegations against members of the security forces? Why don't we have groups consisting of trusted lawyers, religious and authentic community leaders to monitor the activity of the security forces in sensitive areas? It would help to scotch allegations about police partiality and abuses of power and would do a world of good to improve the image and reputation of the police.

25
We Forgive You
(1990)

IN NOVEMBER 1990 a hotel outside the small town of Rustenburg, Transvaal, was the site of the first conference in thirty years to bring together the leadership of the white Dutch Reformed Church (DRC) and the "anti-apartheid" South African churches. It included many other churches, making it probably the most widely representative gathering of church leaders in South Africa's history. This extract from Tutu's opening sermon sketched the background.

We have been on a kind of roller-coaster ride, reaching the heights of euphoria that a new dispensation was virtually here, and then touching the depths of despair because of the mindless violence and carnage that seemed to place the whole negotiation process in considerable jeopardy.

And just as we were recovering our breath, the God of surprises played his most extraordinary and incredible card. God said, "My dear children, you who are Christians must get together in conference, and despite all your denominational differences and hostilities." If anyone had predicted in September 1989 that in November 1990 virtually all the churches in South Africa would be gathered together in a national conference, most of us would have been looking for a good psychiatrist for that madman. There can be no question at all that this conference, as has already been described by the co-chairman, is a miracle. And we must celebrate that fact, that as Jesus told his disciples nothing is too difficult, too impossible for God, we are here because the God of surprises has surprised us all with his grace and mercy. And so we must thank God and praise and adore his Holy Name.

The issues of confession, forgiveness and restitution for the wrongs committed against black South Africans became the central theme of the conference, in part as a response to this observation in the sermon.

If there is to be reconciliation, we who are the ambassadors of Christ, we to whom the gospel of reconciliation has been entrusted, surely we must be Christ's instruments of peace. We must ourselves be reconciled. The victims of injustice and oppression must be ever ready to forgive. That is a gospel imperative. But those who have wronged must be ready to say, "We have hurt you by this injustice, by uprooting you from your homes, by dumping you in poverty-stricken homeland resettlement camps. By giving your children inferior education. By denying your humanity and trampling down on your human dignity and denying you fundamental rights. We are sorry, forgive us." And the wronged must forgive.

Those who have wronged must be ready to make what amends they can. They must be ready to make restitution and reparation. If I have stolen your pen, I can't really be contrite when I say, "Please forgive me," if at the same time I still keep your pen. If I am truly repentant, then I will demonstrate this genuine repentance by returning your pen. Then reconciliation, which is always costly, will happen. When even a husband and wife quarrel, until one of them can say, "Sorry, forgive me," they can't really restore their former relationship. It can't happen just by saying, "Let bygones be bygones."

Professor Willie Jonker, a theologian at the University of Stellenbosch, responded by departing from his text in an address the following day to "confess before you and before the Lord, not only my own sin and guilt, and my personal responsibility for the political, social, economic and structural wrongs that have been done to many of you and the results [from] which you and our whole country are still suffering, but vicariously I dare also to do that in the name of the NGK [the white DRC], of which I am a member, and for the Afrikaans people as a whole." The archbishop gave a spontaneous reply.

Professor Jonker made a statement that certainly touched me and I think touched others of us when in public he made a confession and asked to be forgiven. And I believe that I certainly stand under pressure of God's Holy Spirit to say that, as I have said in my sermon, when that confession is made, then those of us who have been wronged must say, "We forgive you," and that together we may move to the reconstruction of our land. It is not cheaply made and the response is not cheaply made.

But a dispute developed over the confession. The white Dutch Reformed leadership endorsed it, citing decisions made by their recent general synod. But leaders of the black Dutch Reformed churches disputed the significance of the synod's decisions and rejected any suggestion that the archbishop could accept the confession on behalf of the conference. He made another intervention.

We are at a moment in the life of our country that we had not expected. It is in many ways quite shattering and I think we need to keep quiet for a moment to give thanks to God, for now that [the confession] is a statement made on behalf of the church by the official representatives . . .

I heard people say that I had no mandate in a sense to have accepted a confession on behalf of anybody except myself and I believe that it is right for people to say so. It is the height of presumption for me to have suggested that I was speaking on behalf of anybody, though I need also to say that I have been ministered to by very many people in my life and I want to give thanks to God for that. Malusi Mpumlwana [a priest of the Order of Ethiopia] stood up here to tell you about his experiences of detention and torture. When I was General Secretary of the South African Council of Churches, Malusi Mpumlwana came to Johannesburg on one occasion. He has said here that he had difficulty forgiving, but I want to tell you that on that occasion he said, "You know, Father, when they torture you, you look on them and you say, by the way, these are God's children," and he said, "and you know they need you," meaning himself, "to help them recover the humanity they are losing." He spoke out of that kind of pain, and I listened to him, as a young person ministering to me on the meaning of forgiveness.

Malusi was at a funeral in King William's Town and they found someone they suspected to be a police informer. Malusi called on a number of us to please come, because they were going to kill that man. Malusi and others held hands to ward off people who were angry. The man who was going to be killed had not even confessed, but Malusi took his life in his hands as he stood against that crowd.

I was part of a South African Council of Churches delegation when we went to Mogopa, a village which was being demolished, and the people were going to be uprooted. The church leaders went to Mogopa to pray with the people before their removal. As we prayed in the rain at about midnight, one of the old men in the village whose home was about to be demolished, whose schools had already been demolished, whose churches and clinics had been demolished, stood up and prayed a prayer that I will never understand. The man said, "Thank you, God, for loving us." I have never understood that prayer.

And then I have been with men like Walter Sisulu and others who have been in jail for twenty-five, twenty-seven years for having the audacity to say they are human . . . They come out of that experience and they have an incredible capacity to love. They have no bitterness, no longing for revenge, but a deep commitment to renew South Africa. I am humbled as I stand in front of such people, and so, dear friends, I think I am convicted by the Holy Spirit of God and by the Gospel of our Lord and Saviour Jesus Christ [in offering forgiveness].

There are no guarantees of grace. When Jesus Christ looked at Zaccheus, he had not guaranteed that Zaccheus would respond to the grace of his forgiveness and love. We are people of grace who have to have the vulnerability of our Lord and Saviour Jesus Christ on the Cross. Jesus Christ, in accepting Zaccheus, released Zaccheus so that Zaccheus could then say, "I will make restitution."

God has brought us to this moment, and I just want to say to you, I am deeply humbled, and I speak only for myself. I cannot, when someone says, "Forgive me," say, "I do not." For then I cannot pray the prayer that we prayed: "Forgive us, as we forgive." Our brothers in the

NG Church [the DRC] came to me and said, "It is going to be up to us to show the genuineness of what we have said, in actions."

But my church has to confess, too. My church has to confess its racism. I have to confess as a black person. How many times have I treated others in my own community as if they were less than the children of God? What is my share in our common sin?

I just pray that all of us will know that we are being led by a gracious God, the God of grace, and that we will see God putting us at the start of wonderful things for this land. Pray, God, that we will respond to your grace graciously.

The "Rustenburg Declaration" adopted later in the week included an extensive section on confession and restitution. The conference was given wide local and international media coverage. Afterward it became apparent that parts of the Afrikaner community were reevaluating Tutu, who for years had been the man most white South Africans "loved to hate." An interview which he gave in Afrikaans for a religious news program on the SABC became the subject of news reports in the Afrikaans press and was rebroadcast. This is a translation of extracts from the original recording.

I have never hated Afrikaners. I have always said I do not hate white people and I do not hate Afrikaners. What I oppose is apartheid. And I have always, always asked and pleaded that our people should work together, because we have such a wonderful country. There are very many good Afrikaners who have tried to work for justice. I know how many of them felt during the years when we had the "poor white" problem, when they did such wonderful charitable work.*

---

*The "poor whites" were typically inadequately educated Afrikaners who had been forced to leave the land and struggle to make a living in towns in the early twentieth century. Their impoverishment began after the war between the Afrikaner republics and the British from 1899 to 1902, called the Boer War by the British and the Second War of Liberation by the Afrikaners. It was later exacerbated by factors such as drought and crop failure. Allister Sparks, in *The Mind of South Africa*, quotes Professor Gwendolen M. Carter of Northwestern University as estimating that up to 60 percent of Afrikaners were "poor whites" by the 1930s Depression (in *The Politics of Inequality*, Praeger, New York, 1958). The phenomenon helped to fuel the growth of the hard-line Afrikaner nationalism that produced apartheid.

I have no doubt that if we hold hands with one another, accept God's grace and remember that Christ is our peace, then we can work together. It is already happening at so many levels; we have people of different races in this country who are working together against injustice, against poverty, people who are showing mercy to others.

I pray that one day we will understand fully that we are God's children, all of us, that we belong to him as one family, God's family.

26
Something Has Gone Desperately Wrong
(1991)

AFTER THE *initiatives of February 1990, most of the rest of 1990
was spent in removing obstacles to talks on a new constitution. A law
that granted indemnity from prosecution for political offenses was
passed, allowing many exiles to return, and the ANC suspended its
armed struggle. The government moved toward desegregating public
amenities and abolishing racial classification. Negotiations resulted in
the phased release of more than 1,000 political prisoners from 1990 to
July 1991.*

*Despite the progress, new obstacles were thrown up by the spread of
violence. Clashes between supporters of the African National Congress
and the Inkatha Freedom Party continued unabated. The leaders of the
two parties, Nelson Mandela and Mangosuthu Buthelezi, met for the
first time in January 1991 after intensive interparty wrangling over
preconditions for a meeting. They made a joint appeal to their supporters to cease the attacks against one another, but strife continued. Several people died in different parts of the country the weekend before
Easter, prompting Frank Chikane to warn that violence was escalating
despite peace talks between politicians. He said that either the political
parties had failed or the violence was beyond their control.*

*Against this background the archbishop appealed to Anglicans to in-
tensify prayer and fasting for an end to violence during Holy Week, the
most important period of their church calendar. He asked them to ini-
tiate ecumenical prayer services on March 27 and delivered this homily
at St. George's Cathedral, Cape Town, on that day.*

It seems as if the culture of violence is taking root in our society. We are becoming brutalized and almost anesthetized to accept what is totally unacceptable. If this kind of violence that keeps erupting at regular intervals continues, then the new South Africa may dawn—and that is doubtful—but it may dawn and there will be very few around to enjoy it; and those who survive will do so only because they are tough, on the basis of the laws of the jungle: survival of the fittest, eat or be eaten, devil take the hindmost.

My friends, yes, there are many reasons why there is violence.

In periods of transition there is the violence due to the instability of transition, as we have seen in parts of Eastern Europe.

Yes, South Africa has never really had a culture of tolerance. The government and its supporters have used dastardly and nefarious methods to deal with their opponents, ranging from the vilification and pillorying of these, as still happens on SABC-TV and radio and government-supporting media, up to the physical elimination of people such as has now been confirmed through the death squads of such as the CCB. Consequently, people have learned that those who differ with you are enemies and the only way to deal with enemies is to liquidate them.

Yes, that is true.

Some of the violence is due to sociopolitical and economic deprivation, and sociologists will tell you that when you think your life will end in a cul-de-sac, that you won't make it in the rat race, then the level of your frustration rises and you break out violently. (See what happened in Britain in those riots against the poll tax. A great deal of the violence was at the hands of whites who felt that they were going to be the left-behinds in the rat race.)

Yes, that is true.

It is true also that we are reaping the horrible harvests of apartheid through the migratory labor system and its ghastly single-sex hostels. It was an explosion waiting to happen, placing virile men in single-sex hostels cheek by jowl with townships where they saw other men leading normal lives with their families. And these hostel dwellers were alienated from those township communities.

Yes, all that is true.

It is true that the police and the security forces have on the whole behaved disgracefully, being accused on all sides of a lack of professionalism as a peacekeeping force totally unbiased, and sometimes it might be true that some of them have sought to foment the violence.

Yes, that has added fuel to the fire.

Yes, that is all true. But it is not all the truth.

A lot of the violence is due to political rivalry. Political groups in the black community are fighting for turf and they do not seem to know, or certainly some of their followers don't seem to know, that a cardinal tenet of democracy is that people must be free to choose freely whom they want to support. To coerce, to intimidate, is to admit that your policy can't persuade on its own merits. People must be free to choose freely whether they want to participate or not in boycotts, in mass action. That is an irreducible, an incontrovertible aspect of democracy.

Something has gone desperately wrong in the black community. We black people must of course point to all the causes of violence I have pointed out and to others that I have not referred to.

But ultimately we must turn the spotlight on ourselves. We can't go on forever blaming apartheid. Of course it is responsible for a great deal of evil. But ultimately, man, we are human beings and we have proved it in the resilience we have shown in the struggle for justice. We did not allow ourselves to be demoralized, dehumanized. We could laugh, we could forgive. We refused to be embittered at some of the worst moments in the struggle.

What has gone wrong, that we have seemed to have lost our reverence for life, when children can dance round someone dying the gruesome death of necklacing? Something has gone desperately wrong when our leaders are not listened to by their followers. There is much to admire in our political organizations, but there is much also which is not right. Some of those who belong to these organizations are totally undisciplined and you can't wage a struggle unless you are dedicated and disciplined. Our organizations need to go back to the grass roots and instill discipline from the lowest ranks up.

It seems to me that we in the black community have lost our sense of *ubuntu*—our humaneness, caring, hospitality, our sense of connectedness, our sense that my humanity is bound up in your humanity. We are losing our self-respect, demonstrated, it seems to me, most graphically by the horrible extent of dumping and littering in our townships. Of course we live in squalor and in slum ghettos. But we are not rubbish. Why do we seem to say that is what we are when you see how we treat our already poor environment?

There are some things that I want to suggest we can do.

The first is that all of us must help to develop the culture of tolerance: live and let live. Let us practice the motto: I disagree with what you say, but I will defend to the death your right to say it. Let us learn to agree to disagree. Those who disagree with us are not necessarily enemies, otherwise there would be very few husbands and wives around.

Two, our political organizations need to put their houses in order; to instill discipline in their members; to adopt at least a minimum code of conduct that says these are the parameters beyond which we will not stray in conducting our political activity.

Third, the authorities must disarm all groups. It is nonsense, utterly unacceptable to speak about traditional weapons. Traditional weapons kill. And it is quite wrong to allow certain groups blatantly to move around armed.

Fourth, let the police become a truly professional peacekeeping force that upholds the rule of law and order without fear or favor. And one hopes that they can begin to be flexible . . . [so they will not insist] on the observance of a law that many of our people refuse to obey, that relates to meetings and demonstrations.

Fifth, I urge that all political leaders stop their killing talk; stop their belligerent, bellicose utterances that incite others to violence whatever the intention of the speaker might have been. There is already legislation available and I urge the government to use it. Why do they allow people like Dr. Treurnicht to get away with the kind of language that they are using so openly? Can you imagine what would have happened to blacks if they said the kind of things that he has been allowed to say? There is legislation to stop organizations such as the AWB [Afrikaner Resistance Movement] making vilifying, denigratory, insulting utterances, racist remarks, that hurt people. The government ought to stamp on such action and do so firmly and quickly.

Sixth, I want to suggest that the municipalities, city councils, local councils, the churches, community organizations, political groupings, participate in a campaign with the people in the townships to clean up those townships. Perhaps our people may then begin to regain a self-esteem, self-respect and pride that they are losing.

And, with others, finally I suggest that all of us, perhaps at midday, pause to pray not just for our country, for all of Africa. And there is a simple prayer that many of us use, and I would suggest that is a prayer that ought to be learned by people everywhere. It is a straightforward prayer, composed by Trevor Huddleston:

> God bless Africa
> Guard her children
> Guide her rulers
> And give her peace.

Part Six

A SPIRITUALITY
OF TRANSFORMATION
Toward Democracy

27

Nurturing Our People

(1992)

SOON AFTER the Holy Week address, talks between the ANC and the government broke down over the government's failure to meet demands aimed at curbing the violence. After a government-organized "peace summit" was boycotted by many organizations, church and business leaders took charge of the process and, during three months of discussions, brokered a National Peace Accord between nearly all of the country's major political forces. In the same period laws regarded as the pillars underpinning apartheid were repealed, including the legislation governing race classification, the 1913 Land Act and the Group Areas Act. Police powers of detention were circumscribed.

Soon after the signing of the peace accord in September, Desmond Tutu, having served five years as archbishop, took four months of sabbatical leave in the United States. While he was away, based at the Candler School of Theology at Emory University, Atlanta, Georgia, the politicians at home began democracy talks at the Convention for a Democratic South Africa (CODESA) in Kempton Park, near Johannesburg.

When Tutu returned, he began to outline the effect of his reading and thinking on his priorities for the remainder of his term in office. Central to his ideas was the development of a "spirituality of transformation," referred to first in an address to his fellow Anglican bishops at a meeting of the Synod of Bishops in April 1992.

The Nature of Christian Leadership

It has taken a very, very long time for it to dawn on me what the true nature of Christian leadership is. I have read the accounts in Mark 9 and 10 and parallels, as well as John 13, with a conventional and possibly cerebral understanding about being properly humble. Recently I have been reading John 13 again and been amazed at the thread that runs through that, connecting it with John 2 as well as the Marcan passages referred to, and with Philippians 2:5–11.

Note how in John 13 authority and power and glory are linked very closely with service, with a pouring out of self for the sake of others, and how that in turn is connected fundamentally with suffering, passion and dying. Authority, power, leadership, glory, in Christ's understanding and his living out what he taught, have everything to do with service, with being a servant, with being the least, with serving and not being served, with giving one's life to be a ransom for others. Is that not what he says in Mark 9 and 10? And does this not echo extraordinarily what the Christological hymn of Philippians 2 reveals about Jesus, who, although he be God, does not snatch at equality with God but empties himself, pours himself out as a libation and takes on the form of a servant (really a slave) and becomes obedient unto death, even the death of the Cross?

But that, paradoxically, is the way to glory, the only way to glory. Doesn't the Lucan Christ on the road to Emmaus remonstrate with his two companions: was it not necessary for the Christ to suffer and so to enter into his glory? There is no other way to Christ's kind of glory, the glory that he had with the Father before the foundation of the world. It says something about the way God is God—that God can be God only as a kenotic, a self-emptying God, the Father pouring forth all his being to the Son, who returns this self-donation and kenosis in equal measure, and the dynamic exchange between them is the Holy Spirit, always proceeding from the Father and the Son.

The seed must fall on the ground and die. Only then will it bring forth the fruit we look for. But without that dying it must remain alone.

That is why the good shepherd must show his genuineness by the infallible sign of laying down his life for the sheep.

I have been reading a remarkable little book by Elizabeth Stuart, called *Through Brokenness,* on the sacraments [Fount Paperbacks, London, 1990]. She says God is not a God who is concerned about his rights, his dignity, etc. He is like the prodigal son's father, who, unmindful of whether he is dignified or not, rushes out in ecstasy to welcome his returning wayward son. Jesus upsets the prim and proper ones by keeping disreputable company. She points out that when Jesus talks about our becoming as children it is not out of a sentimental regard for children, but as without any rights that they could flaunt, and as those who were utterly dependent for everything on others. We can have no claim on God, we have no rights and can only throw ourselves on his mercy and he is always more ready to give than we to receive.

I am coming to understand this a little better—to be on the right-hand side of Jesus in his glory, you must drink the cup which he will drink and be baptized with the baptism with which he will be baptized. It is to walk the Via Crucis, the Via Dolorosa. It is to be crucified. Unless you take up your cross you cannot be my disciple—it is not just a figure of speech. If you are to be a Christlike leader then you must say with Paul: We preach Christ crucified and ourselves as your servants for Christ's sake. Suffering is not optional. It is of the essence of Christian discipleship and leadership. It is the badge of all our tribe (à la Shylock in *The Merchant of Venice*). You will have noted that in John 2, after performing the sign at Cana of turning water into wine, i.e. serving others, Jesus, it is reported, thereby showed his glory.

It appears, then, that the last thing I should want to be is a leader after our Lord's pattern, for it involves existing for the sake of others, emptying oneself, serving others, suffering and even dying as the only way to Christ's kind of glory. One of the pieces I read on the Transfiguration during my sabbatical pointed out that this event is linked very closely to our Lord's prediction of his passion and the necessity of his disciples to deny themselves and to take up their cross to follow their Lord and Master. The divine voice commanding that Peter and company should "Hear Him" was to admonish them to take seriously Jesus' teaching about true discipleship—that they would be vindicated only after following in the path that he trod of suffering, passion and death as the only way to God's glory . . .

We have all been greatly blessed by God in the privilege we have had to witness and minister against apartheid. And sometimes we have had our witness, all of us, authenticated by different kinds of suffering. We have tried to witness for justice and equity. We will still have to be around to be the voice of those who will be marginalized and voiceless in new dispensations in our countries, when we may have to speak critically against those whom we championed previously. That will be costly but we cannot afford to be co-opted or to become this or that party at prayer. We must have a critical solidarity but have the space to be the church able to say prophetically, "Thus saith the Lord . . ." for those who may be popularly and democratically elected are still but mortals who may succumb to the blandishments of power, so that yesterday's oppressed become tomorrow's oppressors. We are going to need to be vigilant as the new dispensations come into being.

The Pain of God

I have been moved, especially during Passiontide, to consider the pain of God. I have thought of the anguish of parents when their offspring have been wayward. For Leah and me, it has been a recent experience as our charming and often incredibly generous Trevor has got into scrapes.* That has been a feeble analogy for God's pain as God has looked on the frightful mess that we have made and are making of things, particularly with the continuing carnage and violence in the black townships of South Africa and the awful killings by Renamo in Mozambique, and what has been happening in Somalia, the Sudan, Burundi, Liberia and the uncertainties in Swaziland and Lesotho.

I ask that we enter during this Episcopal Synod more deeply into the anguish, desolation and pain in the heart of God to bring before the throne of grace those persons and situations of concern, to hold up for

*Trevor Tutu, the couple's only son, was convicted under anti-hijacking legislation over a publicity stunt at an airport and an argument with airline employees on an aircraft.

blessing and healing especially those we may think are the perpetrators. Perhaps we may want to miss lunch one day and spend the lunch hour in prayer and silence.

Speaking about entering into the divine life brings me to my next point. Someone has suggested to me that we need much more contemplation than activism today. This person has said she thinks that I should say I have been quite active and robustly so but that I should now consider deepening my contemplative side. We obviously have not been beguiled by much-loved dichotomies as between secular and sacred, activism and contemplation. But I think she is talking about the balance being weighted more and more in favor of the hidden, the inner life, for the sake of all that we hold dear and for which we have prayed and striven and continue to do so.

Perhaps we have been manning the barriers, being in the front line in the struggle, and we have been privileged to do so. In the course of this feathers have been ruffled, hurts inflicted by what many have experienced as abrasive and turbulent. I don't think that could be avoided and in any case the Gospel is almost always disturbing of comfortable status quos. But I hope we can have a different emphasis—that of seeking to strengthen the inner life of the church, of pouring oil and balm on wounds, of nurturing our people for the tasks of transformation. This is not being pietistic. It is to cultivate an authentic spirituality of transformation in the transition period of much flux, bewilderment, violence and turbulence.

This change in emphasis led to concerted attempts to be less in the forefront, as explained in an interview with John Evenson of Southern Africa Church News *in June 1992.*

I personally would want for us, maybe for me, to be spending a great deal more time where people are hurting. My high-profile other operation made it more difficult to have been there. I don't in a way regret that: one had to be doing that because people had to speak and tell the story about our people. Now I want to be more present with people where they are. And you can say what happened in the first phase makes this other one more credible, that one is able to give hope to people in a hopeless situation. I don't know why they should think so, but when one visits in situations of that kind, people seem to be given a sense that they are important and so it is affirming people and helping in the very difficult, testing time of transition.

I am really a pastor and we are going to be going through a crucible. The level of expectation in some ways is probably unrealistic, and when you think of the major problems we face in housing, in education, in health, employment, we may be going into a situation where there is actually going to be a great deal more turmoil. The church has got to be there, assisting people in a bewildering time because some of the landmarks and signposts have been shifted . . .

When you go into these extraordinary informal settlements and meet up with the people in shacks, when you are expecting that, living in such dehumanizing circumstances, people would have lost the sense of personhood, it's really always such an incredible experience. The nurture I am receiving from them is remarkable—the humanity, the humaneness, the dignity, the capacity to laugh, the capacity to be clean, to love, to rear children, in circumstances that by rights ought to make all of that impossible.

On the Brink of Disaster

(1992)

H A R D L Y H A D the move away from being "abrasive and turbulent" been confirmed than a visit to "where people are hurting" led to new controversy.

In March 1992 the white electorate spurned extreme right-wingers and voted in a referendum by a margin of two to one to endorse negotiations for a constitutional settlement. Emboldened by its mandate, the government proposed at the second full meeting of the Convention for a Democratic South Africa (CODESA II) that such issues as whether the country should be a unitary or a federal state should be decided by a 75 percent majority in the constitutional forum. The ANC, strongly in favor of a unitary state, rejected the demand and began a program of "rolling mass action," including street demonstrations, to back up its position.

In the midst of the political crisis created by the deadlock at CODESA II, during the night of June 17, 200 to 300 men armed with axes, knives, spears and automatic weapons moved through an informal settlement at Boipatong, in the Vaal Triangle south of Johannesburg, slaughtering forty-six people. The attackers were later found to have come from a nearby migrant workers' hostel dominated by IFP supporters. Boipatong residents alleged that some policemen had acted in collusion with the attackers. When F. W. de Klerk tried to visit the area to express his sympathy, he was chased away by angry residents. After he left, police opened fire on a crowd, reportedly killing up to eight people. The ANC withdrew from CODESA, blaming the government for violence.

The archbishop, Bishop Michael Nuttall of Natal and Bishop Peter Lee, in whose diocese Boipatong was located, visited the area with other church leaders on June 19. The following extracts are from a sermon preached on June 22 in St. George's Cathedral, Cape Town.

Dear friends, we are back in this cathedral as if February 1990 had not happened. Our country is on the brink of disaster. Many of us have had to anesthetize ourselves to the agony and the suffering of our fellow South Africans. Many of us have had to invoke the kind of defense mechanism that had to see us, we hoped, through this horrendous period of carnage and bloodletting. We had reached dangerous levels when many of us would sigh with relief and say, "Oh, it's only five," or "It's only six or seven people who have been killed. Thank goodness." Only! That is so utterly unacceptable, because those who have been killed, who are being killed are not just cold sets of statistics. Those five or six or seven or eight or ten, hey, that was someone's husband, father, son. That was somebody's brother, somebody's sister, mother. But if we had had to cocoon ourselves against this stark reality of our country, I hope what happened in Boipatong will have shocked all of us out of what might be an indifference or a complacency or worse . . .

The people in Boipatong told a different story [from that told by the authorities] . . . The people say the police escorted the attackers. I did not myself go to this particular house, but they were taking people, church leaders, to a house where they said a Casspir broke this fence so the attackers could have access to the house. One man who was escorting us said a riot vehicle stood over there, and he pointed to a corner of the squatter camp, and shone its searchlight on the squatter camp as if to illuminate it for those who were going to attack.

Now, we are talking not to so-called sophisticated people. It was so-called ordinary people and many of the press say they went there soon after the attack and went right through the township and the story they got was the same story from virtually everybody. When would the people have sat down to concoct that story? How could they all tell much the same sort of thing? And if it was happening only in Boipatong we would have said, *ja*, well, maybe they got it wrong. But you go to Natal and ask, "What happened?" "The police sided with these people." Now, I'm not interested in bashing the police. I just want to say that when we went to Phola Park after 32 Battalion, the people again reported what were said to be allegations and we got the usual knee-jerk reaction of the government that it is not true. And then Goldstone goes in and discovers that it is exactly as the people say.* Why should they tell a lie? Why should the mother of a woman who was seven months pregnant and was hacked to death by these people, why should she tell a lie? She's already in such pain, why exacerbate that pain by telling a lie? If our authorities could give us even a modicum of intelligence.

The State President goes to Boipatong and the people throw him out. He says they did that because they saw on television pictures of people saying he's a murderer . . . The State President is behaving exactly as his predecessor: that black people are so stupid that you need maybe a white person, you need somebody to come and tell you, "Did you know that you have a toothache," and you say, "Ah, I have a toothache, you told me, I didn't know I had a toothache."

I wrote a letter to one of his predecessors and warned him that Soweto was going to explode. I said that a few weeks before June 16, 1976. I wrote a letter but then the Prime Minister of this country said in his response to me, "You were got up to all of this really by the Progressive Party," because I am really a kaffir [a derogatory word for blacks] and we are basically stupid. And that hurts me. It hurts me that they think our people actually don't feel pain; that our people have got to be told by others that they are suffering, then they discover that they are suffering.

I hurt for my people. I thought Mr. de Klerk was a man of integrity. This is his last chance. I am going to be saying some of the things I am asking him to do. If he doesn't, I will tell the world that I believe he is not a man of integrity. I am not saying so yet. The onus is on him to

*Phola Park was an informal settlement east of Johannesburg where 32 Battalion, a military unit of foreign troops employed by the South African Army to fight in Namibia and Angola, had carried out widespread beatings on April 8. In the words of a joint statement issued with the local Anglican leader, Bishop David Beetge, "reports indicate that 32 Battalion descended to the level of a generalized revenge attack on the people of Phola Park in retaliation for an attack on them by individuals." An investigation headed by Judge Richard Goldstone of the standing commission of inquiry into violence called for the battalion, one of the country's most controversial, to be withdrawn from township duty. The unit was abolished soon after.

give me evidence that he is a man of integrity and not like all of them, looking for how he can deal with our people.

Can you tell me how—if it is mass action that provoked this particular carnage—can they maybe tell us how something that was itself peaceful could bring about this kind of reaction? But even more, how did the so-called mass action affect the dwellers in this particular hostel, that they should in reaction to it feel they were so affected that they should go and kill, not the people who are involved in mass action, kill nine-month-old babies? How does a nine-month-old baby have anything to do with mass action? Why must it be people in those shacks? Can somebody tell me? Ah, supposing in fact it was so, supposing it was. So what! Didn't this government tell us that they were concerned for the maintenance of law and order? If I get up here and say you have annoyed me and I boink you one in the nose, and we fight outside in the street, does the government say, "No, no, we have nothing to do with that"? They would never do that. They would say you are breaking the law.

It is the responsibility of the government to deal and deal effectively with the violence, whoever causes it, whatever the reason for it . . . In the days of the state of emergency [the police] were able to ferret out people who were being surreptitiously introduced into the country. They thought nothing of demolishing shacks if they thought there was one of these terrorists in there. They were telling us about our funerals. They would tell us when the funeral must happen, where it must happen, who must speak, how many people must attend a funeral. They used to be there to ensure that you did what they told you. Now these fellows, suddenly now they become so inept they can't even arrest people who have been apprehended by people who are not armed, people who were caught on the trains. [Gunmen who, in other recent attacks, had opened fire indiscriminately on commuters on suburban trains had been seized by passengers but had not appeared in court.] Where are those people who were arrested on the trains? Where have they gone? You see, what this government does, they know people get very, very concerned but your attention span is very short. They will arrest people, and then you'll say, ah yes, they have arrested people. Maybe even take them to court and then they disappear and we say they've dealt with it. They are smart.

They are smart but we've kept telling them, we used to tell them before February 1990, "Hey, this is God's world, this is God's world and you've had it." We thought they had changed. They have not changed or they must give us more clear evidence that they have changed. I don't think they have changed. They were looking for a way of getting the world to reduce its pressure on them. And I am saying this with a very sore heart because we were the first black leaders to meet with Mr. de Klerk, with Allan [Boesak] and Frank Chikane, and we said, "This man is different, he can listen." He's got to give me more evidence now.

I call for an end to the bickering and power play at CODESA and for our politicians to stop trading insults and making political capital of the violence. I urge them to meet three demands:

1. The government must bring to justice those responsible for the Boipatong Massacre. This does not just mean that people should be arrested and appear in court: the trial must begin as a matter of urgency and we must see the guilty convicted and sentenced without undue delay. And might I just say, if they are sentenced to imprisonment we mustn't have a computer mistake that ensures that they are released very soon after they have gone to jail.

2. There must be interparty agreement, either through the mechanisms of the National Peace Committee or through CODESA, on the immediate constitution of an international monitoring force. The deployment of such a force is becoming increasingly inevitable, whatever the government may say for public consumption, and if we allow the situation to deteriorate much further, we will end up with a Yugoslavian nightmare in which international observers will come too late to prevent outright civil war.

3. We must have agreement, again either through the Peace Committee or CODESA, on immediate multiparty control of the security forces. Pending the implementation of this agreement, Mr. de Klerk must take over personal responsibility for the security forces, particularly the functions of Minister of Law and Order.

If at least one of these demands is not met before the Olympic Games begin, then the South African team to the Olympic Games must withdraw. [South Africa was scheduled to participate in the Olympic Games in 1992 for the first time after being expelled for apartheid in

1964.] When we return to the Olympic Games, we must be able to do so in a spirit of celebration and unity. We cannot do it with the country in a state of national mourning for our dead and while we are caught up in a deepening political crisis. Those who choose to insulate themselves from the suffering and grief caused by this horrific slaughter must realize that they cannot have both a Boipatong and Barcelona.

If our Olympic Committee does not withdraw the team, then it must be expelled from the forthcoming games and we want to say much the same about the pending rugby tour by the All Blacks, that they too will come only if at least one of these demands that we have made is met. I am calling today on our friends around the world to begin a campaign to achieve that end.

I had hoped those days were behind me. I should tell you that before embarking upon this course I intended to seek an interview with Mr. de Klerk to discuss the violence with him and to warn him that I intended returning to the international community if he did not act immediately. But his gross insensitivity in leaving the country [and visiting Spain] during such a crisis has persuaded me that it would be wasting valuable time to wait for Mr. de Klerk to return from his jaunt.

There are two last things I want to say. I hope somewhere, somehow it will sink into the consciousness of most of our white fellow South Africans that we are human beings. Just a simple thing: we are human beings. We are not animals. We are human beings who have feelings, we are human beings who cry when our children die. We are human beings and please, you our white sisters and brothers, can you hear? Our cry is for you to recognize that God has created us as God has created you. Our cry is that God has given us a land that is large enough for all of us. And we want to share it with you. When you walk around and you see people stunned and people who have done nothing are killed so that some politicians can make political capital, you say there is evil abroad. It is diabolical. But we appeal to you white South Africans, stand up and say this can't be done in your name, for, you see, we still, even now, cannot vote. This government is not our government. We have respected them only because we wanted to have some order. They are not our government. We didn't elect them. They're your government. Can you tell them that all we want is to be able to live harmoniously in our country? In our country. We allowed you white people to come here and because of our stupid hospitality now we sleep in shacks.

We ask you white South Africans, who have said virtually nothing about all the corruption in this country. Billions of our money have been wasted. On the whole you have said nothing. Can you really keep quiet any longer? We ask you.

It is going to be difficult for us to keep saying to our people, "Please, please, please don't want to revenge." That is what we said to the people in Boipatong. We said, "Please, please don't let them make you want to be filled with bitterness." And our people respond. Please, please, we ask you how long do you expect us to be able to say, "Cool down, please be calm"?

How much more must still happen before all of you white people get up and say, "We've had enough"? How many more billions must disappear? And nobody, nobody is accountable. People become rich with our money and not one is found guilty. And we sit and do nothing . . . I call on you, my dear sisters and brothers who are white, the people you have elected are destroying this country. We said so long ago, and we were saying it appears they have changed and there is going to be the possibility of talking. We made a mistake in supporting the referendum because as soon as the result of the referendum happened, an intransigence and an arrogance entered into the government. They thought you were supporting them.

Whether you do or don't stand up, let us tell you again what we have said so many times: We are going to be free, we are going to be free. We are going to be free despite all of this that they are doing. We are going to be free. We want you to be with us when we are free. We want you to share with us, we want you to be human with us, we want you to walk tall with us. Will you? Will you stand up?

Well, actually, I am asking you, can you please stand up and keep a moment's silence for the people of Boipatong who were killed? Thank you.

The call for an Olympic boycott fell away when the archbishop, following a meeting with De Klerk, decided that the government had moved substantially toward meeting the conditions he had proposed. But the political deadlock continued and the ANC and its allies intensified mass action. The archbishop expressed doubts about it, saying anger was running at such a high level that he was concerned leaders would not be able to keep control of demonstrations. Later, after a successful work stay-away on August 3, he conceded that the protests had been largely peaceful.

However, the spiral of confrontation was broken only after troops of the Ciskei homeland opened fire on a crowd of 70,000 protesters outside their capital, Bisho, on September 7, killing twenty-nine and injuring more than two hundred. Unlike most of the massacres since 1990, which had been carried out surreptitiously, often at night, the attack at Bisho took place with dozens of political leaders, journalists and peace monitors in the line of fire. It had also been predictable: the day before, Tutu had telephone consultations with both De Klerk and the ANC in an unsuccessful attempt to promote a compromise suggested by local church leaders to avoid confrontation. The shock brought the country back from the brink and the ANC and the government negotiated a new understanding over the way ahead.

29

We Offer to You These Children

(1993)

AFTER THE *breakdown of 1992, constitutional talks were reestablished at what became known, in the absence of agreement on a name to replace CODESA, as the Multiparty Negotiating Forum. Church leaders were not party to negotiations and their activities in public life as the country moved toward a constitutional settlement in 1993 were directed to two overriding and related objectives: bringing about unity among black leaders and promoting peace.*

As the common interests of the government and the ANC brought them together in an uneasy working relationship, leaders such as Chief Mangosuthu Buthelezi and some of the heads of the "independent" homelands began to forge an opposing force. Church leaders responded by trying to bring together black leaders on opposite sides of the split. Much of the work went on behind the scenes, through visits to Buthelezi in the kwaZulu capital of Ulundi and President Lucas Mangope in "independent" Bophuthatswana, and discussions with leaders such as Nelson Mandela. One of the high points in these efforts was the organization by Tutu and Bishop Stanley Mogoba, Presiding Bishop of the Methodist Church of Southern Africa, of a top-level summit between the ANC and the IFP in June 1993.

However, the public ministry of church leaders was concentrated on responding to crises brought about by continuing conflict. The National Peace Accord of 1991 was the basis for successfully defusing tensions and checking the spread of violence. But the causes of conflict proved too deep-rooted for quick solutions, particularly in areas of Natal.

Early in the morning of March 2, 1993, gunmen stopped a light de-livery vehicle carrying twenty children to school near Imboyi, outside the provincial capital, Pietermaritzburg, on an uphill stretch of a wind-ing dirt road. The assailants then opened fire with weapons, including automatic rifles, killing six children and injuring seven. Their ages ranged from nine to eighteen. The parents of some were officials of the Inkatha Freedom Party. This was an off-the-cuff prayer said during a pastoral visit to the site of the killings.

O God, we come to you . . . wondering what has happened to our peo-ple that anyone, for whatever reason, could mow down children in cold blood in this fashion. What could have got into those of your children to perform such a dastardly deed? We come here, Lord, asking you to drive away this evil as you drove out demons from those who were pos-sessed, as you drove out death, as you triumphed on the Cross against all that was against your love, your compassion and your caring.

Please, God, you have placed us in this land, such a beautiful land, a land which is so richly endowed with all of your gifts, a land that is being soaked so much with blood. Please, God, cleanse it, strengthen all of us to stand up against evil of every kind. Please, God, end this violence and bring to being this new dispensation when your children will be able to live in peace and harmony . . .

God, we bring before you the families of those children who have been killed and those who have been injured. We ask you to give them the comfort of your Holy Spirit. We pray that we in a small way may be able to console and to comfort when we meet with some of them.

We pray also for those who have carried out this evil deed, for no matter how evil they are, they remain your children. We just pray that awareness of being your children will touch their hard hearts, make them repent and stop them from ever being guilty of something of this kind again.

We pray for those who have been injured and we offer to you these children who have died. May their sacrifice be a sacrifice that will en-sure that freedom and peace will reign in this land. For Jesus' sake, amen.

His Death Is Our Victory

(1993)

SOUTH AFRICA was thrown back to the verge of civil war on Holy Saturday, April 10, 1993, when Janusz Waluz, a fanatically anti-Communist Polish immigrant, assassinated Chris Hani, the General Secretary of the South African Communist Party and a member of the ANC's national executive committee. The Communist Party was banned in 1950 but had operated in an alliance with the ANC since the 1960s and had been unbanned with the ANC and PAC in 1990. Waluz used a pistol supplied by Clive Derby-Lewis, a leader of the Conservative Party. In a 1992 opinion poll Hani had been judged to be second in popularity to Nelson Mandela and was a hero to militant young black people.

After the assassination the ANC made vigorous efforts to control the anger of its supporters and Mandela assumed the role of a head of government, making national radio and television appeals for calm. Up to 2,500,000 people took part in eighty-five events during a national day of mourning on April 14. Violence was reported at three places, with up to seventeen reported killed. In Cape Town most of the crowd was disciplined, but rioters on the fringes injured people, smashed cars and windows and looted shops.

Much of the country came to a standstill on April 19, the day of Hani's funeral. Four million people were estimated to have stayed at home. Twenty-five people were killed, nineteen of them in random hit-and-run attacks at night in Sebokeng, south of Johannesburg. More than 100,000 attended the funeral at a Soweto soccer stadium, where the following address was delivered to the cheering and responsive crowd.

I greet you in the name of our Lord Jesus Christ; good day. [In Xhosa, repeated in seSotho, Afrikaans, Shangaan and English.]

To the Hani family, we the whole community and nation bring you our condolences and sympathies. We ask God to give you his Holy Spirit and to wipe the tears from your eyes. We, too, have suffered a great loss. May God comfort you in your great loss. [In seSotho and Xhosa.]

I bring messages of sympathy and condolence from the Archbishop of Canterbury, from the Presiding Bishop of the Anglican Church in the United States and the Archbishop of Ireland.

St. Paul, in the Letter to the Romans, chapter 8, verse 31, says, "If God be for us, who can be against us?"

We have come to bury a great son of the soil. Is there anyone here who doubts that Chris was a great son of the soil? ["No."] I don't hear you. ["No."] Is there anyone here who doubts that Chris was a great son of our soil? ["No."] Well, of course you will then hear people say, "Ah, no, no, no, no, no. He was a Communist." I want to say: I loved him, I loved him for his warmth and his laughter. At Bisho he stood next to me as we were singing, "Lizalis'idinga lako Thixo nKosi yenyanyiso" ("Fulfill your promise, Lord God of truth"), and he belted it out with a wonderful baritone, singing all the verses off by heart. And then at the end I asked him, "Hey, Chris, how can a Communist sing and sing so lustily a Christian hymn?" And he laughed as he alone can laugh.

Whether he was a Communist or not, secondly he was dedicated to peace, to reconciliation, to negotiation. In the very week of his death he was speaking about a peace corps, speaking about how everyone must become a combatant for peace. He was a man of transparent integrity, for when he advocated peace, it was not because he was a coward. He had been head of the MK [Umkhonto we Sizwe, the ANC's military wing], but it was because of his integrity that when circumstances changed, he changed his position even if it might lose him support.

We have a crazy country with people obsessed with their anti-Communism. If a Communist were to say, "Hey, it is raining outside. Don't go out, you will get wet," then they expect everybody else to say, "Ai, no, no, no, no, a Communist has said you are going to get wet. We must say no, you won't get wet because it is Communist rain."

For us he was a hero and a great leader, irrespective of whether he was a Communist or not. After all, as we have said before, those who oppressed us were not Communists. We were oppressed by those who claimed to be Christians such as we are. Those who invented apartheid were not Communists, they were Christians. And remember, when they wanted to praise Mr. de Klerk in recent times for suggesting the initiative of change, then they said as a form of high praise, "Oh, Mr. de Klerk is the Gorbachev of Southern Africa." And Gorbachev was a Communist and they were naming him as a form of praise.

Dear friends, we have come to bury our hero, our leader, a man of peace, a man of justice and reconciliation, a man for negotiation. Chris Hani died on the most sacred weekend of the Christian calendar. Chris died between Good Friday and Easter Sunday. Let us recall that God extracted out of the death of Jesus Christ a great victory, the victory of life over death, that God showed in the victory of Jesus that goodness is stronger than evil, that light is stronger than darkness, that life is stronger than death, that love is stronger than hate. God is telling us the same message in the horrible death of Chris Hani. His death is not a defeat. His death is our victory.

His death is the victory of truth, the truth of liberation, that liberation is stronger than the lie of apartheid, that liberation is stronger than the injustice of apartheid, of its oppression and exploitation.

The death of Chris Hani gives this country yet another opportunity. It gives the government and all the key players another chance. We want to make a demand today. We demand democracy and freedom. When? We demand democracy and freedom. When? ["Now."] They don't hear you in Pretoria. They don't hear you in Cape Town. We demand democracy and freedom. When? ["Now."] We demand a date for the first democratic elections in this country. When? ["Now."] We demand the date for a new, for the democratic, first democratic elections of this country, when? ["Now."] Now. When, when do we want that date? Now. ["Now."]

We want a transitional authority with multiparty control of security forces, when? ["Now."] Now. We demand a transitional authority, when? ["Now."] We want peace and security and safety for everybody in this country, when? ["Now."]

My friends, we are marching to victory. We are marching to the victory of freedom over the oppression of apartheid. We are marching to victory, the victory of justice over the injustice of apartheid. We are marching to victory, the victory of light over the darkness of apartheid. We are marching to victory, the victory of life over the death of apartheid. We are marching to victory, the victory of truth over the lie, the corruption, the deceit of apartheid. We are marching to victory, the victory of goodness over the evil of apartheid. We are marching to victory, the victory of gentleness, of kindness, over the harshness of apartheid. We are marching to victory, the victory of goodness, of compassion, over the cruelty of apartheid. We are marching to victory, the victory of compassion and sharing over the competitiveness, the selfishness of apartheid. We are marching to victory, the victory of peace and reconciliation over the violence and alienation of apartheid.

We will be free! We will be free in this country! We are going to rule this country! We are going to be the government of this country. We, all of us, black and white, all of us are going to live in peace and justice and friendliness in this country.

And so, dear friends, we commit ourselves, each one of us, we commit ourselves to discipline, we commit ourselves to peace, we commit ourselves to negotiation and reconciliation.

For we are the rainbow people of God! We are unstoppable! Nobody can stop us on our march to victory! No one, no guns, nothing! Nothing will stop us, for we are moving to freedom! We are moving to freedom and nobody can stop us. For God is on our side.

And so . . . We raise our hands, we raise our hands and we say: We will be free! ["We will be free."] All of us. ["All of us."] Black and white together. ["Black and white together."] We will be free! ["We will be free."] All of us. ["All of us."] Black and white together. ["Black and white together."] For we are marching to freedom. [Cheers, whistles.]

The Bottom of Depravity

(1993)

THE VAST majority of the victims of violence during the transition to democracy were those who had been the victims of apartheid: black South Africans. In June 1993 constitutional negotiators set a provisional date for the country's first democratic elections, then confirmed the date on July 2. Between July 2 and 13 more than 220 people died in violence on the East Rand, east of Johannesburg, and at least 50 in Natal. Upsurges of violence were often linked to breakthroughs in negotiations, leading to speculation that the violence was deliberately instigated by right-wing elements intent on preventing change.

With conflict concentrated in black townships, most whites were not directly threatened except by a sense of fear and insecurity. However, there were some racist attacks in predominantly "white" urban areas, the worst of which was that on St. James Church, in Kenilworth, Cape Town, on July 25. Four men burst into a Sunday evening service, lobbed hand grenades among the pews and sprayed the 1,000-strong congregation with automatic-rifle fire. Eleven people died immediately and more than fifty were injured.

The massacre drew condemnation across the board and the ANC urged its supporters to join the hunt for the assailants. Thousands of Capetonians of all races gathered at the City Hall on July 29, at the invitation of Mayor Frank van der Velde, to call for peace. The meeting took the form of an interfaith rally including Christian, Jewish and Muslim leaders.

My dear sisters and brothers:

Rampant evil is abroad. Evil men perpetrate vile deeds of darkness, of violence, of death, with breathtaking impunity. They have reached the bottom of depravity in attacking and so desecrating a place of divine worship and adoration, God's sanctuary.

A creeping despondency and sense of impotence want to cover our beautiful land like dark, threatening clouds. We must not let that happen. We, the people of Cape Town, say "No" to that. Let us not let it happen. God will not let it happen.

Our God is a God who is an expert at dealing with evil, with darkness, with death. Out of the darkness and chaos before creation, our God brought into being light, life, goodness and a created order, and when he beheld it, he declared it to be: "Very good."

And out of the despair, the evil, the darkness, the pain of slavery, God, our God, brought about the great deliverance, the Exodus. God, our God, created out of a rabble of disorganized slaves his own special people whom God led out of bondage into the promised land, because God, our God, is a God of freedom. Our God is a God of justice, of peace and goodness.

Supremely, God, our God, did his stuff in the awfulness of the Cross, its violence, its darkness and its death. For out of this ghastly instrument of death and destruction, our God produced the glorious victory of Jesus Christ in the Resurrection—a victory that was victory of life over death, of light over darkness, of goodness over evil. And you and I must grasp that fact, that we have a God, as the chorus says: "What a mighty God we have!"

We used to say in the darkness of repression, in the most awful times of apartheid's suppression: *"Moenie worry nie, alles sal regkom"* ["Don't worry, everything will be okay"]. Because our God is a God who will bring justice out of injustice. And they thought we were dreaming. *Nou hier's dit!* [Now here it is!] We are going to have a new South Africa! We are going to have a South Africa where all of us, black and white, will be truly free.

And we, the people of Cape Town today, united in this kind of way against this atrocity, are saying "No" to violence. To all violence! Because we revere each human being. One death is one death too many.

["Yes."] We say "No" to intimidation, we say "Yes" to freedom! We say "Yes" to peace! We say "Yes" to reconciliation.

If these people who did what they did on Sunday, if these people who do what they do in [black townships like] Katlehong, Daveyton and Thokoza, think that they have succeeded in separating us, let us say to them, "No! You have failed, you have succeeded in bringing us together."

And we, as we have always said, are the rainbow people of God. ["Yes!"] We are beautiful because we are the rainbow people of God and we are unstoppable, we are unstoppable, black and white, as we move together to freedom, to justice, to democracy, to peace, to reconciliation, to healing, to loving, to laughter and joy, when we say: This South Africa belongs to all of us, black and white!

α Miracle Unfolding

(1994)

BRINKMANSHIP in constitutional negotiations and continued violence remained the dominant features of public life during the final
stages of South Africa's transition to the first democratically elected
government in its history.

In November 1993 the multiparty talks adopted an interim constitution despite a boycott by Inkatha and white right-wingers. In December exclusive white rule ended with the establishment of the Transitional Executive Council, which monitored the government during the
period before the elections and had the power to make government decisions affecting the elections. The tricameral parliament approved the
interim constitution later in the month. The constitution created the
Government of National Unity (GNU), to rule for five years after the
April 1994 election, with all major parties represented in the administration. During these five years the final constitution would be written.

In another attempt to curb violence, church leaders convened a new
summit of black leaders in December 1993 and made a symbolic visit
during the meeting to two communities at war with one another on the
East Rand. Intensive efforts by politicians to bridge the gap between the
Inkatha Freedom Party and the parties which had agreed to the interim constitution failed, with the IFP holding out for more autonomy
in the kwaZulu/Natal region, which it believed it dominated. Chief
Buthelezi did not attend the December summit and Tutu returned to
Ulundi shortly before Christmas to ask whether he could do anything
to bring the parties closer.

As electioneering got under way early in 1994, violence surged once again in kwaZulu/Natal, and tensions built up in the "independent" homeland of Bophuthatswana. Tutu and Bishop Stanley Mogoba visited Lucas Mangope, the President of Bophuthatswana, in a desperate attempt to bring him into a settlement. Within weeks his administration had toppled to a popular uprising, and white right-wingers who intervened to prop up his regime were chased away by his security forces in a humiliating defeat.

As the conflict in Natal grew worse, a state of emergency was declared, supported by the ANC but vigorously opposed by the IFP. During a march to demand greater autonomy, more than fifty sympathizers of the IFP were killed in unprecedented scenes of fighting on the streets of Johannesburg. Some were killed when unidentified gunmen shot marchers from rooftops, others when guards at ANC headquarters opened fire in response to what they said they believed to be an armed siege.

In the controversy about the causes of conflict during the transition, representatives of the outgoing government repeatedly pointed to findings by Judge Richard Goldstone's commission of inquiry that most clashes were between supporters of the ANC and the IFP. But while this was how much of the violence manifested itself, long-held suspicions about what triggered it off in volatile conditions were given new substance when Judge Goldstone uncovered preliminary evidence revealing, on the face of it, that top police generals had been involved in a strategy of destabilization. Three officers, including the second-in-command of the South African Police, were effectively withdrawn from duty.

Three weeks before the elections, F. W. de Klerk, Nelson Mandela, Mangosuthu Buthelezi and King Goodwill Zwelethini of the Zulus met to try to break the constitutional deadlock and bring the IFP into the elections. When they failed, they called in international mediators, including Dr. Henry Kissinger, but they could not reach an agreement on the terms of reference for the mediation. Church leaders, fearing that Natal would be overwhelmed by violence during the election, traveled to kwaZulu under the auspices of the National Peace Accord and made an impassioned plea to King Goodwill at least to make a public appeal for peace. The King responded favorably and called upon "each and every Zulu" to stop the violence, whether they supported the ANC or the IFP.

In succeeding days a Kenyan mediator who had remained in South Africa after others had returned home continued his brokering role.

A week before the election, De Klerk, Mandela, and Buthelezi reached an agreement on the status of the Zulu kingdom and monarchy, clearing the way for the IFP's participation. By coincidence, Desmond Tutu was at Union Buildings, the seat of government in Pretoria, when the breakthrough occurred. He was called out of another meeting to congratulate the leaders. His jubilation was reflected in a sermon preached in St. George's Cathedral, Cape Town, the following Sunday, April 24, in a pre-election service which was broadcast nationally.

My text is from Psalm 77, verse 14, where the psalmist exults and says: "You are a God that works wonders." Yes, all of us would say "Amen" to that, especially after the miracle of last Tuesday, which saw the IFP joining the electoral process, and even more so when we see where we are today. For next Wednesday and Thursday we will hold our very first democratic elections in South Africa. Wow! How utterly unbelievable! How wonderful! Yes, what a mighty God we serve! The God of surprises, the God who lets miracles unfold before our eyes.

On those momentous days coming you and I, all of us, black and white, will be voting, most of us for the very first time ever. You and I, all of us South Africans, black and white together, will make a cross. Nearly 2,000 years ago, God made his Cross, for God gave us his only begotten son to die on that Cross. St. John the Evangelist declares, God so loved the world that God gave his only begotten son, this son the good shepherd, to lay down his life for us. The Cross is God's mark that God has chosen to be our God, that God has chosen to be on our side against evil, against sin, against death, against the devil. The Cross is God's mark of the depth of his love for us, for you, for me.

You are very special to God. You are of infinite worth to God. God loves you not because you are lovable, but you are lovable precisely because God loves you. And that is a love that will never change. God loved you and that is why God created you, created me. God loves you now, God will always love you, for ever and ever. His is a love which will never let you go. Your name is engraved on the palms of God's hands. The very hairs on your head are numbered. You and I, all of us, are known by name. Each one of us is of infinite worth because God loves each one of us, black and white, with his infinite, everlasting love.

The Cross is God's mark demonstrating God's victory on Good Friday, a victory made more clear in the glorious resurrection of Jesus on Easter Sunday. The Cross declares that God has overcome evil and injustice, sin and death. On the Cross Jesus cried out in triumph: It is finished, it is accomplished, I have achieved what you, Father, sent me to do. By his death he has destroyed death as we sing in the preface before the Sanctus. When Jesus died, the curtain in the Temple separating mortals from God was torn from top to bottom, signifying that we were no longer separated from God. Jesus has effected reconciliation between us and God. We are now God's friends. We can now call God Father because we have received the spirit of Jesus, the spirit of adoption. We, mere mortals, sinful, sinful as we know ourselves to be, can call the King of Kings, the Lord of Lords, he who dwells in light unapproachable, we can have the incredible privilege, the incredible intimacy, to call God "Abba"—Daddy God.

For all of us, black and white together, belong in the family of God. We are brothers and sisters, we are one. With his Cross God has effected reconciliation among us all. Jesus, so says the Epistle to the Ephesians, is our peace. He has broken down the middle wall of partition. And the Epistle to the Galatians says: In this Jesus now, there is neither Jew nor Greek, slave nor free, male nor female. Through the Cross God has said "No" to racism and its injustice and oppression. For racism is a sin and that is why we call on all of our people not to vote for parties which exploit racist fears and prejudices . . .

There is life after April 28. We are all wounded people, traumatized, all of us, by the evil of apartheid. We all need healing and we, the Church of God, must pour balm on the wounds inflicted by this evil system. Let us be channels of love, of peace, of justice, of reconciliation. Let us declare that we have been made for togetherness, we have been made for family, that, yes, now we are free, all of us, black and white together, we, the Rainbow People of God! And let us make a success of this democracy. And we are going to make it. For we have a tremendous country, with tremendous people. Our God, who makes all things new, will make us a new people, a new united people in a new South Africa. And when we make it—not if we make it but when we make it—it will be because God wants us to succeed, for we will be a paradigm for the rest of the world, showing them how to solve similar problems. Hey, if God be for us who can be against us!

As churches throughout South Africa prayed for a free, fair and peaceful election, right-wing forces began a last-ditch campaign to disrupt the process. Within earshot of worshipers in central Johannesburg, a car bomb exploded near ANC headquarters, killing nine people and injuring ninety-two. The next day, in Germiston, east of Johannesburg, a bomb at a taxi rank serving black commuters killed ten. Two people died in a blast in Pretoria and bombs were detonated in other parts of the country, some at polling stations. On April 26, the day on which voting started for people in special categories—such as the aged and infirm— another car bomb injured sixteen people at Johannesburg's international airport.

But as voting gathered momentum, millions of South Africans showed that nothing would stop them from voting. Thousands of people joined long lines on April 27, some waiting the best part of a day to vote, and an extraordinary peace settled on the country. Desmond Tutu described his feelings in the draft of an article written for the German publication Die Zeit.

What an incredible week it has been for us South Africans. We all voted on April 27 and 28 in the first truly democratic election in this beautiful country. We are still on Cloud Nine and have not yet touched terra firma. Our feelings are difficult to put into words. I said it was like falling in love. That is why it seems the sun is shining brighter, the flowers seem more beautiful, the birds sing more sweetly and the people—you know, the people are really more beautiful. They are smiling, they are walking taller than before April 27. They have suddenly discovered that they are all South Africans. And they are proud of that fact. They are no longer the pariahs they used to be.

They stood in the voting queues together—white, black, Colored, Indian—and they discovered that they were compatriots. White South Africans found that a heavy weight of guilt had been lifted from their shoulders. They are discovering what we used to tell them—that freedom is indivisible, that black liberation inexorably meant white liberation. We have seen a miracle unfolding before our very eyes—it is a dream coming true. It is a victory for all South Africans. It is a victory for democracy and freedom.

I am looking forward to the post-election celebrations. We all deserve them after the ghastly repression, injustice, deprivation and brutality of apartheid, one of the most vicious systems since Nazism. We could not have reached this point of liberation without the support of all our friends in the international community, the anti-apartheid movement, the churches and many, many others. We have won a great victory and you in the international community have a substantial share in that victory. Thank you, on behalf of millions from South Africa, for all your prayers, concern and support. Join the celebrations. You deserve it too . . .

We must now all work together for confession, forgiveness, restitution, reconciliation and peace. The interim constitution will assist in this process because we are compelled to have a Government of National Unity which will be a multiparty administration that will operate on the basis of consensus and compromise. The system of proportional representation ensures that virtually every constituency in the country will have a hearing in the national and provincial legislatures. Nelson Mandela, in his post-election statements, is stressing reconciliation and that he wants the post-apartheid processes of governance to be as inclusive as possible.

The level of violence has been unacceptably high. Much of it is due to the machinations of a Third Force. The Goldstone Commission in its latest report says there is prima facie evidence to link high-ranking police officers to a conspiracy to destabilize the black community by fomenting sectarian violence. Mercifully none of the violence has been ethnic. [In Natal it has been Inkatha-supporting Zulu pitted against ANC-supporting fellow Zulu.] It is not even by and large racial, except for that emanating from a lunatic fringe of the white right wing. A legitimate government, democratically elected, will be able to rehabilitate the police and army so that those organs of state can deal effectively with the violence because they have become more credible as neutral law enforcement and peacekeeping agencies. As it is, contrary to gloomy forecasts, the violence subsided quite considerably during the election [apart from the bombs planted by white right-wing elements]. Indeed the violence in Natal dipped dramatically with the entry of the IFP into the electoral process.

Apartheid has left us a horrendous legacy represented by massive homelessness, with seven million living in ghetto shacks, a huge educational crisis, unemployment, inadequate health care largely inaccessible to the most needy. The rural areas are poverty-stricken, without running water, electricity or proper sewerage, so that cholera epidemics happen in a country that pioneered the heart transplant. It is quite bizarre.

People have perhaps unrealistically high expectations that democracy will mean a job and a good home overnight. Unfortunately no one possesses a magic wand to bring paradise immediately. But the new government will have to move quickly to improve the quality of life of the most disadvantaged to make it quite clear that there is a qualitative difference between living under an unjust dispensation and living in a democracy. Resources that were wantonly wastefully invested in the defense budget to engage in unnecessary military adventures in Angola or to destabilize our neighbors will, with a drastically reduced defense budget, be available for this necessary social spending. But people will also need to be told to be patient and to reduce their expectations to more realistic levels. The economy will need to be stimulated to create jobs. [Many will be available if the state and the private sector engage in the building of houses and similar projects.]

We are certain our friends abroad will now want to return to invest massively. Democracy in South Africa must succeed for the sake of the sub-continent, indeed for the sake of the continent, since South Africa can become the locomotive to drive Africa's economic train. Africa needs a few success stories. It has been suggested that the West might well consider a financial aid package for the sake of democracy akin to the one it provided for President Yeltsin's Russian Federation . . . Be our partner in this exhilarating enterprise.

On the Sunday after the election, part of a sermon at a celebration of the Mothers' Union of St. Luke's Church, Salt River, Cape Town, likened God to a mother bringing the new South Africa to birth.

St. Paul in Galatians speaks about "in the fullness of time"—when the time was just right. In the fullness of time. And don't mothers know the fullness of time? The baby growing in the womb, and in the fullness of time, nine months later, the baby is born. In the fullness of time, the baby is weaned. In the fullness of time, the baby walks. In the fullness of time, the baby goes to school. But for all of that to keep happening, this baby must be cared for, nurtured, fed, loved, brought up in all of these stages, dependent so utterly on mother.

I was just thinking as I prepared this sermon: "Yes, for our country too, it is a kind of 'in the fullness of time.' " It is as if God was like a mother, preparing this country, preparing it through pain, through suffering, preparing different kinds of people, nurturing them, making sure that one day there would be an F. W. de Klerk, who would meet with a Nelson Mandela, and somehow there would be an understanding. But in the fullness of time. It would probably not have been right five, ten years ago. Things were not quite as they should be.

In the fullness of time South Africa is now ready for this gift. South Africa is like a baby that was in a womb, nurtured by the love and the caring of God. In the fullness of time this new South Africa is brought to birth. In the fullness of time we come as a new people . . . For it is the fullness of time and God has brought us to birth.

South African public life was overwhelmed by a series of "firsts" in 1994. On May 9, after the ANC had won the election, the first democratically elected legislature in South African history, the National Assembly, held its first meeting. Desmond Tutu wept as he watched the election of the first black head of state. Also elected was the first woman speaker in the country's history.

Nearly five years earlier, at the end of the 1989 march for peace, Tutu had addressed a demonstration on Cape Town's Grand Parade from a city hall balcony. During his speech he had invited F. W. de Klerk to join the gathering, and at the time forces calling for democracy were demanding the return of exiled leaders and the release of political prisoners. On May 9, 1994, after the National Assembly had met, Tutu returned to the Parade to act as master of ceremonies at a celebration. From a city hall balcony, he first welcomed the new Executive Deputy

President F. W. de Klerk. Then he welcomed an exiled leader who had returned: Executive Deputy President-elect Thabo Mbeki. Finally he welcomed a political prisoner who had been released.

Friends, this is the day that the Lord has made and we will rejoice and be glad in it. This is the day for which we have waited for over three-hundred years. [Cheers] This is the day of liberation [Cheers] for all of us, black and white together. [Cheers] This is a day of celebration. [Cheers]

My fellow citizens—Hey, I can rightly call you fellow citizens, for on April 27 and 28 South Africa voted and millions of us voted for the very first time. And a miracle happened. We discovered that we were South Africans [Cheers] and we have discovered that we are proud of that fact. [Cheers] Yesterday at the FNB Stadium [First National Bank soccer stadium in Johannesburg] I sang "Die Stem" [The Voice of South Africa, anthem of the previous government and now one of two official anthems] for the very first time in my life, and I loved it. Who will ever forget the picture of a Tokyo Sexwale [a former ANC military commander and now premier of a regional government] taking the salute as the South African Police and the South African Defense Force filed past? A new South Africa has come to birth.

We have said a resounding no to racism. What have we said to racism? ["NO!"] What have we said to injustice? ["NO!"] What have we said to oppression? ["NO!"] What have we said to hatred? ["NO!"] What have we said to violence? ["NO!"] What have we said to alienation and division? ["NO!"] And we have said a loud and reverberating YES to freedom. What have we said to freedom? ["YES!"] What have we said to reconciliation? Yes! ["YES!"] What have we said to forgiveness? ["YES!"] What have we said to peace? ["YES!"] What have we said to unity? ["YES!"]

We of many cultures, languages and races are become one nation. We are the Rainbow People of God. And one man embodies this new spirit of reconciliation and unity. One man inspires us all, one man inspires the whole world. Ladies and gentlemen, friends, fellow South Africans, I ask you: welcome our brand-new State President, out-of-the-box, Nelson Mandela!

The Making of a Peaceful Revolution   *267*

To a roar from the 70,000-strong crowd, the President-elect emerged onto the balcony to say that South Africa had voted for change, "and change is what they will get . . . Our plan is to create jobs, promote peace and reconciliation and to guarantee freedom for all South Africans."

President Mandela was inaugurated at the Union Buildings in Pretoria the following day, in front of what journalists described as the largest gathering of heads of state and government since John F. Kennedy's funeral. Religious leaders who had served on the National Inauguration Committee, wanting to demonstrate that South Africa was a multifaith society in which religious tolerance would be promoted, included Christian, Hindu, Jewish and Muslim readings and prayers in the ceremony. The religious segment of the proceedings ended with the following prayer from the archbishop.

Thank you, O God our Father, that by the death and resurrection of your only begotten Son Jesus Christ Our Lord and Saviour, you have overcome sin and death and evil, injustice and oppression, hatred, separation and alienation.

Thank you, O God, for having brought us to this point in the history of our beautiful motherland, South Africa. Before our very eyes we see a miracle unfolding and our dreams becoming reality as the sun shines on a new dawn for us all, black and white together.

Thank you, O God, for freeing our country from racism and oppression and for liberating all our people. Thank you for the courage of those who initiated change. Thank you, O God, for those who sacrificed their freedom and even their lives in the struggle for justice. Thank you for bringing those who were previously enemies around the same table to achieve a negotiated settlement. Thank you for the miraculous way in which you transformed the election into a corporate act of nation-building.

Thank you, O God, for all those, here and overseas, who have supported us with their prayers and love.

Thank you, O God, that you have chosen this your servant to be the first President of a democratic South Africa where all of us, black and white together, will count, not because of irrelevancies such as race, gender, status or skin color but because of our intrinsic worth as those created in your own image, as redeemed by the precious blood of Jesus, as being sanctified by the Holy Spirit.

Bless our President with wisdom, good health and all the gifts necessary for this high calling.

Bless his colleagues the executive deputy presidents and members of the Government of National Unity.

Bless this beautiful land with its wonderful people of different races, cultures and languages so that it will be a land of laughter and joy, of justice and reconciliation, of peace and unity, of compassion, caring and sharing. We pray this prayer for a true patriotism in the powerful name of Jesus who died and rose again and now reigns with you, O Father, and the Holy Spirit, one God, forever and ever. Amen.

Prayer for Africa [adapted]:

> *God bless South Africa*
> *Guard her children*
> *Guide her leaders*
> *And give her peace for Jesus Christ's sake.*
> *Amen.*

Editor's Acknowledgments

Desmond Tutu's ministry rests to a considerable degree on the generosity, strength and self-sacrifice of his wife, Leah. Similarly, the work that has gone into this collection would not have been possible without the patience and understanding of my wife, Liz.

Many other spouses have made sacrifices as a result of the demands of the archbishop's ministry, among them Terry Crawford-Browne, Carol Esau, Pat Jones, Jacqui McQueen, Nomahlubi Ndungane, Dorrie Nuttall, Anne Owens and Zingi Tisani. Thank you also to colleagues Chris Ahrends, Bishop Merwyn Castle, Sid Colam, Lavinia Crawford-Browne, Matt Esau, Robin Harper, Colin Jones, Bishop Michael Nuttall, Bishop Njongonkulu Ndungane, Michael Owens, Rowan Smith, Mazwi Tisani and Nolan Tobias for helping to shape my perspectives, for companionship while traveling and for camaraderie in difficult situations. I owe more than I can express to my parents, who laid the basis for a rejection of the racial prejudice that was characteristic of much of the community in which we grew up.

An enormous effort has gone into typing sermons, speeches and transcripts of tape-recordings over the past seven years. Thanks to Estelle Adams, Nonzame Sodladla, Lavinia Crawford-Browne, Simone Noemdoe and Kerry Ward in Cape Town, to Cheryl O'Neal and Peg Arey at Emory University, Atlanta, and to Liz Allen for her voluntary typing and proofreading services.

Gratitude is also due to members of the Provincial Standing Committee of the Anglican Church in Southern Africa, who have had to find the money to finance the extraordinary ministry of a Desmond Tutu, including the employment of a media secretary, and to the Parish of Trinity Church in New York City, which paid for my initial employment. A number of pieces in this collection are drawn from a manuscript compiled during a sabbatical the archbishop and I spent at Emory University, Atlanta. Thanks to the Carnegie Corporation of New York, which helped to fund the sabbatical, and to Dr. Jim Laney, Dean

Kevin LaGree, Gary Hauk, Tom Bertrand, Nancy Seideman and their staff at Emory; also to Frank Ferrari of New York, now in Johannesburg, and Charlie and Lynn D'Huyvetter of Atlanta, who also helped make the sabbatical possible.

Without Lynn Franklin, our literary agent in New York, this book would not be. We are deeply indebted to her and to Tom Cahill at Doubleday for their belief in it. Thanks too to Carolyn Brunton in London, Sally Gaminara at Doubleday U.K., and Trace Murphy, Juliette Shapland and Maron Waxman in New York.

Finally, thank you Father Desmond for your remarkable trust in and generosity toward those who have the daunting but privileged task of supporting your ministry.

Bibliography

A History of South Africa, Leonard Thompson, Yale University Press, 1990.

Mandela, Tambo, and the African National Congress, edited by Sheridan Johns and R. Hunt Davis, Oxford University Press, 1991.

Naught for Your Comfort, Trevor Huddleston, William Collins, 1956; reissued by Collins, Fountain Books, 1977.

South Africa: A Modern History, T. R. H. Davenport, Macmillan, 1991.

South African Review, edited and compiled by South African Research Service, Ravan Press, Johannesburg, 1983.

Stormkompas, edited by Nico J. Smith, F. E. O'Brien Geldenhuys and Piet Meiring, Tafelberg, Cape Town, 1981.

A Survey of Race Relations in South Africa, South African Institute of Race Relations, various editions.

The Apartheid Handbook, Roger Omond, Penguin, 1985.

The Mind of South Africa, Allister Sparks, Mandarin Paperbacks, 1991.

Through Brokenness, Elizabeth Stuart, Fount Paperbacks, London, 1990.

Tutu, Voice of the Voiceless, Shirley du Boulay, Penguin, 1989.

Index

Addis Abada, 11
Afghanistan, 93
Africa, 5, 9–10, 157–59, 265
"African," as classification, 4. *See also* Blacks
African Bursary Fund, 32
African Methodist Episcopal Church, 170
African National Congress, 4, 16, 41, 91, 91*n*,
  92, 97–98, 99, 108, 110, 125, 129, 133,
  139, 146, 147, 154, 170, 187, 196, 204,
  205, 206, 215, 252, 263
  Bisho massacre and, 248
  clashes with Inkatha, 209, 210, 211, 227,
    249, 259, 260, 264, 265
  at constitutional negotiations, 241
  flags of, 195, 196
  Hani killing and, 251
  Johannesburg violence and, 260
  mass action campaign of, 241, 248
  outlawed, 5
  St. James killings and, 255
  suspension of armed struggle, 209, 227
  talks with government, 199, 235
  Tutu's talks with, 152
  unbanned, 191
  wins election, 266
Afrikaans language, 13, 105
Afrikaner Brotherhood, 75*n*
Afrikaner Resistance Movement, 230
Afrikaner Weerstandsbeweging, 50
Afrikaners, 7–9, 47, 50, 54, 125, 142, 154. *See
  also* Whites
Aksie Eie Toekoms, 50
Alaska, 74
Albertyn, Charles, 182
Alexander, Ray, 196
Alexandra Township, 35, 51, 108, 124
All Africa Conference of Churches, 157–59
All Blacks rugby team, 246
Amin, Idi, 129, 165
Amos, 29
Anglican Church, 5, 105, 154, 157, 203,
  212–13, 252
  blacks in, 6, 113
  meetings with De Klerk, 216
  political parties and clergy of, 203
  South African Council of Churches address
    to, 27–40
  township wars and, 210
  Tutu on finances of, 119–21
  Tutu on rites and practices of, 117–18

Tutu on unity and, 59–63, 64, 118, 119
  Tutu's address to bishops of, 235–39
  Tutu's Holy Week appeal to, 227–28
  See also Tutu, Desmond
Anglican Students' Federation, 205–6
Angola, 93, 158, 200, 243*n*, 265
Anti-apartheid movement
  attitudes toward, 38, 51–52
  beach protests, 172–74
  Biko's death and, 15–16
  black consciousness and, 15, 16
  church leaders in, 25, 139–40, 156, 169–70,
    171–76, 179, 185, 191, 203–6. *See also*
    South African Council of Churches
  Defiance Campaign, 169–70, 176, 179–80,
    200
  educators and, 140, 175, 179
  government reaction to, 5, 53, 97–98,
    113–14, 139–40, 141, 164, 170, 172–74
  multiracial support for, 102
  in 1960s, 5
  1980 protests, 41
  students in, 13, 41, 86, 91, 105, 106, 110,
    175
  treatment of leaders of, 139, 172, 179–80,
    182
  violence and, 10–11, 85–86, 90–91, 97, 98,
    99–101, 129–30, 175–77, 179, 180,
    185–86
  women in, 52
  See also African National Congress;
    Apartheid; South Africa; Tutu, Desmond
Apartheid
  in early union, 3–4
  family life under, 87, 88, 89–90
  international response to, 97–98
  laws implementing, 4–5
  racial classifications of, 4, 89, 227, 235
  reforms, 26–27, 53, 113, 191–92, 227, 235
  roots of, 225*n*
  statistics regarding, 87, 88–89, 163
  theological justification for, 56, 65–66
  versus "separate but equal," 148
  See also Anti-apartheid movement; South
    Africa; Tutu, Desmond
Asingeni Fund, 34
Associated Press, 130
Athlone, 100*n*
Attenborough, Sir Richard, 16
Atteridgeville, 107–8

Australia, 186
Azanian People's Organization, 139
Azapo, 139, 206

Baboon-fetus incidents, 217
Banning, 16, 34–35, 51, 55, 90, 139, 164
Bantu Administration and Development, 88*n*
Bantustans. *See* Homelands
Beeld, 84
Beetge, David, 243*n*
Beirut, Lebanon, 215
"Beirut" (in Sebokeng), 214
Belfast, 11
Berlin, 199
Biafra, 11
Bible, 72, 142
    apartheid contrary to, 147–48
    on government, 151–52
    New Testament, 27, 28, 30–31, 37, 40, 60,
        62, 63, 65, 67, 70, 78, 92, 94, 121, 127,
        134, 140, 148, 150, 151, 152, 162, 224,
        236, 237, 252, 261, 262, 265–66
    Old Testament, 17, 28, 29, 36, 37, 38, 59–61,
        68–69, 70, 71, 114, 116, 149, 150, 161,
        162, 213, 261, 266
    on oppressors, 169–70, 171
    social justice and, 148–52
    See also God; Jesus
Biko, Ntsiki, 20
Biko, Stephen Bantu, 15–21, 25
Bill, François, 123
Bisho, 248, 252
Bishopscourt, 113, 186
Bishop's House, 217
Bizos, George, 124
Blackburn, Molly, 125
Black People's Convention, 15, 16
"Black peril" politics, 49–50
Blacks
    in churches, 54. *See also* Dutch Reformed
        Mission Church; South African Council of
        Churches
    in government, 91
    government support among, 155–56
    in municipal elections, 156
    political rivalry among, 229, 230
    President's Council and, 48, 49
    as separate nations, 8
    tribalism, 211, 213, 215–16, 264
    violence among, 97, 98, 99–100. *See also*
        Townships
    in World War II, 52*n*, 154
    See also Apartheid; Homelands; South
        Africa
Black Sash, 52, 102, 124
Bloubergstrand, 172
Boer War, 3, 7*n*, 225*n*
Boesak, Allan, 54, 85, 102, 140, 141, 143, 186,
    188, 191, 204, 245
Boipatong, 241–43, 244, 245, 246, 247
Bombings, 263, 265

Bonhoeffer, Dietrich, 100
Bophuthatswana, 27, 249, 260
Boraine, Alex, 111
Botha, Dominee Dawid, quoted, 69–70
Botha, P. W., 35, 39, 83, 97–98, 119, 125,
    126–27, 143, 186, 201
    failures of, 47, 51, 53, 110–11
    letter to Chikane, 154
    meeting with South African Council of
        Churches, 41–45, 106–7
    reforms of, 26–27, 53
    reply to church leaders, 146
    Tutu and, 108, 145–56
Botha, R. F. "Pik," 8, 97, 111, 130, 196
Botho, 125
Braamfontein, 31
Brandfort, 34
Brink, C. D., 151
British Broadcasting Corporation, 139
British Embassy, 179
Browning, Edmond L., 161
Buchanan, Duncan, 213
Buitenkant Street church, 185
Burger, 84
Burundi, 238
Business leaders, 98, 235
Buthelezi, Mangosuthu, 133, 209, 227, 249,
    259, 260, 261
Buti, Sam, 41

Canada, 5, 100, 186, 210
Candler School of Theology, 235
Cape Colony, 3, 7*n*
Cape Town, 100*n*, 109, 113, 170, 175, 179,
    217, 251, 265
    protests in, 41, 139, 169, 175, 176, 180,
        186–89, 191, 195
    reception for Mandela in, 194
    September 1989 protest march in, 186–89,
        191, 195
    squatters in, 50–51
    violence in, 185–86, 255
Cape Town, Diocese of, 105–11, 217
Cape Town, University of, 81, 171, 196
Carlin, John, 216
Carlton Hotel, 48
Carter, Gwendolen M., 225*n*
Catholic Church, 140
Ceres, 195
Chardin, Teilhard de, 64
Chase Manhattan Bank, 97
Chikane, Frank, 154, 191, 204, 210, 227, 245
China, 173
Chinese, 48
Christian League of Southern Africa, 75*n*, 107
Church leaders
    in anti-apartheid movement, 25, 139–40,
        155–56, 169–70, 171–72, 173–75, 179,
        185, 191, 203–6
    forgiveness issue and, 222–25
    peacemaking efforts of, 136–37, 206, 209,

210, 211, 212, 213, 214–15, 216, 235, 248, 249, 259, 260
  reconciliation of, 221–25
  See also South African Council of Churches; Tutu, Desmond
Church of Reconciliation, 36
Church of St. Stephen and St. Lawrence, 130
Church of the Province of Southern Africa, 113.
  See also Anglican Church; Tutu, Desmond
Ciskei, 27, 248
Citizen, The, 212
City Hall (Cape Town), 194, 255–57, 266
City Press, 210
Civil Cooperation Bureau, 217, 228
Cold War, end of, 199
Collaborators, 97, 98, 99
Coloreds, 4, 48, 186
  in churches, 54
  1983 constitution and, 81–84, 85, 87, 99, 108
  rugby participation of, 49
  in school boycotts, 41
Committee for the Defense of Democracy, 140
"Common purpose" doctrine, 145
Communism, 93, 100, 130, 252–53
  downfall of, 200–1
  Tutu accused of, 146, 147, 150, 152, 153, 154
  Tutu on, 100, 252–53
Congress of South African Trade Unions, 133
Conservative Party, 81, 83, 251
Convention for a Democratic South Africa, 235, 241, 245, 249
Cowley House, 33
Craven Week, 49
Cricket, 83
Crossroads, 35, 51, 124
Cry Freedom, 16
Cull, Francis, 117

Daveyton, 257
Debayle, Anastasio Somoza, 165
Defiance Campaign, 169–70, 176, 179–80, 200
De Klerk, F. W., 181, 193, 197, 201, 204, 211, 245, 246, 253, 266
  as executive deputy president, 266–67, 269
  1989 protest march and, 186–87, 188
  1990 concessions of, 191–92
  talks with Mandela, 199
  talks with Zulus, 260, 261
  violence and, 209–17, 241–48
Delmas trial, 124
Denmark, 26, 39
Dependents' Conference, 33
Depression, Great, 225n
Derby-Lewis, Clive, 251
Detainees' Parents Support Committee, 102, 114
Detention, 16, 55, 92, 97, 114, 122–23, 124, 130, 156, 235
  Tutu on, 89–90, 164

Diakonia House, 31
Disenfranchisement, 87
District Six, Cape Town, 126, 194
Duduza, 98
Duncan, Sheena, 32
Durand, Jaap, 65–66, 66n
Durban, 195, 209
Durban education conference, 110
Dutch Reformed Church, 8, 52, 66, 70, 88, 151, 154, 186
  forgiveness of, 222–24, 225
  ousted from world body, 54, 56, 74
  relations with anti-apartheid churches, 73–74, 221–25
  support for, 75
Dutch Reformed Mission Church, 54, 65, 85, 140, 223

Eastern Europe, 196, 199, 217, 228
East Rand, 86, 210, 255, 259
Edendale, Pietermaritzburg, 133
Edendale Valley, 209
Educators, 140, 175, 179
Eloff, C. F., 54, 107, 152
El Salvador, 93
Emory University, 235
End Conscription Campaign, 102, 124
English language, 13
Episcopal Church, 161. *See also* Anglican Church
Episcopal News Service, 161
Eritrea, 157
Esau, Matt, 130, 186
Ethiopia, 10, 158, 223
Evenson, John, 239
Exiles, 266. *See also* African National Congress

Family Day, 87
Federal Theological Seminary, 36
First National Bank Stadium, 267
Flags, 170, 195
"Foreign Natives," 82
Fort Hare University, 106
France, 3, 100, 186
Franco, Francisco, 165
Funerals, 98, 107, 111, 211–12, 244, 251–54

Geldenhuys, Frans O'Brien, 73
Geneva, 35
Germany, 3, 186
Germiston, 263
Gerwel, Jakes, 141, 175
Glasnost, 201
God, 27, 55–56, 66–67, 236, 237, 238, 256, 266. *See also* Bible; Jesus
Goldstone, Richard, 213, 243n, 260, 264
Gorbachev, Mikhail, 201, 253
Government of National Unity, 259, 264, 269
Gqubule, Simon, 139
Grahamstown, 15
Grand Parade (Cape Town), 194, 266

Great Britain, 3, 7n, 84, 145, 186, 228
Group Areas Act, 51, 113, 147, 235
Guguletu township, 175

Hani, Chris, 251–53
Harms, Louis, 217, 218
Hazendal, 170
Herstigte Nasionale Party, 50
Heyns, Johan, 65, 66n
Hindus, 268
Hitler, Adolf, 88, 129, 165
Holy Spirit, 114–15, 236
Homelands, 8, 35, 39, 51, 87–88, 110, 133, 248
    established, 4
    independence of, 26–27
    leaders of, 249
Huddleston, Trevor, 5, 231
Human Sciences Research Council, 99
Hunger strikes, 155, 170
Hyde Park, 187

I Found My Brother (Woods), 16
Imbali, Pietermaritzburg, 205
Imboyi, 250
Independent, The (London), 216
India, 5
Indians, 4, 48
    in churches, 54
    1983 constitution and, 81–84, 85, 87, 99,
        108
Information, Department of, 26, 75n, 107
Inkatha Freedom Party, 209, 250
    clashes with ANC, 209, 210, 227, 241, 249,
        260, 264, 265
    1994 elections and, 259–61, 265
    Zulus in, 211
Inkatha Yenkululeko Yesizwe, 133, 137, 205–6.
    See also Inkatha Freedom Party
Irish Republican Army, 99
Israel, 10, 36

Jabulani Stadium, 211–12
Jerusalem, 10
Jesus, 7, 33, 39–40, 42, 54, 159, 253
    baptism of, 114
    before Pilate, 151, 171
    crucifixion of, 17–18, 261, 262
    forgiveness and, 224
    glory of, 236–37
    humanity of, 27–29, 55, 67
    as liberator, 36–38, 56
    as man of God, 30
    on nonviolence, 176–77
    as reconciler, 55, 56, 61–63, 65
    as redeemer, 162
    resurrection of, 256
    on salvation, 117
    on social justice, 150–51
    Transfiguration and, 115, 237
    See also Bible; God
Jews, 88, 255, 268

Johannesburg, 35n, 36, 41, 191, 195, 217, 235,
    263
Johannesburg, Diocese of, 5
Johannesburg airport, 263
Johannesburg Bantu High School, 4
Johannesburg Stock Exchange, 98
Jones, Colin, 171, 174, 175, 180, 182, 185
Jonker, Willie, 222–23
Journal of Theology for Southern Africa, 32

Kagiso, 210, 211
Kairos, 32
Kampuchea, 93
Kant, Immanuel, 66
Katlehong, 210, 211, 257
Kempton Park, 235
Kenilworth, Cape Town, 255
Kennedy, John F., 268
Kenya, 124–25, 261
Kerk en Stad (quoted), 69–70
Khotso House, 76, 155
King, Martin Luther, Jr., 214
"Kingdom of God and the Churches in South
    Africa, The" (Botha), 70
King William's Town, 224
Kinshasa, Zaire, 157
Kissinger, Henry, 260
Klerksdorp, 3
Kohl, Helmut, 145
Koornhof, Piet, 26, 35, 51
Korea, 93
Kotze, Pen, 51
Kragdadiagheid, 50
Kruger, Jimmy, 16, 31, 51
KTC (squatter camp), 86–87, 123
kwaNdebele, 110
kwaZulu, 249, 259–60
kwaZulus. See Zulus

Labor Party, 81, 83, 84
Land Act, 4, 235
Latin America, 93
Lay Ecumenical Center, 133
Lebanon, 215
Lebombo, 129
Lebowa, 110n
Lee, Peter, 242
Lesotho, 12, 25, 108, 212, 238
Liberia, 238
Lindsay, Orland, 161
London, 5, 154, 187
Louw, Lionel, 182, 185
Lusaka, 108, 153
Lutheran Church, 69, 74
Luthuli, Albert, 91n

Madibane (Bantu) High School, 4
Malan, Magnus, 43, 217, 218
Maluleke, Elias, 210
Mandela, Nelson, 34, 41, 113, 133, 204, 249
    Hani killings and, 251

inauguration of, 267–69
jailed, 5
meets with Buthelezi, 227
Natal and, 209
as president, 264
release of, 191, 192–93, 194, 196
talks with De Klerk, 199
talks with Zulus, 260–61
Tutu on, 201
Tutu's welcome to as president, 267
Mandela, Winnie, 34
Mangope, Lucas, 249, 260
Maputo, 130, 132
Marcion, 37
Marriage, interracial, 4, 89, 113
Marxism, 29. *See also* Communism
Mass Democratic Movement, 169–70
Mau Mau, 124
Mbeki, Thabo, 196, 199, 267, 269
Merchant of Venice, The, 237
Methodist Church, 26, 108, 139, 185, 249
Metropolitan Methodist Church, arrests at, 180
Middle East, 93
Migrant workers, 9n, 209–15, 228, 241
Military service, 38, 52, 102, 124–25
Mind of South Africa, The (Sparks), 4, 225n
Mkhatshwa, Smangaliso, 123
Mogoba, Stanley, 108, 249
Mogopa (village), 224
Moi, Daniel arap, 125
Mosothos, 213
Mothers' Union, 265
Motlana, Nthato, 51
Moutse, 110
Mozambique, 93, 113, 129, 158, 238
Mpumlwana, Malusi, 223–24
Mulder, Connie, 88n
Multiparty Negotiating Forum, 249
Muslims, 255, 268
Mussolini, Benito, 165

Naidoo, Archbishop Stephen, 140
Namibia, 33, 42, 45, 92, 113, 199, 200, 243n
Natal, 3, 97, 205, 242
    church leaders' intervention in, 137, 209, 210
    Tutu's sermon in, 133–37
    violence in, 133, 136, 137, 206, 209, 210,
        217, 242–43, 249, 255, 259–60, 264–65.
        See also Townships
National Assembly, 266
National Forum Committee, 85
National Inauguration Committee, 268
National Party, 4–5, 34, 47, 49–50, 81, 83, 84,
        97, 186
National Peace Accord, 235, 249, 260
National Peace Committee, 245
National Security Management System, 53
Native Corps, 218
"Natives," 82, 122. *See also* Blacks
Natives Land Act, 4, 235
Naudé, Beyers, 16, 102, 185

Nazism, 88, 100, 142, 154
"Necklacing," 97, 126, 229
Nederduitse Gereformeerde Kerk. *See* Dutch
    Reformed Church
Nederduitse Gereformeerde Sendingkerk. *See*
    Dutch Reformed Mission Church
Netherlands, 3
NGK. *See* Dutch Reformed Church
Nicaragua, 93, 161, 165
Nigeria, 11
Nobel Peace Prize, 86, 91, 99, 107, 157
Noriega, Manuel, 161
Northern Ireland, 11, 93, 98, 99, 217
Northwestern University (U.S.), 225n
Nuttall, Michael, 205, 242
Nyanga, 51

Oliver, Gordon, 186
Olympic Games, 245–46, 247
Orange Free State, 3
Orange Free State, University of, 106
Orlando West High School, 13
Ossewa Brandwag, 52n
Ottawa, 54
Ox Wagon Sentinels, 52n

Paarl, 174
Pageview, 126
Pan Africanist Congress, 5, 16, 92, 99, 125,
        191, 205, 206, 215, 251
Panama, Tutu's sermon in, 161–65
Parliament, 3, 111, 169, 259
    marches on, 139, 142, 145, 146, 147, 151,
        179–80
    1983 changes and, 81–84, 85, 87
    nominations to, 48, 49
Pass laws, 4, 5, 11, 35n, 43, 91, 99, 110, 141,
        218
Pavlov, Ivan, 141
Peers, Michael, 161
Peninsula Technikon, 175
Pensioners, 123
People's Congress, 70, 151
People's Rally, 173, 174
Perestroika, 201
Peterson, Hector, 13
Philip, Archbishop, 117
Phola Park, 243
Pietermaritzburg, 205, 133–37, 209, 250
Pilgrimage of Hope, 35
Plessis, Barend du, 107
Poland, 91n
Political prisoners, 38, 227, 266, 267
Popieluszko, Jerzy, 91n
Population Registration Act, 89, 147
Port Elizabeth, 15
Port Elizabeth, University of, 106
Portugal, 10
Power sharing, 81
Presbyterian Church, 10, 123
President's Council, 48, 49

Pretoria, 15, 41, 261, 263, 268
Progressive Federal Party, 43, 51, 83, 105, 111,
　123, 243
Prohibition of Mixed Marriages Act, 89
Property rights, 11
Public facilities, 4, 113, 227

Qoboza, Percy, 16, 41
Quislings, 99

Racial classifications, 4, 89, 227, 235
Radio Freedom, 147, 152
Rand Daily Mail, 34
Reagan, Ronald, 84
Relocation forced, 25–26, 51, 224
Renamo, 　, 238
Rent increases, 85–86, 91
Resettlement, 35, 39, 43, 55, 87–88, 92, 107,
　123
Restrictees, 170, 171. *See also* Banning
Retief, Johan, 180
Rhodesia, 39, 42. *See also* Zimbabwe
Riebeeck, Jan van, 200
Rivonia trialists, 191, 196
Robben Island, 33, 34
Robbins, James, 139
Rockman, Gregory, 186, 188
Roger, Brother, 35
Rommel, Erwin, 52
Rugby, 8, 49, 246
Russell, Philip, 105
Russia, 265
Rustenburg, church meeting at, 221–25

St. Augustine of Hippo, 60
St. George's Anglican Church (Silvertown), 176
St. George's Cathedral, 113, 139, 140, 156, 171,
　194, 195
　arrests at, 180
　memorial service in, 186
　police desecration of, 185
　pre-election service at, 261–63
　service to replace People's Rally, 173–75
　Tutu's Boipatong sermon in, 242–47
　Tutu's homily at, 228–31
St. Helena, 113
St. James Church (Cape Town), 255
St. James Church (New York), 74
St. Luke's Church (Cape Town), Tutu's speech
　at, 265–66
St. Mary's Anglican Church, 175
St. Mary's Cathedral, 6, 12–13, 36
St. Michael and All Angels Church (Sebokeng),
　sermon at, 213–14
St. Paul's Cathedral (London), 154
Sales tax, 91
Salt River, Cape Town, 265
Sandton, 124
Sanhedrin, 151
Sathekge, Emma, 107
Scandinavia, 100

Schlebusch, A. L., 26
Schoombee, Pieter, 180
Sebokeng, 210, 212–15, 216, 251
Secheba, 147
Second War of Liberation. *See* Boer War
Security Police, 9, 15–16, 152, 179. *See also*
　South Africa, police
Seko, Mobutu Sese, 157
Selassie, Haile, 11
Senate, 48
Senatle, H. B., 213
Seven Days' War (Natal), 209
Sexwale, Tokyo, 267
Shakespeare, William, 237
Shalom, 60
Sharpeville, 5, 91, 97, 98, 213
Sharpeville Six, 145, 146
Shultz, George, 145
Shylock, 237
Silvertown, 176
Simon, Jack, 196
Sisulu, Walter, 196, 204, 224
Six-Day War, 11
Skosana, Maki, 98
Slabbert, Dr. van Zyl, 111
Smith, Ian, 42, 125
Somalia, 238
Somoza, Anastasio, 165
Sonn, Franklin, 175
Sophiatown, 126
South Africa
　athletic boycotts of, 83, 108–9, 181
　border wars, 38, 53, 92, 110
　citizenship in, 43, 88–89, 267
　Cold War and, 200–1
　democracy talks, 235
　democratic constitution of, 227, 241, 249,
　　259, 263
　democratic elections in, 253, 255, 259, 263,
　　266
　democratic government of, 241, 259
　democratic legislature meets, 266
　economic sanctions against, 97–98, 101,
　　102–3, 105, 108–9, 111, 126, 200
　education in, 4–5, 43, 49, 88–89, 91, 92,
　　105, 107, 124, 213
　emigration from, 125
　European settlement of, 200
　financial crisis in, 98
　formation of, 3
　government "peace summit," 235
　international relations of, 9–10, 16, 50,
　　97–98
　justice system in, 9, 90–91, 92, 97, 110n,
　　123–24, 130
　labor laws in, 4, 8, 26, 34, 48, 87, 88, 92,
　　141–42, 211, 228
　media in, 83, 84, 107, 113–14, 130, 146,
　　164, 180, 196, 212, 228
　military expansion of, 53
　municipal elections in, 156

1981 elections, 49–50
1983 constitution, 81–84, 85, 87, 91, 108
1984 elections, 85
peace accord in, 235, 249, 260
police and security forces in, 9, 15–16,
    123–24, 152, 171–72, 179, 181, 211–19,
    228–29, 241–43, 245, 253–54, 260, 264,
    267
politics in, 49–51, 81–85, 110–11, 186, 229,
    230, 241
right wing in, 75n, 107, 216–19, 255, 259,
    260, 263, 264, 265
security measures of, 97, 113–14, 152
states of emergency in, 97, 110, 113, 260
strikes in, 86, 133, 185
talks with African National Congress, 199,
    235
torture in, 123
violence in, 113, 114, 123, 133, 137, 141,
    209–17, 248, 251, 260, 263
voting rights in, 3, 4, 81–84, 85, 87, 99, 267
withdrawal from British Commonwealth, 5
See also Anti-apartheid movement; Apartheid;
    Tutu, Desmond
South African Broadcasting Corporation, 84,
    107, 146, 196, 228
Tutu interview with, 225–26
South African Catholic Bishops' Conference,
    123
South African Communist Party, 146, 154, 191,
    206, 251
South African Council of Churches, 25, 86, 92,
    155–56, 223, 224
activities of, 30–38, 63
allegiance of to God, 54–55, 57–58
commitment to liberation, 36–38
dialogue with others, 73–74
Dutch Reformed Church and, 73–74
finances of, 53
government harassment of, 155–56
government investigation of, 53–54, 75–76,
    107, 152
and hunger strikes, 152
interracialness of, 35–36
joins anti-apartheid movement, 25
legitimacy of, 56–57
meetings with Botha, 41–45, 106–7
militarization and, 73
and municipal elections, 156
openness of, 75
peacefulness of, 71–73
peacemaking role of, 206
secular versus divine authority over, 55,
    57–58
spiritual nature of, 73–74, 76
support for, 75, 76
Tutu's statements about, 27–40, 54–79
South African Defense Force, 45, 52, 86, 110,
    123, 124, 216–19, 243n, 267
South African Institute of Race Relations,
    114

South African Native National Congress, 4. *See
    also* African National Congress
South African Press Association, 186
South African Review, 53
South African Students' Organization, 15, 16
South African Supreme Court, 110n, 130, 152,
    185
South Eastern Transvaal, Diocese of, 205
Southern Africa Church News, 239–40
South Western Townships. *See* Soweto
Soviet Union, 200
Soweto, 6, 13, 43, 85, 105, 106, 110, 123–24,
    210, 211, 243, 251
Sparks, Allister, 4, 225n
Spear of the Nation, 170
Sports administrators, 140
Squatters, 51, 86–87
"Standing for the Truth," 155, 169, 179
Stellenbosch, University of, 51, 222
"Stem, Die," 267
Stormkompas, 65, 66n
Strand (beach), 172, 173, 195
Stuart, Elizabeth, 237
Sudan, 11, 158, 238
Swapo, 42, 110
Swart gevaar ("black peril") politics, 49
Swaziland, 113, 238

Taizé, 35–36
Temple, William, 71
Thatcher, Margaret, 145, 179
Theological Education Fund, 6
Thiart, Hendrik Marinus, 218n
Third Force, 216, 217, 264
32 Battalion, 243
Thokoza, 210, 211, 257
Through Brokenness (Stuart), 237
Tiananmen Square, 173
Tower of Babel story, 61
Townships, 124, 257
appearance of, 229–30, 231
tribalism in, 211, 213, 215–16
violence in, 85–86, 172, 175, 209–19, 228,
    238, 243n, 255
Trade unions, 4, 6, 26, 50, 133, 139, 179, 196
Train attacks, 244
Transitional Executive Council, 259
Transkei, 27, 51
Transvaal, 3, 209–10, 217, 221–25
Transvaal Congress, 47
Transvaler, Die, 84, 212
Treurnicht, Andries, 13, 49, 81, 230
"Trojan Horse" incident, 100n
Tswanas, 8
Turfloop University, 106
Turnhalle talks, 42
Tutu, Desmond, 3, 4, 185
and accusations of Communism, 146, 147,
    150, 152, 153, 154
at Anglican Students' Federation, 205–6
archbishopric sermon of, 114–25

attempts to enter into dialogue, 106–8
at beach protests, 172–73
on Biko's death, 16–21
Bisho massacre and, 248
on black consciousness, 19
on "black-on-black" term, 98, 217
on Boipatong killings, 242–47
and Botha, 8–9, 39, 41–45, 47–51, 106–7,
    108, 110–11, 126, 145–46
on brotherhood, 117, 118–21
Cape Town diocese speech of, 105–11
and Cape Town protest march, 186–89,
    266–67
career of, 5, 6, 12, 25, 26, 85, 99, 113, 157,
    235
Central America visit of, 161
on Christian leadership, 236–38
on Christians as witnesses, 130–32
on Cold War ending, 200–2
on "conditional reflexes" of language, 140–42
on corruption, 246–47
on Defiance Campaign, 169–70
on dehumanization of blacks, 122–24,
    174–75, 246
and De Klerk, 191–204, 211, 216, 217,
    243–47, 266
on democratic elections, 253
on democratic South Africa, 201, 237–38,
    240, 264, 265
on divine missions, 114–15
on divisions within church, 37–39
on doom of apartheid, 58, 140, 143, 164, 171,
    174, 199
on earthly rulers versus God, 151–52
on economic sanctions, 37–38, 101, 102–3,
    105, 108–9, 111, 126, 200
Eloff commission statement of, 54–79
on emphasis on inner life, 238
encouragement to marchers at St. George's,
    181–83
on evilness of apartheid, 56, 58, 64–67,
    147–48
feast-day remarks of, 130–32
on forgiveness, 222, 223–25
on God, 55–56, 66–67, 115–17, 158,
    161–62, 169, 174, 195, 197, 201, 213,
    236, 237, 238, 256, 261–62, 266
government investigation of, 152
on government repression, 141, 142, 162–64,
    174
growing prominence of, 26
and Guguletu protests, 175
at Hani's funeral, 252–54
harassment of, 217
on Harms commission findings, 217–19
on his lower political profile, 203–5
on his own church's racism, 224–25
Holy Week homily of, 228–31
on hopes for negotiations, 191, 193–94
on human rights abuses in Africa, 157–58
on human spirit, 240

on inequity of apartheid, 87
Inkatha and, 249, 261
and international community, 91, 101, 102–3,
    108–10, 111, 126, 265
on Jesus, 7, 17–18, 27–30, 37–38, 39–40,
    55, 56, 61–62, 63, 64, 67, 68, 70–71,
    77–79, 146, 147, 150, 158, 162, 171, 177,
    224, 236–238, 253, 256, 261, 262, 268,
    269
on justice system, 89–91, 140–43, 170–71,
    244, 245
on legacy of apartheid, 265
on legality versus morality, 141–42
on liberation, 36–38
at Mandela's inauguration, 268–69
at Mandela's reception, 194
on Mandela's release, 192–93, 196
Mangope visit of, 260
marked for death, 217–18
on martyrdom, 132
media and, 109, 212
on mixing religion and politics, 67–72, 203–6
Mothers' Union sermon of, 265–66
Mozambique remarks of, 129–30
Natal sermon of, 133–37
National Forum Committee and, 85
on need for global peace, 92–94
on need for step-by-step change, 43–45
on 1983 constitution, 81–84, 87, 108
on 1990 changes, 196–97
on 1994 election day, 261–64
Nobel lecture of, 86–94, 129
passport taken away from, 109
peacemaking efforts of, 136, 152–53,
    210–11, 249
at People's Rally replacement service,
    173–75
on police and security forces, 217–19,
    228–29, 230, 242–43, 245, 252–53, 264
on political groups, 229, 230
on politicians, 243–44, 245, 247–48
on pollution in townships, 229–30, 231
post-election article of, 263–65
on prayer, 231, 238–39
pre-election sermon of, 261–63
on "rainbow people," 175, 187–88, 254, 257,
    262
reaction to election-day violence, 186
reaction to Mandela's election, 266
reaction to Sebokeng violence, 212
on reconciliation, 55–56
reevaluation of by Afrikaners, 225
on revolution, 142
on ridiculousness of apartheid, 163
on right-wing activity, 216–19, 265
on rule of law, 170–71
at Rustenburg church conference, 221–26
sabbatical leave of, 235
sabotage against, 132
St. George interfaith address of, 140–43
Sebokeng sermon of, 213–14

Security Police march of, 171–72
on signs of hope, 102
on South African "birth process," 265–66
on South African Council of Churches,
  27–40, 54–79
on South African pride, 197, 263, 267
Southern Africa Church News interview with,
  239–40
on special treatment accorded to him, 182
on "spirituality of transformation," 238
on suffering, 77–79, 236–37, 239–40
at Synod of Bishops, 235–39
synod-opening speech of, 217–19
thanskgiving sermon of, 194–97
on tolerance, 230
on transfiguration principle, 121–22
treason charges considered against, 130, 132
on treatment of his family, 101
on tribalism, 211, 215–16, 264
in Ulundi, 259
United Democratic Front and, 85
United Nations speech of, 99–103
on unjust rulers, 164–65, 196
on violence, 10–11, 19–20, 86, 90–91, 92,
  98, 99–101, 105–6, 109–10, 125–26,
  129–30, 134–36, 142–43, 173, 176–77,
  181–82, 195, 210, 211–12, 213–14,
  230–31, 238, 244, 245, 250, 256–57,
  264–65
and Vorster, 6–14, 105–6, 107, 243
on weapons, 230
welcomes democratically elected officials,
  267–68
West Point lecture of, 199–202
on white fears, 10, 101–3, 124–25, 201–2
on whites, 7–8, 10, 38–39, 73, 100–1,
  225–26, 246–47, 263–64
Tutu, Leah, 179, 238
Tutu, Trevor, 101, 238

Ubuntu, 125, 229
Uganda, 11, 158, 215
Uitenhage, 102
Ulster, 93
Ulundi, 249, 259
Umkhonto we Sizwe, 170, 252
Unemployment, 91
Union Buildings, 142, 261, 268
Union Defense Force, 154, 218
United Democratic Front, 85, 97, 102, 133, 136,
  139, 143, 169, 174, 179
United Nations, Botha in, 8, 16, 99–103
United States, 16, 84, 97, 145, 186, 200, 235
United States Military Academy, Tutu's lecture
  at, 199–201
United States Supreme Court, 148
Universities, Tutu's visits to, 106
Urbanization, 110–11

Vaal Triangle, 85–86, 145, 210, 241
Vaderland, 84

Van der Merwe (stock figure), 135
Van Rooyen (stock figure), 135
Velde, Frank van der, 255
Venda, 27
Verkramptes, 49
Verwoerd, Hendrik, 5, 51, 105
Vietnam, 10, 11, 93
Viljoen, Gerrit, 191
Villa-Vicencio, Charles, 171
Vlok, Adriaan, 140–41, 142–43, 171, 181
"Voice of South Africa, The," 267
Volkskongres, 70, 151
Vorster, B. J., 26, 42, 43, 47, 52*n*
  Tutu's letter to, 6–14, 105–6, 107, 243
Vrye Weekblad, 189

Waluz, Janusz, 251
Washington, Denzel, 16
Washington Times, 146–47
Webb, Eddie, 218, 218*n*
Western Cape, University of, 140, 141, 173, 175
Western Province Council of Churches, 176,
  182
West Germany, 145
West India, 83
West Rand, 210
Whites, 4
  anti-apartheid movement and, 51–52, 102
  killings of, 255
  political division among, 50
  poor, 225
  Tutu on, 7–8, 9–10, 38–39, 73, 101–2,
    225–26, 246–47, 263
Williamson, Craig, 152
Windhoek, 42*n*
Witwatersrand, 86, 210, 212
Women, in politics, 266
Women's groups, 140
Woods, Donald, 16
Wordsworth, William, 59
World, The, 16
World Alliance of Reformed Churches, 54, 56,
  188
World Conference on Religion and Peace, 152
World Council of Churches, 5, 38
World War II, 4, 52, 100, 154, 218

Xhosas, 8, 211, 213, 215

Yeltsin, Boris, 265
Yugoslavia, 245

Zaire, Tutu's sermon in, 157–58
Zambia, 98, 108, 152
Ziet, Die (Germany), 263–65
Zimbabwe, 39, 93, 125
Zulus, 8, 133, 211, 213, 215, 249, 259, 260,
  261, 264. *See also* Inkatha Freedom Party
Zweledinga, 25
Zwelethini, Goodwill, 260